David Gardner is Chief Leader Writer and Associate Editor at the *Financial Times*. He was the paper's Middle East Editor from 1995–1999. In 2003 he won the David Watt prize for political journalism for his writing on the Arab world.

'At last, a book that goes to the heart of the eternal Middle East Crisis. David Gardner writes courageously and candidly of the west's 'support and indulgence' of corrupt Arab tyrannies, an indulgence that far from securing stability, breeds extremism. He also spells out how US and UK support for Israel has solidified even in the face of Israel's strengthening grip on the Palestinians and the occupied west bank. This is a book that should be in the hand baggage of every one of President Obama's Middle East negotiators.' — **Jon Snow, Channel Four News**

'David Gardner's book is the most lively, well-informed and controversial overview of the Middle East to appear for several years. It will instruct, entertain, but also infuriate many readers, because his rapier thrusts invariably strike home. To understand this turbulent region, this is a <u>must</u> read. David Gardner is one of Britain's leading foreign affairs experts. His sources are unique, his range awesome and his indictment of Arab tyranny and Western connivance devastating and unanswerable.' — **Patrick Seale, author of** *Asad of Syria*

'timely, absorbing, and deeply disturbing...*Last Chance* is central to any understanding of the problems and prospects of the Middle East in the twenty-first century' — **Avi Shlaim, Professor of International Relations, St Antony's College, Oxford**

LAST CHANCE

The Middle East in the Balance

DAVID GARDNER

I.B. TAURIS

LONDON · NEW YORK

Published in 2009 by I.B.Tauris & Co Ltd
6 Salem Road, London W2 4BU
175 Fifth Avenue, New York NY 10010
www.ibtauris.com

Distributed in the United States and Canada Exclusively by Palgrave Macmillan
175 Fifth Avenue, New York NY 10010

ISBN: 978 1 84885 041 5

A full CIP record for this book is available from the British Library
A full CIP record is available from the Library of Congress

Library of Congress Catalog Card Number: available

Designed and Typeset by 4word Ltd, Bristol, UK
Printed and bound in Great Britain by CPI Antony Rowe, Chippenham

FSC
Mixed Sources
Product group from well-managed
forests and other controlled sources
Cert no. SGS-COC-2953
www.fsc.org
© 1996 Forest Stewardship Council

for SAMIA

Contents

Acknowledgements

This book began life as a paper I gave on Arab governance at the United Nations university in Tokyo in January 2002, in the wake of 9/11, while I was living in Beirut. It continued in the form of a series of reported essays I wrote about the Arab world for the *Weekend FT* and *FT Magazine* in the following three years. Those helped me put back on the boil the essential ideas of the book, which had crystallized during my time as the Middle East editor of the *Financial Times*, in 1995–9. Those themes kept bubbling away in my head. I had a first stab at setting them down in book form, in the autumn of 2005 in Dubai. But not until last summer, in Oxford, did they settle into a form that I felt really made sense, at least to me. We shall see whether my sense of this extraordinary region is shared by others.

In the course of acquiring such feel as I have for this unique part of the world, I have accumulated huge debts to a very wide range of people across the Middle East and its neighbouring countries. Even though I am, by profession, a journalist, I have never ceased to be amazed at the way perfect strangers are prepared to devote their time and invest their stock of patience in instructing foreigners in the ways of their world. In the Arab world this is often done with a generosity I have seldom encountered, in ways that turn some of those strangers into firm friends. You all know who you are.

I have been fortunate over the years to meet many of the region's leaders, some of them several times. Of all those encounters and interviews, I particularly recall: my second meeting, in 1995, with the late King Hussein, a man of exquisite courtesy who was always trying to think through the future; an interview, earlier that year, not long before he was murdered, with Yitzhak Rabin, the gruff soldier trying uncomfortably to adjust to his role as peacemaker; the third time I met Hassan Nasrallah, shortly after the 1998 al-Qaeda attacks on US embassies in east Africa, when he excoriated Bin Ladenism and the Taliban and predicted it would be the example set by the reformist President

Mohammad Khatami in Iran that would light the way forward for Islam; or my final of over a dozen conversations with Rafiq Hariri, in late 2004, which returns to my mind in every detail each time I am reminded of his vile assassination a few months later.

Where relevant, bits from these encounters are cited in the book. But as any journalist knows, it is through the middle to senior cadres of a regime – and the most perspicacious of its opponents – that one usually acquires the best information and understanding. They will more rarely be quoted by name in this book; even when speaking on the record, it seems to me prudential not to associate them with controversial theses. They, too, know who they are.

At the *Financial Times*, I am extremely grateful to Lionel Barber, the editor, and Dan Bogler, managing editor, for giving me the time off to finish this book. I am grateful to earlier FT editors, Andrew Gowers and Richard Lambert, for giving me the run of the Middle East. I also thank John Lloyd and Graham Watts, editors of *FT Magazine* in its early period, for giving me generous chunks of their space to write.

A particular thank you to two dear friends and colleagues, Robert Graham of the FT and Phil Bennett of *The Washington Post*, for reading the manuscript with an encouraging but critical eye and making helpful suggestions, and to Bhavna Patel of the FT library for research support.

At I.B. Tauris, I am grateful to Iradj Bagherzade, chairman and publisher, for investing this project with faith. I owe huge thanks to Abigail Fielding-Smith, my editor, for her unvarying support and invaluable suggestions. Thank you, Abbie.

In Oxford, I am enormously grateful to Dr Eugene Rogan, director of the Middle East Centre, and to Professor Margaret MacMillan, Warden of St Antony's College, for arranging for me to become a Senior Associate Member, and for the ideal working conditions in which I was able to complete this book. I could not have had a warmer and more encouraging or stimulating welcome than from Eugene and his MEC colleagues: thank you for granting me temporary membership of your tribe.

I owe one debt to my late father, Terry Gardner, for having the great foresight to bring me up (partly) in the Middle East, in Kuwait, Cairo and Beirut. But my greatest debt of all is to my wife, Samia Nakhoul, for her love and encouragement, her courage and patience, and through whose eyes I have seen this region illuminated.

Preface

Among the many urgent and formidably difficult tasks facing Barack Obama at the outset of his historic presidency, by no means the least of them will be the long, uphill struggle to restore America's reputation in the world and, in particular, to recover a position of legitimacy in the Arab and Muslim worlds.

As revealed by poll after depressing poll, the USA (and the West in general) no longer has any moral standing among Arabs and Muslims – even, tragically, the instinctively pro-western among them. This is almost certainly the last chance for a very long time for the USA to reclaim its role as the lead custodian of an international order founded on freedom and the rule of law.

President Obama, in speech after spellbinding speech before taking office, gave every indication he understood this. As he told the vast crowd at his victory rally in Chicago:

> To those who would tear the world down – we will defeat you. To those who seek peace and security – we support you. And to all those who have wondered if America's beacon still burns as bright – tonight we proved once more that the true strength of our nation comes not from the might of our arms or the scale of our wealth, but from the enduring power of our ideals: democracy, liberty, opportunity and unyielding hope.

The election of Obama has brought hope in abundance to the wider Middle East. He has promised 'tough and principled diplomacy' in place of the bungling and bad faith that marked George W. Bush's catastrophic eight years of misadventure in the region. Unless that translates quickly into transformative policy change, however, it will evaporate. The main signals of western intent that must be sent are: even-handed but assertive US mediation in the Middle East conflict that seeks security for the Israelis and justice for the

Palestinians; for the USA and Europe to seek a grand bargain with Iran, offering security to Iran's neighbours but giving Tehran a stake in the stability of the region; and through a structured and orderly withdrawal from Iraq that ends the US occupation and confronts Iraqis with the need to compromise on the essential elements of a shared future. It is no accident that leaders in Israel, Iran and Iraq were nervous about the election of Obama: it confronts them with difficult choices.

It should also, by now, be obvious that there is a connection between all the policies mentioned above. It is not just that it will be almost impossible to establish stability in Iraq without Iran; the invasion of Iraq and overthrow of the Sunni order there has so enhanced the power of Shia Iran that almost no problem in the region – Palestine, Lebanon and Afghanistan as well as Iraq – is soluble any longer without Tehran's support or, at least, quiescence. Yet, even if all that is done, if the West continues to collude in the survival of tyranny across the region, it will abet the onward march of jihadi extremism.

That is why this book will have a great deal to say about despotism. It is about the particular forms of Arab autocracy that have led the Arab peoples to political failure and to fall badly behind on almost every index of development, and about the way the western powers, led by the USA, have abetted this tyranny. Its central thesis is that unless the Arab countries and the broader Middle East can find a way out of this pit of autocracy, their people – roughly two thirds of them under 25 – will be condemned to bleak lives of despair, humiliation and rage for generations, adding fuel to a roaring fire in what is already the most combustible region in the world. Support for autocracy and indulgence of corruption in this region, far from securing stability, breeds extremism and, *in extremis*, failed states.

It will, of course, be primarily up to the citizens of these countries to claw their way out of that pit. But the least they can expect from the West is not to keep stamping on their fingers.

Any shot fired in the Middle East echoes around the world. No crisis there can any longer be purely regional if, indeed, any ever has been. That is not just because the region sits on just under two thirds of the world's proven oil reserves or because of its strategic geopolitical position. Any conflict in the Middle East registers within minutes in the oil market, and we have, through experience, come to fear the spillover effects, regionally and internationally, that now come in waves as well as ripples.

The misbegotten adventure of the invasion and occupation of Iraq, for instance, has not only immeasurably increased the power and influence of Iran, it has uncorked the long-fermenting conflict between Sunni and Shia Muslims from the Levant to the Gulf and across to the Indian subcontinent, as well as proliferating the anti-western bigotry and messianic jihadism associated with Osama bin Laden.

What we now face is a broader crisis between the West and the world of Islam, with the Arab world at its core. This is not – *pace* Samuel Huntington, Bernard Lewis and a host of lesser Islamophobe commentators, and despite the self-serving claims of the 'they hate us for our freedoms' industry – because there is an endemic and intrinsic conflict between Christians and Muslims. It is because a majority of Muslims is convinced that the West, interested only in a stability based on regional strongmen, the security of Israel and cheap oil, is engaged in a war against Islam and bent on denying them the freedoms it claims for itself.

At the heart of that crisis are not only the unresolved conflicts in which the West has taken a position perceived as hostile – Israel–Palestine, Iraq, Iran, Lebanon–Syria, Afghanistan–Pakistan and, more peripherally, Chechnya, Kashmir and Xinjiang – but the plague of tyranny that has created an Arab Exception. This has left the Arabs marooned as the tide of democracy of the past 30 years has swept across almost every other region in the world, from Latin America to central and eastern Europe, or from south-east Asia to sub-Saharan Africa.

We have been complicit in that tyranny and it is the contention of this book that this has been every bit as effective at turning an entire civilization against the West as the disastrous ways in which we have intervened in these lands. There is no other part of the world – not even China – where the West operates with such lethal condescension and so little regard for the human and political rights of local citizens.

The autocracies we have supported differ from country to country but rest on essentially the same foundations: a monopoly of power, based on the army as the backbone of the state and, within that, the Mukhabarat, the omnipresent security services, which keep the ruler in power and the people in political chains. The security establishments in these national security states are pivotal. The hydra-headed Mukhabarat in effect mediates the information flow between the ruler and the ruled, the better to manipulate both. As we shall see, the powers of the autocrat are circumscribed, to the extent that the president is the prisoner of his praetorians; Roman emperors, not to mention Islamic sultans, would recognize the syndrome. In overtly theocratic regimes, whether an ally such as Saudi Arabia or an adversary such as Iran, power also flows from the clerical establishment. But that is not unique to them.

As I will argue, so completely have the Arab regimes repressed political activity across the spectrum, that they have left their opponents no rallying point except the mosque. This has been one of the principal factors in the violent rebirth of Islamic revivalism. The other has been the collapse in legitimacy of Arab rulers, which we shall examine in the first three chapters. Yet, the retreat into Islam, as many Arab and Muslim writers have pointed out, was not the first choice of the peoples of the region. Despotism and intervention – and our part in both, which left the region's dwindling band of liberals out on a limb – left them little other choice. But precisely because Islamism became almost the only means for these societies to regroup, nearly all the region's dictators have been forced into some degree of reliance on their clerical establishments. This, they believe, enables them to win legitimacy and outflank the Islamists – from the right – but in countries such as Egypt it also abets a creeping theocracy. That too, as Muslim Brotherhood strategists have long understood, is a form of power.

The West, tainted by its connivance in tyranny and manipulation of the politics of the region for its own ends, often appears blind to the effect it has in encouraging this and other dangerous trends in the region. Its leaders are particularly resistant to the idea of dealing with Islamists when they do, against the odds, triumph at the polls: most recently in Palestine, Iraq, Lebanon and, to an extent, Egypt. Those who argue for democracy, moreover, often do so in the mistaken belief it will bring stability to the region. It may not, especially if the West and its Israeli ally continue to wreak chaos through blundering and selectively applied military might that has discredited the freedom agenda of the recent administration of George W. Bush in Arab and Muslim eyes.

Democracy, indeed, could open a long period of illiberal politics that may be inimical to stability. Yet, to me, it is inescapable that the West's only realistic choice is to foster, or at least not actively obstruct, the right of Arabs to decide their own future, in whatever form they wish. That form is likely to be heavily influenced by Islamism. The freedom agenda proclaimed by Bush, not to mention the liberal internationalism espoused by his erstwhile British acolyte, Tony Blair, have been discredited by their duplicity and naïve belief in the efficacy of military force. Yet it is of the utmost importance that this should not diminish the validity of the insight brought to the West so violently by al-Qaeda in the 11 September 2001 and subsequent attacks: that tyranny, connived in by the West, breeds terrorism and instability, as well as infantilizing politics and public life and holding back development.

The reason for the discredit and lack of moral authority and political influence of the West is that, for most practical purposes, that insight has not led to a fundamental change of policy, which is still in danger of retreating into a shallow realism, despite the advent of Barack Obama.

What the USA and Europe have to do is to cease propping up Arab despots, to stop uncritically supporting dictatorship in Egypt and absolute monarchy in Saudi Arabia, and to find ways to open up these societies to what their citizens still find attractive about the West. In practice, that should mean favouring civil society options such as the funding of education, the empowerment (and education) of women, the building of functioning institutions and a law-based society, and adopting a blatant bias towards democracy and its brave defenders rather than, say, financing the Egyptian army or supporting Israel's violent assaults on its neighbours such as in the 2006 Lebanon war.

The clear support of democratic values is the core of what Joseph Nye, in 'The Paradox of American Power', calls soft power: 'getting others to want what you want' rather than coercing them with military and economic might. Anything less than clear support dissipates soft power and erodes influence, signalling that Arabs and Muslims are to be denied democracy in case they support Islamists, just as many Latin Americans, Asians and Africans had to put up with western-endorsed dictators in case they supported communists, real or supposed.

While democracy is an intrinsic human and public good, however raucous or inefficient, its value as the cornerstone of good governance is priceless, as a series of Arab development reports produced by the UN Development Programme from 2002 well illustrated. While these show that there is no causal link translating democracy into high economic growth and income, they also demonstrate that democracies are better at avoiding war, civil conflict and the failure of states and societies and, most of all, that the construction of institutions and the rule of law – the underpinning of democracy – does yield great development rewards, including stability. That is where the West should concentrate its fire. While, obviously, people need to want democracy if it is to have a chance of working, the West's job is to demonstrate it really wants people to 'want what we want'. It has not done so.

In the course of this book, I will examine aspects of the Arab political order that to me best explain and illustrate the persistent failures of Arab countries, either to deliver development to their people or to recover Arab lands and give the Arabs a respected voice in the world. There is no absolute model, and I do not intend to wrench different experiences into a shape that fits one. The recent history of the region is a tortuous tale of the twists and flows of power, the surges and the blowbacks. The precise context is different in Cairo, Beirut or Riyadh, but the overarching imperative of political change is common. I attempt to preserve the particular features of different regimes – and non-Arab experiences to which they can usefully be compared, in Iran, Pakistan and, most promisingly, Turkey – while selecting aspects of their behaviour and interaction with the West that add up ultimately to failure to achieve much beyond regime survival, the accumulation of pent-up rage among their citizens, and foreign intervention. Throughout, I shall insist on the role of despotism as the main structural impediment to advance, and the malign role of western policy in strengthening its resilience.

That role has to change. It is not a question of 'regime change', or of actively destabilizing the existing order. Instead of propping up tyrants for short-term (and often illusory) gains, western policy needs to find ways of stimulating and aiding those elements in Arab and Muslim society that might, eventually, replace them. Arabs and Muslims, at the very least, have the right to expect that the USA and its allies do not actively support those who deny them their freedoms.

Strategic thinking must replace sloganeering. Superficially muscular and rhetorically determined slogans such as 'Staying the Course' are mere obfuscation: the Titanic stayed the course; lemmings stay the course. It is the 'Course' that needs urgently to be re-charted. The blunderbuss imprecision of the 'Global War on Terror' is another lamentable example that, furthermore, diplomatically enabled Moscow, Delhi and Beijing to reclassify regional disputes involving Muslims in Chechnya, Kashmir and Xinjiang as part of it. As the November 2008 terrorist assault on Mumbai showed, Kashmir, for example, has as a result ceased to be a regional dispute with potentially tractable grievances and been stitched into a broader confrontation with international jihadism.

There is a precise and identifiable enemy – international jihadism – that must be isolated and crushed before it makes further inroads into the Muslim mainstream. As I shall argue, Osama bin Laden at least did us one favour in shattering a near century-long status quo: after 9/11 it is no longer politically tenable to base Middle East policy on networks of Arab strongmen and unconditional support for Israel.

The West starts from a historic low in the broader region. It has to regain its moral standing among Arabs and Muslims. The USA and its allies, whether by sins of commission or omission, operate policies that continue to alienate and often enrage 1.2 billion Muslims, at a time when they need to confront huge strategic challenges such as the rise of China and revival of Russian nationalism, or the threat of climate change and energy security (to say nothing of what is shaping up as the worst financial and economic crisis for almost a century). In the Arab and Muslim worlds, they desperately need to regain legitimacy and moral authority. They will not do this through support for tyrants, through wars of choice, or complicity in Israeli land grabs.

As mentioned earlier, clear signals of western intent must be sent: through the USA acting finally as the even-handed mediator of an outcome to the Middle East conflict that gives security to Israelis and justice to the

Palestinians; through the USA and Europe burying the visceral animosities of the past and reaching a grand bargain with Iran; and through a structured and orderly withdrawal from Iraq that ends the occupation.

There are grounds for hope. Turkey, for example, has shown that political Islam can evolve. Its ruling Justice and Development Party was rebuilt from the wreckage of two failed Islamist parties and broadened out to evolve into a sort of Muslim equivalent of Christian Democracy. It is widely admired in the Arab and Muslim worlds, not as a model but because it works. Success sells.

Islamism in the Arab heartland is more likely to evolve in ways that are consistent with viable state institutions and a functioning rule of law, moreover, if the new US administration and its allies rethink their policies in the broader Middle East. Part of this rethink should be an audit of US relations with this world that reveals another pernicious aspect of what I call (inadequately) the Arab Exception. Unlike in its dealings with almost all other countries, Washington does not have *institutional* relations with Arab (and bordering) countries. It deals, preferentially, with rulers and regimes – frequently in currencies such as oil and arms. This applies, too, in non-Arab parts of the region, where the relationship was with the Shah in Iran or General Pervez Musharraf in Pakistan, with predictable if differing levels of disarray once the strongman had fallen.

The fatal western attraction to autocrats is neither attractive nor, except episodically, successful. Those who hanker after the status quo that existed before Bush chose his peculiarly destructive and incompetent way to shake the region up should be aware of two things: it is no longer available; it had become a machine inducing, at best, paralysis, and at worst pushing towards breakdown. Allied autocracies of the importance of Egypt and Pakistan are flirting with failure as states. Letting the wider Middle East plod on in a recognizably messed up way in the belief that it is better simply to manage periodic crises is not a policy option; it is a dangerous fantasy. The stakes are now just too high.

If we continue to connive in the survival of tyranny, moreover, then, as I have said, we abet the onward march of the jihadis, for whom western policy is their most consistently reliable ally. We also condemn the broader Middle East to violence, stagnation and possible state failures, for which we will also pay a heavy price. There is not much time left to try to get this right. We must start now.

The Arab Political Jungle

F ew people in the world find *The Lion King* politically controversial, but those who do are likely to be functionaries of the Arab world's hydra-headed intelligence services.

Producers at the Lebanese film company that dubbed the Walt Disney jungle opera into Arabic can tell you why. For a start, the dubbers were banned from using two words at the heart of the story: namely 'lion' and 'king'.

In the eyes of the censors of the Mukhabarat, as the intelligence services are generically known, any use of the normal words for lion and king – *assad* and *malik* – would amount to the crime of *lèse-majesté*. Assad, of course, is the name of the present and former president of Syria, Bashar al-Assad and his late father, Hafez al-Assad. Alongside this republican dynasty, moreover, there are real kings who could be affronted in Saudi Arabia, Jordan and Morocco.

To confer their names or titles on an animal would guarantee a ban on the film, the production company said, describing how it manages to navigate this politico-semantic minefield.

King Fahd, for instance, the late Saudi monarch, would present a double challenge because his name means 'panther'. That word is therefore also banned, one acceptable alternative being *daba'a* – which according to some dictionaries can mean hyena ('The Pink Hyena'?).

'We are forced to change all these names or find some sort of synonym', said one of the dubbing producers – such as 'ruler of the forest' for 'Lion King'.

As a prominent Arab journalist observed at the time: 'words frighten these people almost as much as ideas'. The Disney bestiary appears full of terrors for the lords of the Arab political jungle.

If the local fortunes of the Lion King or the Pink Panther were simply a matter of social mores, this would be a colourful but trivial matter. The intoxicating power and poetry of the Arabic language, furthermore, would inevitably command police attention in a region swept barren of ideas by the autocrats who are its political hallmark.

For the world at large, however, there is nothing trivial about this absolutist political culture in the aftermath of the 11 September 2001 attacks on New York and Washington, and a proliferation of jihadi outrages thereafter. The way most Arab countries are governed – in particular Saudi Arabia and Egypt, Washington's two closest Arab allies, where most of the 9/11 suicide hijackers and their ostensible leader came from – has ceased to be of primarily local or regional concern and become a burning domestic and foreign policy issue across the world.

Put simply, the breathtaking audacity and cruel realpolitik of the 9/11 assault made it no longer possible for the USA, the West and their Arab despot clients to ignore a dictatorial political set-up that incubated blind rage against them. Osama bin Laden had smashed a near century-long status quo in the region.

Western indulgence of and support for a panoply of Sunni Arab strong-men, in charge of often artificial states bolted together from the debris of the Ottoman empire, had become as great an affront to Arab and Muslim sensibilities as western bias towards Israel in the endless battle over how to share Palestine. Policies pursuing stability, cheap oil and the ostensible security of Israel had ended up by incubating Islamist terror.

An ossified political order, invariably incapable of lifting its economies out of stagnation or offering a decent livelihood to the majority of its citizens, had spawned the threat of globalized Islamist hyper-terrorism inspired by bin Laden and al-Qaeda. Resentful of tyranny and humiliated by backwardness, the very young population of the Arab world (where up to two thirds of citizens are under 25) had watched as democratic change embraced Latin America, eastern Europe, and large swathes of Asia and Africa, but passed them by, creating an 'Arab Exception' connived in by the West.

The point that the USA and some of its allies were, at last, beginning to grasp was this: that the habitual tyranny of many Arab regimes was an essential alloy in the alchemy of Islamist terror; and that western indulgence of Arab despotism was an equally important element in that witches' brew.

Condoleezza Rice, US secretary of state in the second term of President George W. Bush, spelt out the new US position in a speech in Cairo in June 2005. For 60 years, she said, the USA had pursued stability at the expense of democracy in the Middle East and had ended up with neither. America, she averred, had learnt its lesson. From now on it would align with those who saw freedom as the indispensable platform for stability, prosperity and security, and against the tyranny that bred despair, rage and terror.

Nearly two years earlier in Washington, in a November 2003 speech to the National Endowment for Democracy, President Bush had castigated the 'cultural condescension' that suggested Arabs and Muslims were unsuited to democracy. He would commit America to a 'generational' struggle for the democratization of the Middle East, just as preceding generations had fought the Cold War.

These are cogent, declaratory speeches. They communicate conviction that despotism has been tried and has failed. But what has been lacking, so far, is action that really demonstrates that the USA – bogged down in an Iraq it believed would be the lever to transforming the 'wider' Middle East – is prepared to take the risks the inevitably messy process of democratization will involve. Instead, Washington and its allies, frightened by the forces they have unleashed by their misconceived and bungled intervention in Iraq, are retreating into a shallow new 'realism', falling back fatally on the old political order that has brought the Arab world and the West to this pass.

Those who affected to remake the Arab world in America's image, moreover, seemed to bring to the enterprise everything except actual knowledge of the countries they targeted for redemption.

Some, exemplified by Ms Rice, brought a Cold Warrior mindset to the job, reading over the transformation of east and central Europe into a wholly different environment in which the West has been backing, as it were, the local variant of Stalinism. Others, typified by the neo-conservative cabal that provided the main philosophical justification for the war in Iraq, appeared to take a ten-pin bowling alley approach to geo-politics in the region: hit the front pin (in this instance, Iraq) hard enough, and the rest would simply be skittled over. No one with experience of the region was invited into the circle of decision makers. As Paul Bremer, the second US administrator of the occupation authorities in Iraq, would sneer to a veteran Central Intelligence Agency man in Baghdad at the time: 'all you people know about is history – we are making history, we are making the future'.[1]

There are three overarching features that define these Arab regimes. First, every Arab country is, to a greater or lesser degree, an autocracy – whether republican or royalist, an absolute or quasi-constitutional monarchy/emirate, whether it has elections or not, or whether it is secular or avowedly religious. There are partial but no complete exceptions to that rule. Infinite variety of form cannot disguise the uniformity of the underlying substance of Arab governance.

Yes, there have been faltering steps towards democracy in the monarchies of the Gulf (Bahrain, Qatar, Kuwait and Oman, for example) and Morocco. Lebanon, with its 'Cedar Revolution' and sectarian political quota system in ferment, is a big but still only partial exception, trapped in its own parochialism and the sectarian gridlock that has gripped the region after Iraq. Egypt and even Saudi Arabia have made recent genuflections to democratic ritual. And, over nearly two decades, there have been flawed and controlled electoral exercises in Jordan and Yemen, or Algeria and Tunisia.

Yet Freedom House, the New York-based monitor of political and civic freedoms, said in its *Freedom in the World* report of December 2001 that the Islamic and Arab nations had diverged with the rest of the world on democracy. In one of the more cogent early reactions to 9/11, it identified the nature of 'the Arab Exception'.

'Since the early 1970s, when the third major wave of democratization began, the Islamic world, and, in particular, its Arab core, have seen little evidence of improvements in political openness, respect for human rights and transparency', the survey said, ranking Iraq, Libya, Saudi Arabia, Sudan and Syria among the ten least free countries in the world.

In those three decades, which saw the end of the Cold War and dictatorships tumbling from Bucharest to Buenos Aires, the Arab world remained marooned in tyranny. In the post-Communist era, moreover, there is no other part of the world – not even China – that is examined by the West with such little regard for the political and human rights of its citizens.

The second defining feature of the modern Arab regime is that autocrats are kept in power by the key institution of the military, including, as the single most important political component, the intelligence services – the ubiquitous Mukhabarat.

So overarching is the military as an institution that in countries as apparently distinct as Saudi Arabia and Saddam Hussein's Iraq there were two armies – a regular army and a praetorian guard (National Guard in Saudi Arabia, Republican Guard in Iraq) for the ruling family. In both these cases that guard was based on tribal networks. And in equally distinct set-ups, such as Jordan and Syria, tribal and clan loyalties underpin state power. But the point is that all that tribal interstitial tissue is worthless unless attached to the hard bone and articulated joints of security establishment and military power.

All Arab countries, moreover, have a plethora of these security services, some of them purely to spy on each other. Syria gets by with six, a relatively lean model, while the Palestinians under Yassir Arafat, even without a state, had a dozen security and intelligence bodies. Arab leaders may make the just rejoinder that the USA, say, has 16 intelligence services. But it is not their primary purpose to keep any individual leader or clan in power.

The third defining feature, and arguably the root of it all, is that most Arab rulers have a problem of legitimacy. That problem has grown over the past three decades, especially in the wake of the disaster of Arab defeat by Israel in the Six Day War of 1967. Such lack of legitimacy has severe consequences in the Arab world, where rulers never change by the ballot but either die with their boots on, or by the bullet.

This book will start by examining this crisis of legitimacy, whose initial beneficiaries appeared to be the feudal monarchies of the Gulf. But the longer-term winners are more likely to be the Islamic revivalists who stepped into this vacuum, picking up the fallen banners of pan-Arab nationalism and portraying their amorphous ideology as a liberation theology.

The Islamists have been the main beneficiaries of stagnation, failure and tyranny indulged by the West. Fortunately, they come in many varieties. This book will argue that one of the main policy challenges facing the USA and Europe will be to separate out irreconcilable jihadis of bin Ladenist conviction from the Islamist movements that are implanted and organized in their societies and wish to play the democratic game, to play in the global marketplace of ideas. There is no conceivable way forward unless the latter are engaged – albeit on clear democratic terms. They cannot be shut out. That is a fantasy.

The fostering of freedom, and, of course, the adoption of a more even-handed policy in Israel–Palestine designed to secure justice for the Palestinians as well as security for the Israelis, will be the key to which way mainstream Muslims tilt – towards the bin Ladens and their jihad against the West or towards representative politics, the rule of law and the development of civil society. For the starting point of any re-examination of policy must be the now irrefutable evidence piled up in poll after poll about how low America's reputation has sunk in the Islamic and Arab world, among notional friends and ostensible foes alike.

In the years since 9/11, the Bush administration and its cheerleaders successfully sold the idea that its jihadi perpetrators 'hate us for our freedoms' and loathe us for our values: for what we are and think, rather than anything that we do. Pause for a moment and recall all those post-9/11 magazine covers and potboilers purporting to answer the question: 'Why do they hate us?' There is something so nearly right in the sheer wrongness of the lethal condescension of most of the answers. Properly formulated, the answer would say: 'they hate us because we have freedoms, but we have found it politically and commercially convenient to back tyrants who deny them their freedom'. In what is ultimately a war of ideas within the Islamic world, there is no idea more damaging than to suggest Muslims and Arabs have no interest in freedom – that they do not bleed just the same as everyone else. Unless we break free from it, radical Islamism will win that war of ideas.

The self-serving fallacies of the 'they hate us for our freedoms' industry were exposed in a host of different books from, for example, the former Central Intelligence Agency official in charge of pursuing bin Laden, Michael Scheuer (the initially anonymously-written *Imperial Hubris*), to the Palestinian–American historian Rashid Khalidi (*Resurrecting Empire*). They and others argued persuasively that it is the policies of the USA and its allies that have ignited Arab and Muslim antagonism.

In September 2004 a comprehensive validation of this analysis emerged from an unusual quarter: the Defense Science Board (DSB), a federal committee of academics and strategists that gives independent advice to the US defence secretary. The DSB found that 'America's power to persuade is in a state of crisis' – not least, it suggested between the lines, because of the Bush administration's unappealing mix of high-handedness, incompetence and attraction to the use of force. Credibility matters, the report said, and 'simply, there is none – the US today is without a working channel of communication to the world of Muslims and Islam'. The polls examined by the DSB are salutary: single digit support for the USA and its policies (for example, a 98 and 94 per cent 'unfavourable' rating in Egypt and Saudi Arabia). Support for the USA in subsequent polls, by the Zogby International group and Pew Global Attitudes Project, among others, was almost undetectable.

The DSB found, nonetheless, that majorities or pluralities *do* support values such as freedom and democracy, embrace western science and education, and like western products and American movies. 'In other words, they do not hate us for our values, but because of our policies', the DSB said, before noting that the surveys showed that hatred of the policies was so corrosive it had begun to tarnish the attraction of the values – a warning if ever there was one that there may not be too much time left to change course. So what is to be done?

In Iraq, state and society have broken apart under a US-led occupation that continued to use disproportionate firepower against an elusive, for a long time barely identified, enemy, causing high civilian casualties. Unable to control an insurgency then being prosecuted by a minority of the minority Sunni, the occupiers committed a seamless catalogue of errors and misjudgements. Their bluster and bungling, and serial own-goals, seemed to be creating strategic disaster, a Balkans-in-the-sands. Arab public opinion watched in anguish as ethnosectarian civil war engulfed Iraq, creating the menacing possibility of a wider sectarian conflict between Sunni and Shia that could suck in Iraq's neighbours, with Shia Iran on one side and Sunni Arab rulers terrified by the empowerment of Iraq's Shia majority on the other.

Meanwhile, US (and British) support for Israel appeared to solidify even while the Israelis continued to strengthen their grip on the immeasurably weaker Palestinians and the occupied West Bank, the summer of 2005 Israeli withdrawal from Gaza notwithstanding. In both these arenas, obsessively observed by Muslims around the world through the relatively new medium of Arab satellite television channels, the events of April 2004 may prove to have been a turning point.

During that fateful month, Arabs and Muslims from Fez to Rawalpindi watched in perplexed horror as US troops destroyed the town of Fallujah, west of Baghdad in the Euphrates valley, and as Israeli forces pulverized Rafah, the Palestinian town in the south of the Gaza Strip. Despite highly restricted media access in both cases, they were sometimes able to watch both infernos simultaneously on split screens, connected up by a plethora of Arab satellite television stations. This was a degree of integration their world had probably not known since the golden days of the Muslim commonwealths so celebrated by today's Islamic revivalists, except that it recalled darker days. It was not uncommon to hear remarks in the vein of: 'this is like watching the Crusades, live on television'.

In the middle of this, on 14 April 2004, President Bush provided Ariel Sharon, Israel's prime minister and the champion of Israeli settlers in the Palestinian territories, with a letter recognizing that Israel would keep virtually all the big West Bank blocs of settlements. Tony Blair, Britain's prime minister, seemed to endorse this new, one-sided and illegal policy, which trampled on several UN Security Council resolutions as well as the Fourth Geneva Convention. To Arabs it looked like a second edition of the 1917 Balfour Declaration through which Britain first identified Palestine as a national home for the Jews.

Then, on top of all that, came the incalculably damaging scandal of prisoner abuse at Abu Ghraib. That threw into high relief worse abuses – amounting to torture – going on at the US facility for suspected jihadis in Guantanamo Bay, Cuba and the Bagram airbase in Afghanistan, as well as a host of other undeclared facilities for the ghost prisoners of the so-called Global War on Terror, across Central Asia, the Middle East and eastern Europe.[2]

Soon enough, it also became clear that the public justifications the USA used for the Iraq war – Saddam Hussein's alleged possession of weapons of mass destruction and a purported link between Baghdad and al-Qaeda – were not true. Indeed, not one of nearly 30 US assertions about Iraq to the UN Security Council by Colin Powell, then secretary of state, in February 2003, was ever substantiated. To most Arabs, US policy looked less the 'forward strategy for freedom in the Middle East' proclaimed by President Bush and more like an American drive to secure forward bases in the region that traditionally provided the West with cheap oil.

The administration's vaunted Greater Middle East Initiative, in this light, looked long on rhetoric and short on action – suspiciously like France and Britain's duplicitous behaviour during their post-First World War carve-up of the Middle East. It did not help that this partnership programme set up its small secretariat in Tunisia, arguably the most efficient police state in the region, whose president, Zine al-Abidine Ben Ali, had just managed to perform yet again the miracle of electoral near-unanimity to prolong his rule.

As a leading Arab editor in Beirut observed around that time, while the year 1989 saw the fall of the Berlin Wall and a new democratic wave burst over east and central Europe, that was also the year of the Taif Accord aimed at ending the 1975–90 Lebanese civil war – used ever after by Syria as the excuse for its creeping Anschluss in Lebanon. 'It seems that in our part of the world', he said, 'West Berlin was taken over by East Berlin'.

It seemed for a while that was at last beginning to change, and in often unpredictable ways. In the course of 2005, in particular, there were tentative grounds for believing that democracy was establishing a toehold in the region – at least at first.

We observed above the paradox that the person most responsible for undermining the status quo in the region was Osama bin Laden. It was his actions that made it impossible to ignore how western collusion with tyrants, who appeared set against both freedom and Islam, incubated Islamist terror. The US administration's response to 9/11 further undermined the status quo, in ways it was not obvious the Bush administration had thought through, for all its laudable declarations supporting freedom across the Arab and Islamic world.

The measured and justified earlier invasion of Afghanistan had denied Osama bin Laden what he sought: a disproportionate response that looked like an attack on Islam and that would incite a worldwide Muslim uprising against the West and its clients (see Chapters III and IV). One year after the Bush administration's war of choice in Iraq, however, Ayman al-Zawahiri, bin Laden's chief strategist, was calling on all Muslims to give thanks to God that the USA had come to Iraq. The USA, as critics of the Iraq war policy (including the present author) repeatedly forecast, had proliferated the bin Ladenist cult of death.

By Zawahiri's reasoning, the USA and its dwindling allies would lose if they stayed and lose if they withdrew. It was hard not to see his logic. The 'damned if they do, damned if they don't' dilemma was real enough. Anything resembling a forced or politically induced withdrawal would enable the jihadis to claim a victory on a scale of the defeat of the 1979–89 Soviet occupation of Afghanistan, achieved with US assistance. Only this time they would claim to have defeated a superpower without the help of another superpower, powered instead by the force of religious zeal.

The option of staying would also further exhibit the limits of America's vaunted power. The US occupation forces, although generally more circumscribed in their use of unbridled force after 2006, were still making more enemies than friends among Iraqis. Persistently perceived as part of the problem rather than the solution by an overwhelming majority of Iraqis, who saw them as occupiers rather than liberators, they were also providing an invaluable training ground for the gamut of urban warfare and terrorism favoured by Zawahiri, al-Qaeda's thinker. By also furnishing a target-rich environment, they served as a recruiting sergeant for international jihadism.

For ultra-jihadis, emblemized by the Jordanian fanatic Abu Musab al-Zarqawi, there was also the reasoned expectation that the civil war he was trying to foment by a campaign of butchery against Iraq's Shia majority would not only catch fire but become a Sunni–Shia conflict across the Levant, down the east of the Arabian peninsula and across to the Indian subcontinent.

After all, once the Pentagon and its Iraq viceroy, Paul Bremer, dissolved the Iraqi army in May 2003, the occupation was left with rapidly worsening options. It had broken the backbone of the state but also destroyed Iraq's main national institution, which predated Ba'athist rule. Those up to 400,000 soldiers, destitute but armed and trained, swelled the ranks of the Sunni resistance, making the stated US policy of rebuilding a national army from all communities delusional. Instead, Americans and the British were forced to rely on rebadged Shia militia and Kurdish peshmerga. They were thus perceived to be taking sides in a sectarian war. That was what happened to the ill-fated US and French multinational forces in Lebanon in 1983–4, where they were eventually regarded as just another variety of militia in the civil war.

The later 'surge' of US troop reinforcements in 2007–8 did little to dispel that perception. Its most advertised success – the temporary alliance with Sunni tribal militia against al-Qaeda – added another side to this bewilderingly fragmented conflict (which will be examined in detail in Chapter IV).

But at the same time, the presence of the most powerful army in the world as a frontline power in the Arab heartland has undoubtedly had other consequences too.

Local autocrats trod with more care and circumspection. In Egypt, President Hosni Mubarak allowed others to stand against him for the fifth presidential term he secured in September 2005 with a mere 88 per cent majority. In parliamentary elections two months later the banned Muslim Brotherhood was able to demonstrate it was nevertheless the only organized opposition force in Egypt. In Saudi Arabia that spring the kingdom held its first, men-only, partial, municipal elections. The Bush administration banked these modest developments as signal successes. More plausibly, it hailed the January and December 2005 elections in Iraq, and that spring's civil uprising against Syrian rule in Lebanon, as decisive evidence of 'freedom on the march'.

Beyond question, the millions of Iraqis who defied savagery and intimidation to vote in a provisional government and constituent assembly showed extraordinary courage. This heroism, by a people ground down by three horrific wars, 13 years of draconian sanctions, and over three decades of Saddam Hussein's brand of fascism, struck a deep chord among Arabs, who watched on satellite television and wondered if at last Iraqis had begun to wrest back control of their future.

The triumphalists in Washington who then claimed total vindication for their almost totally bungled strategy were right to point out – up to a point – that these and subsequent elections would not have taken place under Saddam. They conveniently ignored that the reason they took place was the insistence of Grand Ayatollah Ali al-Sistani, the foremost Shia spiritual leader, who had vetoed three successive schemes by the US-led occupation authorities to postpone or dilute them, frightened at what democracy might unleash. Sistani was the man who held the Iraqi ring.

In Lebanon, Rafiq al-Hariri, the towering political figure of post-civil war reconstruction, had also tried to hold the ring, usually in alliance with the Syrian overlord he eventually turned against. His assassination in February 2005 – almost certainly by the mafia of Lebanese–Syrian security services that ran the country – was a massive error of judgement. It was the detonator for a civil intifada and the completion of Syria's regional and international isolation. But the frustration that poured onto the streets of Beirut was a response to Syrian, not American, policy.

As with the Iraqi voters, moreover, the sea of demonstrators and cedar flags was being watched live on satellite television around the region. This, more than a purported USA policy *volte-face*, was what was shaking the foundations of each and every Arab tyranny. Little wonder that Egypt and Saudi Arabia, Washington's leading allies as well as the region's leading dictatorships, furiously told Bashar al-Assad to get out of Lebanon, the sooner to get Lebanese protesters off the streets.

That said, in the same way Arabs resent America not for what it is but for its policies, they *do* notice and react when those policies appear to change.

They noticed when Secretary Rice snubbed Egypt after the arrest of opposition MP Ayman Nour in early 2005, and related it to President Mubarak's surprise decision to allow multi-candidate presidential elections (but they also noticed when Mubarak got away with thumbing his nose at Washington's demand for international election monitors and coasted comfortably to victory, and when Cairo used thuggery and trickery to rob Nour of his seat in parliament and subsequently jailed him).

They took note too as France and the USA worked together through the UN Security Council to strengthen Lebanese hands against Syria (but remember all too well that when Syria sided with the USA in the first Gulf war against Iraq, and subsequently entered ultimately sterile peace negotiations with Israel, it was left unmolested to consolidate its occupation of Lebanon).

But Arabs also quite logically saw the summer of 2006 Israeli war on Hizbollah in Lebanon as a logical extension of the USA's misguided misadventure in Iraq: a loss of nerve in response to the spectre of an arc of (mostly) Shia radicalism under the leadership of Tehran, from Iran through Iraq to the borders of Israel.

This was not just Israel lashing out, as it episodically does, by allowing itself to be suckered back into asymmetric warfare by weaker but wily opponents. The American and British refusal to call time on Israel's 34-day assault on Lebanon will never be forgotten or forgiven. The attempt to destroy the Shia Islamist movement and militia seen in Washington and London (and Sunni Arab capitals such as Cairo and Riyadh) as the spearhead of Iran in the Levant, was regarded as a regrettable but necessary price to pay to roll back Tehran's perceived ambitions in the region. That is why Israel got away with razing south Lebanese and eastern Bekaa villages, with levelling Beirut's southern suburbs, and with, in short, vandalizing Shia Lebanon.

Naturally, that was not the public narrative, which was George W. Bush's freedom confronting terror, or Tony Blair's arc of extremism. Prior to Iraq, however, there was no arc, just an archipelago of disjointed radicalisms and unresolved rejectionisms.

The Anglo-American approach, with, in this case, Israeli assistance, helped join these up, adding a failing state on Israel's northern border to the failed would-be state of Palestine to its south, with the broken state of Iraq to its east.

The Lebanon fiasco was to continue and compound the failure in Iraq where, as Anthony Cordesman, the US strategist and supporter of the invasion of Iraq, observed in 2006, 'we essentially used a bull to liberate a china shop'.[3]

It was also a policy that was hopelessly inconsistent, for anyone who saw past the cant about arcs and freedom, adding further to Arab and Muslim perception of western hypocrisy. In Lebanon, a Shia Islamist militia allied to Iran that was also (then) part of an elected government, Hizbollah, had to be destroyed. In Iraq, by contrast, a Shia Islamist militia allied to Iran, the Badr brigades of the Supreme Council for the Islamic Revolution in Iraq (SCIRI), was part of an elected government that Washington supported. Inconsistencies of this sort have a habit of stewing for a bit, but then they boil over.

The 2006 summer war underlined the extent to which the debacle in Iraq, far from enabling the USA and its friends to pursue a radical new freedom agenda in the region was throwing the whole process into reverse. In the course of this book we will keep coming up against the limits of the West's appetite for (Arab) democracy. But we should immediately notice three effects from this episode.

In licensing Israel's wanton assault on Lebanon, Washington and London had correctly noted the growing alarm of their Sunni Arab allies at the way in which the Iraq adventure had immeasurably enhanced Iran's influence. There was, at the beginning of the war, even some not altogether private satisfaction in Cairo, Riyadh and Amman at the beating ostensibly being administered to Hizbollah, an organization seen as an Iranian proxy. Saudi officials warned against confusing 'legitimate resistance' with 'irresponsible adventurism', while the kingdom's Wahhabi clerics counselled the faithful against sympathy for the idolatrous Shia. But Israel's unbridled destruction of Lebanese lives and livelihoods changed all that.

Arab leaders, it soon emerged, feared the reaction of their peoples at least as much if not more than they fear Iranian influence in the Levant and the Gulf. King Abdullah of Saudi Arabia, a close US ally who in 2002 got the Beirut Arab summit unanimously to offer a comprehensive peace to Israel in return for all the Arab land it seized in the 1967 Six Day War, was saying by late July 2006, two weeks into the last Lebanon war, that 'patience cannot last for ever'. Since the patience of Arab rulers in the face of Israeli expansion has proved legendary, one can but surmise he was referring to the gathering rage of his people. In his stated view, the stakes had never been higher: 'If the peace option fails because of Israeli arrogance, there will be no other option but war'.

A second effect of the Lebanon fiasco, in which Israel, like the USA in Iraq, gave a mercilessly public exhibition of the limits of its military might as Hizbollah stood its ground, was that Tehran was able to create the perception that through its allies it could create a balance of terror – and deterrence – across the Lebanese–Israeli border. That was an important consideration should the stand-off with the West over Iranian nuclear ambitions eventually turn violent.

But the third and most obvious consideration was how Hizbollah's state-within-the-state inside Lebanon had acquired a position in which it could almost replace the state, or at least checkmate it. The month-long war dangerously aggrandized Hizbollah while lethally wounding the pro-western and – rare for the Arab world – democratically elected coalition government of Fouad Siniora.

It was not just that Sayyed Hassan Nasrallah, the charismatic Hizbollah leader, had become a hero on the Arab street, for Sunni as well as Shia, of the stature of Gamal Abdel Nasser, his incendiary tapes outselling the pop diva Nancy Ajram. Arab governments to whom Washington professed friendship could only take due note. Friends and foes in the region had to conclude that the Bush administration – already regarded as dangerous adventurers in the region – would always back Israel unconditionally, even at the risk of creating another failed state.

We shall see later how such a failure came nearer in May 2008, after the internal stalemate in Lebanon that followed the last war was broken when Hizbollah overran West Beirut in a single morning.

Before this, however, Arab public opinion was offered a marked contrast by the different way the USA and leading European countries were dealing with the Ba'athist regimes of Iraq and Syria.

The Iraq adventure was seen in the region as the epitome of US unilateralism, powered by a deadly combination of arrogance and ignorance, which has both proliferated jihadism and primed a sectarian time bomb in the heart of the Arab world. Arabs are shocked but not so much awed as disgusted and enraged by this bloody fiasco.

The Syria-in-Lebanon experience offered an important and, for a time, potentially beneficent contrast to the Iraqi carnage. Change in Lebanon, which occasionally looked as though it might reach into Syria itself, was at one stage being brought about by multilateralism rather than unilateralism (US- and French-backed UN pressure), civilian rather than military action (Lebanon's civic intifada), and was introducing in a highly visible and exemplary way democratic values of the rule of law and accountability (through the UN-mandated investigation that with its forensic relentlessness was humbling the Syrian–Lebanese security services).

The future of the Arab world still hangs to an extent on these two fascinating processes of change – the bungled and brutal, but also episodically heroic, Iraqi adventure, alongside the Syria-in-Lebanon saga, part slow-motion train wreck, part mesmerizing court drama. But a great deal also rested on how the USA managed and promoted change across the region as a whole.

The Arabs' experience of the past 60 years will not be erased by high-minded declarations. That experience tells them that, in the interests of short-term regional stability and cheap oil, the invariable US default position in the

Middle East has been to defend the status quo and shore up whatever local strongman comes to hand (Saddam Hussein, after all, was once seen by Washington as an indispensable ally). It does not help that so many people in Washington believe that too. How much Arab democracy can America stand? How much, indeed, does it really want?

Democracy is untidy anywhere, but will be very messy in the Arab world. The Iraq enterprise, for instance, has set in train tectonic shifts by empowering its Shia majority, and emboldening Shi'ism across a startled region that – since the collapse of the last Shia government, the heterodox, Cairo-based Fatimid dynasty in 1171 – was used to treating the Shia as a despised and repressed minority. As already remarked, many in Washington and the capitals of Europe have already started to reflect the panic of their Sunni Arab clients at this violent tilt in an age-old balance of power.

Already, moreover, in the most competitive Arab political arenas, in Lebanon and Palestine as well as Iraq, elections have favoured Islamist parties such as Hizbollah, Hamas and the Da'wa. In Algeria, at the beginning of the 1990s, Islamist parties were poised to win power at the ballot box and military suppression of the democratic experiment plunged the country into a vicious civil war. As the partial success of the repressed Muslim Brotherhood in Egypt's parliamentary contest in November 2005 showed, varieties of Islamist parties would certainly do well elsewhere too, if genuine elections were allowed. The contemporary tyrants of the Arab world had laid waste to the entire political spectrum, leaving their opponents no other rallying point but to fall back on the mosque. They thereby made it inevitable the revivalists would emerge as a major political force, and only enlarged the fundamentalist constituency by trying to outflank the Islamists from the right, notably through alliances with reactionary clerical establishments (as we shall see in the next chapter).

The USA fits this pattern. After the euphoria of Iraq's first elections, for instance, there was a long and deadly pause before a government was formed. US officials blamed squabbling Iraqi politicians for the loss of momentum that allowed the insurgency to regain the initiative. That was fair, but it would have been fairer to have acknowledged how panicked American go-betweens tried to prevent Shia Islamist groups from dominating the government, not to mention how they manoeuvred to try to rig the vote against them in the first place.

Or take that ringing keynote speech on democracy Condoleezza Rice delivered in Cairo. No sooner had she finished than, in answer to a question, she said the USA would not be opening lines of communication to the Muslim Brotherhood, Egypt's main organized albeit illegal opposition force.

Democratic reform, to look at it another way, will often be antithetical to short-term stability. That is usually true anywhere. In recent memory, it was true in Latin America and true in eastern Europe, true in sub-Saharan Africa and true in south-east Asia. In the Arab world – where the standing of the outgoing president of the leading democracy, George W. Bush, lies below that of one of the vilest tyrants in recent memory, Saddam Hussein; where liberals tend to be coteries who like whisky and the West but the masses incline towards men in beards; where politics is a conspiracy theory but its practitioners compulsively conspire; and where many countries are a blinding mosaic of tribal, ethnic and religious rivalries not even their leaders fully understand – that will be true in spades.

I will argue in this book that there are big risks. But I will also argue that these are, in the main, risks that have to be taken and got through – if the Arabs are ever to be able to feel they are reclaiming their destiny.

Nearly all who argue for a democracy strategy towards Arab countries do so in the belief it will bring stability to the region. It will not – at least in the short time spans most western politicians are prepared to consider. It will be highly inimical to stability for what will feel like a prolonged and bleak period of often illiberal politics, conducted in large part by a blur of men in turbans. But the West is so tainted by its conniving in tyranny and manipulating the politics of the region for its own ends, and the reaction to this has reached such an explosive pitch, that it has no other choice but to foster, or at least not actively impede, the right of Arabs to decide whatever form of their own future they wish.

It should be highly instructive that Ayman al-Zawahiri – in a videotape broadcast by al-Jazeera television in October 2005 – felt able to assert that 'the Americans will never permit any Islamic regime to assume power in the middle of the Islamic world, unless such a regime is in full collaboration with them, as is the case in Iraq'. But just imagine what it would do to the credibility of the jihadi movement if Zawahiri were proved wrong – if the West and the world did decide to respect the democratic will of the Arabs and the Muslims.

Let us be clear. Any liberalization or political opening in the Arab core of the Muslim world is bound to be heavily coloured by Islamized politics. The idiom and the practice will be strange to us all, not just the Jeffersonian triumphalists and Wilsonian idealists in Washington. Perhaps a working, if imperfect, analogy is to compare the religious nationalist identity that is likely to take hold with Islamism to the nationalisms of the nineteenth century that launched Europe's nation-states on a sort of forced march into the future. As this process gets under way, the trick will be to head off and isolate the equivalently fascist variants of the type that European nationalism incubated in the twentieth century.

15

That should, in theory, be doable. But it requires a re-examination of policy – not just pro forma freedom declarations.

This book will examine policy but look more closely at its end-users, as it were – the interaction of policy and the reality on the ground that so easily escapes the designers of policy models in metropolitan capitals. But it will also emphasize the extent to which policies, US and Arab, have to change for any advance to be possible – and morbid, self-fulfilling predictions about civilizational clash to be avoidable.

In Iraq, the USA needs to spell out credibly that it has no long-term designs on the country in terms of forward bases or oil resources (unlike its British colonial predecessors) and then conduct an orderly withdrawal. Such is the chaos it has created that this could well reignite civil war – a war that is probably in abeyance as America deploys a level of forces it cannot possibly keep up. But only the Iraqis can pull themselves out of this mess – with determined regional and multinational support for everything that pushes in the direction of pluralism and representative government. In Israel–Palestine the requirement is simple: for the USA, assisted much more assertively by Europe, to arbitrate even-handedly. Justice for the Palestinians and security for the Israelis is perfectly attainable – but only if the USA comes to realize that it is no part of its national interest or its founding ideals to enable Israel to colonize Arab land. As for the European Union, its political charade of treating as equals the Israeli occupier and the Palestinian occupied is an unsustainable hypocrisy.

The USA will also have to engage with non-violent Islamist movements, which the DSB study mentioned earlier correctly identified as the emerging centre of political gravity in the region. Those that retain a military capacity, such as Hizbollah or Hamas, will have to be drawn into the political game, using a pragmatic arsenal of carrots and sticks. We will see later how badly the attempt to isolate Hamas – victors in the 2006 elections in which they trounced Fatah, the traditional vehicle of Palestinian nationalism – has failed, at outrageous cost to the people of Gaza.

The speed with which the USA and its allies began showing the limits of their enthusiasm for democratic experiment has rightly caused scandal in Arab and Muslim countries.

In Iraq, as we saw in passing, the 2005 elections disgorged a Shia-led coalition, as expected, and buried Washington's two favourite secular Shii, Ahmad Chalabi and Iyad Allawi. The government was built instead around the Da'wa (Islamic Call) party of Nouri al-Maliki, and the Supreme Council for the Islamic Revolution in Iraq (SCIRI) of Abdelaziz al-Hakim. Yet the biggest winner, in a parliament where two thirds of MPs are Islamists of some stripe, was Moqtada al-Sadr, whose Mahdi army had launched two insurrections in 2004 against coalition forces.

Indeed, for a while it seemed that the democracy the USA was trying to encourage was mainly of benefit to its Islamist enemies and their Iranian patrons. The West recoiled in the face of the electoral advances of Hizbollah and Hamas – though there was no question about their fairness. In a strategically vital country such as Egypt, where the banned Muslim Brotherhood made an electoral breakthrough in the face of government intimidation, the West has not really pressed the democracy argument. No matter what the military-backed regime of Hosni Mubarak does, never has there been any question about the $1.3 billion annually Washington has been giving Egypt's army since it made peace with Israel 30 years ago.

Further afield, when the Turkish parliament, with a majority of the neo-Islamist Justice and Development party (AKP) that opened a new horizon for the coexistence of Islam and democracy after 2002, voted against allowing US forces to open a northern front against Iraq, Washington publicly upbraided Turkey's generals for letting its politicians off the leash. A US aid and loans package worth potentially $24 billion, in the middle of NATO ally Turkey's worst financial crisis since 1945, was promptly cancelled.

Or take Pakistan. The USA and its allies supported (and financed to the tune of $12 billion) General Pervez Musharraf's thinly-disguised dictatorship in the belief that only he (and the army, as Pakistan's last working institution) could prevent his nuclear-armed country falling to the jihadis: the spectre of mullahs with nukes. In practice, General Musharraf's marginalization of the mainstream parties gave an enormous boost to radical Islamists, while Pakistan's federation was being pulled apart by jihadism, insurgency and eth-nosectarian conflict.

Electoral evidence nevertheless suggests that, on ideas alone, Islamists struggle to get beyond 15 to 25 per cent of the popular vote (in Indonesia or Malaysia, post-civil war Algeria and Morocco, Jordan and Egypt) unless they retain the aura of resistance groups (Hamas and Hizbollah, or the Sadrists in Iraq). Their fortunes rise when the West is seen to collude with despotic regimes, especially when this appears aimed at Islam as well as freedom. That is something 'realists' should really think about.

Turkey, under the triumphantly re-elected AKP in 2007, suggests that Islamists make real and enduring breakthroughs once they jettison their radicalism, appeal to the modern mainstream and, in short, become the Muslim equivalent of Christian Democrats (the secular establishment's failed attempt to use the courts to shut down the AKP and ban its leaders in 2008 does not invalidate but underlines this). As I have argued, freedom, in the Arab and

Muslim worlds as elsewhere, is the indispensable platform for prosperity, stability and security. It is tyranny that breeds despair, rage and terror.

What the USA and Europe have to do is cease propping up Arab despots and adopt a blatant bias towards democracy and its brave defenders, rather than, say, bankrolling the Egyptian army. It is not a question of actively destabilizing the existing order (the facile formula of regime change), but recognizing the need to stimulate and serve those elements that might, eventually, replace it. Arabs and Muslims, at the very least, have the right to expect that the USA and its allies do not actively support those who deny them their freedoms. The blundering arrogance of bluntly but selectively applied military might has not only wreaked chaos across the Middle East, it has discredited the freedom agenda proclaimed by Bush (not to mention the liberal internationalism espoused by Blair). But that does not diminish the validity of the insight informing these ideas: that tyranny, connived in by the West, breeds terrorism.

The market in ideas seems not wholly unlike other markets: faced with excess, it not only corrects, it overshoots. That is happening now with the retreat into a shallow and shabby 'realism' that is elbowing aside the democratic aspirations of the Arabs and locking them back into Arab exceptionalism. That, quite simply, will not work.

Certainly, no change in policy means the short-term survival of tyranny and the onward march of the jihadis. That would be a catastrophe. The jihadis are already close to entering the mainstream of Muslim opinion and society. As currently configured, western policy is their most reliable ally. As I have already suggested – and the peremptory title of this book deliberately highlights – we really do not have that much time; what we are starting to live through is not some periodic up-and-down in relations between West and East. Unless policy changes, we can expect at least one generation of conflict, more probably several, between the western and Muslim worlds. A neo-medieval pall will descend upon Arab and Muslim countries – and the shared values of Islam and the West will wither into dust.

II

The Despot in his Labyrinth

*U*neasy Lies the Head was the perhaps inevitable title of the autobiography of the late King Hussein of Jordan. Hussein was not just the West's favourite benign Arab despot. He was the improbable survivor of innumerable plots, coups and uprisings, of three Arab–Israeli wars, two Gulf wars and a civil war with the Palestinians, as well as around a dozen assassination attempts in the 46 years he wore the heavy crown of his improbable desert kingdom.

That kingdom, created by the British as a regional buffer state, was never less than buffeted by predatory neighbours like Israel, Iraq and Saudi Arabia, just as the king himself was vigorously challenged by Arab nationalist rivals such as Gamal Abdel Nasser of Egypt, Hafez al-Assad of Syria, or Yassir Arafat of the Palestine Liberation Organization (PLO).

The Hashemite monarch, descended from the family of the Prophet Mohammed and the Sharifs of Mecca who launched the Arab Revolt against the Ottoman empire, always exuded total confidence in his legitimacy. Yet, although he was the most open of Arab autocrats, what he relied on to stay in power was the military and the Mukhabarat, his ubiquitous secret police. No less than in any other Arab state, the army was the pivotal institution for this elegant and charming authoritarian.

To underline this essential truth is not necessarily to disparage King Hussein's often liberal instincts. Nor is it to ignore the fact that survival in Middle Eastern politics required skills he possessed in abundance: the level head and steely nerves of a tightrope walker; the political colours of a chameleon; the calculated generosity of a tribal patriarch; but also the calibrated ruthlessness of an army commander.

What it reveals is that even a leader willing to experiment with change, a regal populist who could utter the word 'democracy' with a more or less straight face, a monarch who was once prepared to share (a bit of his) power with Islamists, was in the end no different from his peers.

On his deathbed, the king cast aside his confidant and crown prince of 34 years, his bookish and amiable brother Hassan, and instead named as his successor his son Abdullah, the young Sandhurst-trained commander of Jordan's special forces, a general who stood at the confluence of the army and the intelligence services. In spite of the cloud of almost Shakespearian dynastic intrigue that enveloped the palace during the king's last illness, in which Hussein's and Hassan's wives worked busily to press the rival claims of their teenage sons, princes Hamza and Rashid, it was the depressing reality of Arab politics that ultimately tipped the balance.[1]

In an angry letter – unusually made public – King Hussein accused his brother of using his position as Regent to meddle in the army. The patrician, English public school and Oxford-educated Prince Hassan had had as little contact with the army as he had with ordinary Jordanians frustrated at the failure of an unpopular peace with Israel to deliver the better living standards the king had foolishly promised.

Hussein assuredly saw his new heir, politically untested but a blooded major-general, as a safer pilot through the choppy regional waters that surely lay ahead.

If the monarchy is Jordan's defining institution, its continuing existence rests on the army. Tribal in composition, the army is made up of East Bank, or native, Jordanians in a country where perhaps as much as two thirds of the population is originally Palestinian, pushed across from the other bank of the River Jordan, by the creation of Israel in 1948 and Israel's conquest of the West Bank and east Jerusalem in 1967. This army of Bedouin loyalists is the bedrock of Hashemite rule.

It had its origins in the Arab Legion (*al-Jaish al-Arabi*), created, financed and commanded by the British in 1920 to defend the then emirate of Transjordan against Wahhabi marauders from the kingdom of Saudi Arabia then being forged in a 30-year-long jihad to its south. It became the tool for the young King Hussein, who ascended the throne aged 17, to consolidate his shaky hold on Jordan.

But it was only when Hussein in 1956 summoned the strength to Arabize the Arab Legion, responding to simmering nationalist resentment in its junior officer corps by firing its legendary commander, John Bagot Glubb (Glubb Pasha) and his British generals, that the king started to secure his position. 'Hussein's broad political reason for dismissing Glubb stemmed from his fear that if he did not place himself at the head of the nationalist movement, he would be over-whelmed by it', writes Avi Shlaim in his brilliant recent biography of the king: 'The Arab Legion was the single strongest national institution in Jordan, yet it was led by senior officers who could not ignore their loyalty to Britain.'[2]

From that audacious strike – at the age of 21 – against the residual British empire, to his deathbed decree pushing aside his brother Hassan from the throne, such coups would be a hallmark of Hussein's rule, a dexterous author-itarianism sustained ultimately by his army.

Although visibly angered by the palace intrigue in Amman while he was undergoing treatment in the USA for cancer, King Hussein's judgement on the succession was clinical. He had placed a strategic bet on a regional peace in which Jordan, as part of a dynamic sub-region with Israel and the Palestinians, would become a prosperous, middle-income economy. The bet went sour, along with the peace process, after the 1995 assassination of Israeli premier and peace architect Yitzhak Rabin by a Jewish religious zealot, the subsequent election of Benjamin Netanyahu at the head of an irredentist Israeli govern-ment, and overwhelming domestic opposition to Jordan's own 1994 peace treaty with Israel.

Among the most disenchanted with the treaty were the native Jordanians, rather than the Palestinian majority usually regarded as the Hashemites' main domestic security challenge. Prince Abdullah, who as the head of his elite forces suppressed bread riots across the loyalist south of the country in 1996, could be expected to grasp this in a way the thoughtful and loquacious Prince Hassan might not.

As one historian of Jordan has written, from early on King Hussein 'real-ized the nature of his assets and liabilities' and he 'always made a point of operating within his limits'.[3]

In 1989, Hussein had held what were – apart from a brief interlude in 1962–3 – the first elections to Jordan's parliament since 1957, when all sem-blance of democracy had been discarded as the young king and his Bedouin army moved to crush Nasserist agitation and a series of attempts to overthrow him. He was taking a carefully calculated risk.

The victors of this experiment in guided democracy were the Islamists, grouped mostly within the Jordanian chapter of the pan-Islamic Muslim Brotherhood (al-Ikhwan al-Muslimeen), later given formal political identity as the Islamic Action Front (IAF). With 34 out of 80 seats, the Islamists were the largest, and only ideologically cohesive, bloc. In 1990–1, the king went further and brought four Muslim Brothers into the cabinet.

But, first, he bound their leadership into a constitutional consensus through a National Charter. This set out the rules of the managed democracy game. It also established Islam as but one fount of political legitimacy, alongside the parallel claims of Jordanian patriotism, Arab nationalism and universal values.[4]

This Jordanian National Charter was one of the most suggestive political documents to have emerged in the modern Arab world. It bucked the trend in the region.

Syria, for instance, savagely suppressed an uprising by the Brotherhood, razing the city of Hama in 1982 and killing an estimated 20,000 people. Egypt, where the Brotherhood was founded in 1928, would shortly embark on the suppression of a radical Islamist insurgency, which it would use as cover for a further clampdown on the illegal Brothers. Jordan, by contrast, appeared to be saying that mainstream Islamists were a force that had to be addressed, and that they could be co-opted and contained within a democratic framework.

King Hussein, however, always kept his rather overstated democratic ambition firmly anchored to the tribal and military bedrock of his rule. To begin with, his cultivation of the Brotherhood dated from the 1950s and his need for a counterforce to the Nasserist left. While all political activity was suspended from 1957, the Brothers were afforded legal status just short of a party, giving them an informal political monopoly for nearly three decades. The traditional leadership of the Brotherhood in Jordan, moreover, came from the families of East Bank notables.

In 1990–1, furthermore, Jordan faced international and regional isolation. The king took a strategic and domestically popular decision to refuse support for the US-led and Arab-backed coalition to evict Saddam Hussein from Kuwait. But it came at a high price. Hussein was using the Brothers to strengthen the resilience of the system at a time it was about to face great stress.

The minute the Brothers and the IAF began to develop an agenda independently from the Palace, however, King Hussein simply changed the rules of the game, enacting new electoral laws to guarantee future majorities in parliament of Bedouin loyalists and tribal grandees. As the peace with Israel grew ever more unpopular, moreover, so the king rolled back his democratic reforms, limiting change to annual but largely meaningless changes of government (he ran through 56 prime ministers in 46 years).

The importance of this episode amply transcends Jordan. King Hussein's behaviour, whether caused by a failure of nerve or an unwillingness to countenance any real power-sharing, meant an opportunity was lost to develop new forms of legitimacy – democratic legitimacy – by one of the few Arab leaders who had any reserves of this precious political commodity left.

For all that King Hussein offered Jordan's stop–start political experiments as a model for his fellow Arab rulers, they could see well enough what he was up to. As it turned out, he was playing pretty much the same game as markedly less benign despots in the region.

* * * * *

We saw in the preceding chapter that the three overarching features that define Arab political regimes are that: they are autocracies; they are kept in power by the military and the Mukhabarat; and their leaders face a crisis of legitimacy. We have just seen how even a leader such as King Hussein, although ostensibly endowed with politico-religious legitimacy, could not or would not entrust his hold on power to that alone, much less to any democratic lottery, preferring the surer bet of his army. For this crisis of legitimacy to a greater or lesser extent encompasses all Arab rulers and is at the centre of the drama of the region. It is ideological, political and religious.

Ideologically, a vacuum was left by the failure of creeds such as pan-Arab nationalism (under Nasser in Egypt and the Ba'ath parties in Syria and Iraq or, for example, the FLN in Algeria) and 'Arab Socialism' (state capitalism with socialist verbiage and some land reform) to deliver either economic development or Arab rights in Palestine.

Pan-Arab nationalism, it is worth pausing to recall, won a position of political pre-eminence in the Arab world in the roughly three decades following the Second World War to the 1967 Arab–Israeli war. Many of its theorists and some of its leaders – such as Michel Aflaq, the Syrian founder of the Ba'ath (Resurrection) party – were Christians, educated in missionary schools and western universities. Two prominent PLO leaders, George Habash and Nayef Hawatmeh, were Christians. So, too, was George Antonius, author of the seminal *The Arab Awakening* in 1938. The pan-Arab creed was, for a time, seen in a West fighting the Cold War as a useful counterweight to the influence of communism, which had real weight in Iraq, especially among the Shia, and intermittent presence in Syria, Egypt and, to a lesser extent, Jordan, which under King Hussein saw advantage in magnifying its importance as a regional threat. By the same token, pan-Arabism was regarded by Islamic revivalists as an alien attempt, copied from the western Enlightenment and European nation-state nationalism of the nineteenth century, to break the bonds of Islam; the Islamist Da'wa in Iraq, for example, was partly conceived as a response to communism, partly as a riposte to secular, republican nationalism. The pan-Arab 'revolutions' in Egypt, Syria and Iraq – in reality coups d'état accompanied by some directed social upheaval – were nevertheless sufficient to rid these countries of their elites and stifle the normal emergence of a national bourgeoisie and its normal historic accompaniment, bourgeois democracy. Their main replacement would become the social escalator of the army.

These were the new, supposedly indigenous, ideologies and their visionary leaders that were supposed to lift the Arabs once and for all out of colonial rule, enabling them to seize their modern destiny. They reached their high watermark with the Suez crisis of 1956, when Britain and France, in a secret pact with Israel, invaded Egypt following Nasser's nationalization of the Suez Canal, but were forced to withdraw by uncompromising US pressure. It seemed for a moment that a self-determining, modern and republican nationalism, shaking off the European colonial intrusion into the region and in alignment if not alliance with the American republic, had got a firm grip on the Arabs' future. Ten years of bombast and improvisation later, as the Arab leaders clashed with each other, incited their peoples to fever pitch and bobbed on the tides of the Cold War between the West and the Soviet Union, the catastrophic defeat of the 1967 Six Day War with Israel torched the pan-Arab edifice. Pan-Arabism, masking national agendas and the will to power of entrenched new elites, turned out to be a cruel deception.[5]

The Arabs, cursed as much as blessed with so much of the world's oil reserves, have been persistently vulnerable to outside intervention – as well as serial defeats at the hands of the Israelis – against which their economic and political backwardness has offered little defence. The Arab League has failed to create cohesion, foster a constructive and confident identity or give Arabs a respected voice in world affairs. There is, moreover, no leader with the moral authority to speak for the Arabs. The grotesque spectacle of Saddam Hussein, masquerading as the Sword of the Arabs throughout the 1980s and 1990s, who manufactured a lineage from the Prophet and proclaimed himself heir to the conquerors of Jerusalem, Saladin and Nebuchadnezzar, showed how profound was this vacuum, this political nothingness.

Initially, it looked as though the feudal monarchies of the Gulf, and of Jordan and Morocco, would be the beneficiaries of the hollowness of the Nassers and Saddams. But the longer-term winners could prove to be the Islamic revivalists who stepped into this vacuum, picking up the fallen banners of nationalism and portraying their own amorphous ideology as a liberation theology.

But a paradox at the heart of the legitimacy crisis is that the Islamists were helped in this by the very Arab regimes that remorselessly suppressed them. Why? Because Arab autocrats, indulged by the West, mostly failed to build the institutions that sustain successful modern societies and include their citizens. They thereby lent credit to the simplistic siren-call of the fundamentalists, typified by the Brotherhood's slogan that 'Islam is the Solution'. So sweeping, moreover, was their repression of all opposition across the political spectrum that they left their opponents only the mosque as a refuge and a rallying point. Egypt, for instance, was able successfully to crush an Islamist insurgency during the 1990s, but, by the middle of that decade, there had emerged an estimated 40,000 unlicensed mosques in the country.[6]

While it is true that, in an era of fast digital and satellite communications, no Arab ruler can ignore popular sentiment, it is no less true that the way in which Arab regimes have dammed up the political mainstream has given force to the violent tributaries, channelled through mosques, that have given the Islamists a monopoly on dissent. As one Bahraini minister put it, referring to Muslim prayer times: 'No other party has the opportunity to get in touch with the masses, five times a day, every day of the year.'[7]

Second, Arab autocrats also helped politico-religious extremism through opportunist alliances with Islamists – a problem endemic across the wider Middle East for a good half century.

In the 1970s, Anwar Sadat, assassinated by Islamists from his own army in 1981 and regarded by the West and Israel as the gold standard of Arab moderation, used the Islamists – including the embryonic Gama'a al-Islamiyya that went on to launch the 1990s insurgency – to eradicate the left and the Nasserists on Egypt's campuses. King Hussein, we have already seen, co-opted the Muslim Brothers as early as the 1950s as a counter to the Nasserists. In the 1980s, Israel, which has acquired many of the political habits of its Arab neighbours, licensed the Brotherhood in the West Bank and Gaza in order to queer the pitch for the PLO (the Palestinian Brothers, of course, would go on to create Hamas, Israel's most implacable enemy).[8]

The Saudi royal family, which has ruthlessly crushed any Islamist (or other) challenge to its monopoly of power, has for nearly 40 years sought to build influence abroad and legitimacy at home by financing Wahhabi mosques and foundations; just during the reign of King Fahd, Riyadh claims to have established 1,359 mosques abroad, along with 202 colleges, 210 Islamic centres and more than 2,000 schools.

The Saudis also supported Islamist groups and causes (including the Brotherhood) throughout the Muslim world and the West. Indeed, the attack on the great mosque at Mecca in 1979 – leading to a bloody siege that rocked the kingdom and the al-Saud – was carried out by religious extremists influenced by the Brotherhood.[9]

Further afield, the government of Tansu Ciller, darling of the West when she was prime minister of a confident, secular Turkey at the beginning of the 1990s, licensed Islamist paramilitaries in the bitter struggle against Kurdish separatists in the country's south-east – allies of convenience that would later bite back with al-Qaeda style bombings in Istanbul in November 2003.

In Pakistan, army commanders, even the liberals among them, have invested in jihadism for compelling tactical reasons. Islamist militants, seldom numbering more than a few thousand and pressing for Kashmiri self-determination, have managed to tie down an Indian army force about 500,000-strong in the Valley of Kashmir since Pakistan's conventional forces were last bested by India on the battlefield. To the west, in Afghanistan and along Pakistan's lawless frontier, the same jihadi networks led to the Taliban in Afghanistan – a territory many Pakistani generals believe they need for 'strategic depth'.

But the most damaging instance of flirting with fundamentalism was, of course, the US backing and arming, with Saudi financing and recruitment of volunteers, and Pakistani logistics and training, of the Jihad against the Soviet Union in 1979–89. In pursuit of the higher goals of the twentieth century's Great Game, Washington chased its Cold War aims cloaked in the holy war zeal of the Mujahideen. Out of that adventure came the tens of thousands of battle-hardened 'Arab Afghan' volunteers – many recruited under indulgent western eyes by Osama bin Laden – and now known to the world as al-Qaeda, an itinerant international of holy warriors for which the USA can claim much credit.[10]

That, too, is not an altogether new story. When Britain and the USA carried out their successful coup against the nationalist government of Mohammed Mossadegh in Iran in 1953 and reinstalled the Shah, the Central Intelligence Agency induced several ayatollahs from the holy city of Qom to endorse their endeavour as a jihad against Godless communism. The rest is history. After the eventual triumph of the ayatollahs in Tehran in 1979, the West and its Arab allies turned to that strongest of strongmen, Saddam Hussein, backing and financing him in Iraq's 1980–8 war against Iran. The emboldened Saddam went on to invade Kuwait and threaten Saudi Arabia.

The path of opportunism in the Middle East has not always been a fortunate one.

But perhaps just as insidious in the Arab social and political context is another form of opportunism by the region's rulers. Bending with the wind, they have made customary, but rarely credible, public displays of piety. The proliferation of images of President Hosni Mubarak of Egypt and his entourage, or King Abdullah of Jordan and his family, on pilgrimage in Mecca, for example, have set a new norm for official religious ostentation. Islamically correct dress and grooming has become the rule and Islamist televangelists have become the celebrities. Gone are the days when Mubarak could order the demolition of a minaret because it obscured a view of the great pyramids at Giza. Pharaoh has had to learn to defer to the Grand Sheikh of Al-Azhar. For it is upon such clerics that Arab rulers now rely to outflank the Islamists – from the right.

The picture is not uniform. The current Grand Sheikh of Al-Azhar, the former Grand Mufti Mohammed Sayyed Tantawi, came out forcibly against female circumcision, a pre-Islamic, African custom of genital mutilation; backed a (largely ignored) government ban on the veil in girls' primary schools; and wrote a treatise demonstrating that Islam since its inception has supported family planning.

Yet the hierarchy of the millennium-old Azhar university – once a beacon of tolerance in the region – not to mention the entrenched Wahhabi clerical establishment in Saudi Arabia, frequently put a more conservative spin on the Quran than the fundamentalists in their religious edicts, banning books and films, outlawing contact with non-believers, and prescribing and proscribing the tiniest details of social behaviour, particularly between the sexes.

In their increasingly desperate search for a thin veil of legitimacy, many Arab rulers are therefore enlarging the constituency of some of the most obscurantist and obtuse strains of Islamism. At the very least this abets a creeping theocracy and stifles the emergence of a confident civil society, which in many Arab countries is in headlong retreat. At worst, this encourages jihadism.

* * * * *

A torrent of commentary in the wake of the 11 September 2001 attacks on New York and Washington has tended to argue – or sometimes merely assume – that militant Islamism is rooted in economic despair and deprivation. Certainly, until 9/11, that was the assumption that underlay much official US thinking on the phenomenon. The antidote, this near-axiom went, was 'let's build the middle classes and then we'll have some liberals to liberalize with'.[11]

But it is the politics, more even than the economics of the Arab world, that need to be addressed.

True, there are huge socio-economic problems to be confronted. Demographically, for instance, the Arab countries face a destabilizing 'youth bulge' – broadly, of having between half and two thirds of the population under the age of 25, with little or no prospect of a meaningful or dignified job. World Bank economists estimated in 2003 that the Arab economies needed to create about 100 million new jobs by 2020 just to absorb newcomers into the labour force.

Of course the Arab countries need better economic management and more transparent governance. Of course they desperately need modern infrastructure. Of course they need more investment in job-creating activities. And of course they need an overhaul of education and training to emphasize critical, independent thinking and problem-solving skills. Nevertheless, the idea that getting the economics right will cause everything else to fall into place is crudely determinist, when not downright evasive.

At one level, organizations such as al-Qaeda, its Egyptian ally, Jihad, or the mainstream Muslim Brotherhood, are led by, and largely made up of, middle-class, sometimes wealthy individuals. Many of the 9/11 hijackers came from similarly privileged backgrounds, while some recent studies of suicide bombers have highlighted their generally high average level of education. It is misleading to see the Islamists simply as the Wretched of the Earth, a problem to be resolved by a clever economic development strategy.

But the 'economics first' argument is flawed in many other respects. Not only does it provide Arab autocrats with the perfect alibi for putting off political liberalization indefinitely, but, as we shall see, there is little evidence economic reform can succeed in states run by self-perpetuating national security establishments.

Above all, however, the argument is flawed and misleading because the high-octane fuel firing Islamist fury is a volatile compound of humiliation and political despair. Political despair about probably five main things:

- Despair at how Islam, once the pre-eminent civilization and long a world power and creator of empires, has lost out to the West.
- Despair at Europe's colonial legacy, which fragmented the Arab world into often artificial states (with Palestine occupied by what many ordinary Arabs as well as Islamists tend to see as modern Crusaders).
- Despair at the failure of pan-Arab nationalists to match their intoxicating rhetoric with achievement and advance (it is easy now to forget how Nasser, through the Voice of the Arabs radio station in Cairo, once mesmerized the Arab world).
- Despair at US and western support for tyrannical Arab rulers, a particular betrayal for those who had admired the culture and political accomplishments of Britain, France and America.
- Despair at the double standard of Washington's seemingly indiscriminate and invariably unconditional support for Israel (which has much greater weight than Europe's drivelling evasions).

If the Israel–US dimension is here mentioned last, that is not because it is least. For Arabs who over the past decade have watched daily on satellite television the Israeli siege of Palestinian towns, villages and refugee camps, the disproportionate toll of civilians and children killed by Israel's indiscriminate use of heavy weapons, the daily demolitions of Palestinian homes, or the secular erosion of the Palestinian land mass by illegal Jewish settlements, by-pass roads for the settlers, so-called security walls and buffer zones, or even the actual erosion of Palestinian orchards and farmland by the uprooting of crops and trees and the removal of topsoil, this wound bleeds. US administrations appear to pour salt on it, by demanding an end to Palestinian violence rather than to the Israeli occupation that prompts it.

But the question is to what extent the other grievances would exist independently if – by some miracle of statesmanship – the Israeli–Palestinian conflict were resolved. That is the question the Arabs must ask themselves. That is the question any serious policy towards the wider Middle East must address.

It is beyond doubt, revealed in poll after poll, that an honest, even-handed campaign by the USA and its allies to resolve that conflict in a way that offered justice to the Palestinians as well as security to the Israelis would begin to restore America's reputation in the Arab and Muslim worlds. And that is something that is within their power to do.

Equally, there is no doubt that the spur to resistance by Islamist groups such as Hamas in the West Bank and Gaza and Hizbollah in Lebanon was Israel's occupation of Arab land. 'When we entered Lebanon', said the former Israeli prime minister Ehud Barak, 'there was no Hizbollah'. Yitzhak Rabin, the slain former soldier–premier, made the same point, lamenting how the 1982 invasion of Lebanon 'let the genie out of the bottle'. While the constituents of Hamas were already present in Islamist social and religious institutions, it did not come into being until the 1987 explosion of Palestinian anger after 20 years of Israeli occupation of the West Bank, Arab east Jerusalem and the Gaza Strip – an intifada neither it nor, much less, Fatah anticipated. Israel was the actor; they were just reacting. Contact between (Sunni) Hamas and (Shia) Hizbollah, moreover, now painted by Israeli hindsight as part of an Iranian grand design, arose from Israel's deportation in late 1992 of 400 intifada activists to the Lebanese border, which became, one Israeli official ruefully recalled, 'Hizbollah University'.

But Osama bin Laden and his kind, described by some Arab commentators as 'universal Islamists', have and always have had a power agenda quite separate to the Palestinian cause.

For so long as the jihadis can rely on the USA to stand by its dictatorial Arab allies, such as the House of Saud and President Mubarak, and to make strategic blunders like the invasion of Iraq, the evidence suggests they are not whistling in the wind. The bin Laden franchise's monstrous bet that it can foment a clash of civilizations may be evil but it is not wholly mad.

Shortly after 9/11, when sympathy for America was at its peak, the Gallup organization carried out an unprecedented poll of some 10,000 people in nine Muslim countries, five of them Arab. It found two out of three people to be hostile to the USA, a ratio that rose to four out of five in allied Saudi Arabia and Egypt. Since then, as remarked in the last chapter, American support in these countries has either become an underground movement or is almost statistically undetectable.

The nature of Arab autocracy plays its part in this.

So intolerant of challenge are the autocrats that criticism and civility have been divorced. Their official newspapers (rarely is there another kind) spew out anti-western diatribes, as do the mosques, the mass media that reach furthest in their increasingly pious societies. In the same way that these rulers seek a veneer of legitimacy from reactionary clerical establishments, they wear a fig leaf of independence through the faux-critiques of their papers; a tactic, moreover, useful as an alternative to any meaningful democratic expression and as a populist decoy and controlled letting-off-of-steam.

To take one example at random, the editor of Al Ahram of Cairo accused the US Air Force of dropping genetically treated food supplies to poison Afghans during the winter of 2001–2 and the war in Afghanistan. Al Ahram is the principal government newspaper of the main US ally in the region. Its editor is a confidant and appointee of President Hosni Mubarak. Neither the government nor the newspaper had any real quarrel with the Afghanistan war itself, since the country had become an emirate of the perpetrators of not only 9/11 but the 1995 attempted assassination of Mubarak in Addis Ababa.

Another form of licensing non-democratic criticism and opening ostensibly safe channels for popular disgruntlement is to encourage official newspapers and broadcasters to attack Israel. A lot of this is perfectly legitimate criticism of Israel's militarist tactics and occupation of Arab land, which would emerge normally in any halfway democratic environment. But some of it is virulent anti-semitism, which few Arab leaders publicly condone but even fewer publicly condemn.[12]

Real though it is, the unresolved conflict with Israel is one of the many crutches Arab autocrats lean on to justify their illegitimate and lawless behaviour. It is perhaps too much to expect, in the rough and tumble of Middle East politics, that any Arab ruler should disinterestedly pursue the legitimate rights of the Palestinians rather than trade on those rights for his own advantage. Equally, it is difficult to escape the conclusion that a stalemate in the Israeli–Palestinian conflict suits many of them. Even though no Arab country any longer contemplates confrontation with Israel, the unresolved nature of this conflict guarantees for their rulers a system of permanent alert. This is militarily bogus but it justifies fierce political control. It is a tattered pan-Arabism useful to blackmail opponents and impugn critics as traitors – the sort of patriotism Samuel Johnson must have been thinking of when he described it as the last refuge of a scoundrel.[13]

Should we assume that these autocrats know, at some level of their consciousness, that they lack legitimacy? And that it is this knowledge, and fear, that leads them constantly to manipulate and engineer opinion? Is that why Arab rulers pathologically manufacture near unanimity at the polls – plebiscites and parliamentary majorities typically of 95 to 99 per cent – a sort of homage that vice pays to virtue?

* * * * *

In the Arab national security state, the essential requirement from the populace is quiescence. Unlike an ideologically driven fascist or communist state, the Arab autocracy – with the singular exception of Saudi Arabia which we will examine in Chapter V – makes little demand on the conscience of the ordinary citizen, beyond insisting that he or she stay out of the political way. Appearances, undoubtedly, can suggest the contrary. A political culture corroded by hyperbole, conducted in a language given to over-statement, punctuated by choreographed spectacles of breast-beating frenzy in support of the Leader, with majorities at the ballot box worthy of Enver Hoxha's Albania, allied to the long-winded sycophancy of courtly address: obviously all this can be easily misread as a form of totalitarianism. But, as ever in the Arab world, form should not be confused with substance. What Arab rulers require, even in politically meaningless plebiscites of unanimity, is the demonstration of administrative and military control. What you believe is your affair, so long as you don't rock the boat.

Just as important, unlike more familiar models of military rule – the garrison states of Central and South America in the 1970s and 1980s, for example – it is the intelligence services rather than the regular army that rule the roost.

This has become particularly evident in countries such as Jordan and Syria, where the young King Abdullah and his ostensibly republican counterpart, Bashar al-Assad, took over from their fathers amid exaggerated hopes of

31

liberalization and change. In both countries political controls have tightened. The intelligence services call the shots. But that is no less true in older and more practised Arab regimes. It is just sometimes less visible. In all these systems, one veteran student of Arab autocracy observes: 'The Mukhabarat mediates the information flow between ruler and ruled, the better to manipulate both.'

This was true even in Egypt, the country in which both Arabs and westerners had placed great hope for reform. The best that can be said of Egypt is that its 5,000-year tradition of highly centralized and authoritarian rule, based in the past half-century on an all-powerful presidency underpinned by the army and Mukhabarat, has shown some signs of mutation but none of renewal. The regime led by President Hosni Mubarak, who entered his fifth six-year term at the end of 2005, brooks no challenge to its prerogatives.

In 2001 and again in 2002, to take but one example, Egypt jailed the Egyptian–American liberal academic, Saadeddin Ibrahim. He was charged with illegally receiving European Union money for his Ibn Khaldun think tank and democratic advocacy centre – this from a government in receipt throughout Mubarak's rule of an average annual $3 billion of western aid, including $1.3 billion a year for the army from the USA. His real crimes, however, were to examine the regime's use of electoral fraud, to draw attention to the precarious position of minority Coptic Christians and, worst of all, to suggest Mubarak was preparing the ground for his son Gamal to succeed him as president.

Is Egypt, therefore, ultimately so very different from Ba'athist Syria, where two MPs were at that time on trial for the crime of 'trying to change the constitution' – which had just been changed to accommodate Bashar, technically ineligible for the presidency because of his youth?

All this is fairly standard stuff in the Arab political arena. But it is more telling to look at examples that abound in the mundane daily workings of an Arab administration. Look carefully, for instance, at Egypt's sincere and theoretically credible attempts to attract investment over the past decade, to find a formula for high, export-led growth, and you will see why the notion that economic reform unlocks political reform – so safe and comforting to western and Arab governments alike – is bogus in the Arab context.

A centrepiece of Egypt's effort to open up the economy, carefully crafted by gifted technocrats and lawyers over 18 months, yielded what was ostensibly a signal breakthrough, a Eureka moment in the political economy of the region. Egypt's labyrinthine corporate law, in which nothing seemed to have been repealed since Napoleon appeared at the mouth of the Nile in 1798, was amended and streamlined to make registration of a new enterprise automatic, unless the newly configured companies' authority objected within ten days, and on a specified list of grounds. The intent was to reverse the burden of proof that the investor was *bona fide*, and thereby unlock new sources of wealth creation.

The changes, personally ordered by President Mubarak, were never implemented. How could they be? They were a head-on challenge to the discretionary power of the Mukhabarat that kept Mubarak in power. From their point of view, the obvious merits of the reforms were irrelevant. As an author of the changes remarked at the time: 'With anything you try to reform, there is a hidden security element. The security obsession is not really about catching anyone, but about maintaining the power of the security people. That is the reality'.[14]

To repeat: the 'economics first' path of reform is a blind alley. Political reform is the key to all real reform in the Arab world. Put another way, it is not only the obscurantist clerics of al-Azhar to whom Pharaoh must defer; the modern Arab despot is the prisoner of his praetorians.

Mubarak, it should be obvious, is no fool. He does not survive at the top of his pyramid of power by accident. But like most despots in his position, he is dependent for real world information on power structures that are supposed to be dependent upon him. He would certainly know what is going on in the officers' mess, what leading businessmen want, which tribe or clan is on top in which village, what clerics need to be appeased, how much it will cost to co-opt this or that opposition voice in parliament or the press, or what American presidents want to hear from him. But he will rarely know what information is being concealed by his security services, and he will not always discern if he is being fed information by factions seeking a specific outcome. The great Abbasid Caliph, Harun al-Rashid, was reputed to go about eighth century Baghdad in disguise to discover the preoccupations of his subjects. The modern Pharaoh Mubarak spends much of his time relaxing with comrades from his days as commander of Egypt's Air Force or in the Sinai resort of Sharm al-Sheikh, large swathes of which his family has contrived to own.

Let us look at some examples. At one level, a despotism such as Egypt's is too clunkingly inefficient to do the modern equivalent of making the trains run on time. Recent evidence of this includes: apartment blocks put up by crooked builders collapsing; ferries capsizing and airliners crashing; parliament (the Majlis as-Shura or upper house) burning down; rockslides set off by wildcat development burying slum dwellings. Rarely is anyone ever held accountable for the neo-pharaonic plagues Egyptians have to endure. But the screened despotism of the modern pharaoh regularly makes strategic errors too.

In 1994, as the Islamist insurgency in Egypt started to make social and political headway, *Reuters* news agency published a number of reports demonstrating that the vast Cairo slum of Imbaba had become, in effect, a state-within-the-state for the Gama'a al-Islamiyya. No such information was allowed to reach Mubarak until, on a flight back from a series of state visits in the Far East, a concerned adviser pressed copies of the reports into the president's hands. Suddenly, Mubarak jumped up, strode back towards his intelligence chiefs in the plane, waved the reports at them and shouted: 'Do we have this? Is there such a thing?'

Suffice to say that, within days, a force of nearly 25,000 Egyptian troops stormed Imbaba – one side of which faced the Nile – from its three other sides. Initially they entered and met no resistance. But then, once drawn into a labyrinth of narrow streets and alleys, they were pinned down and faced with eight days of fierce, house-to-house fighting. Yes, we did have this, but it took a fluke for Pharaoh to find out.[15]

Reform of Egypt's public sector-dominated and *rentier* economy began in good measure because modernizers around Youssef Boutros Ghali, who would later become the strategist of reform, insinuated small pieces of simple but actionable information into the president's presence. Thus, at the end of 1995, Mubarak stormed into a cabinet meeting, waving more bits of paper, demanding to know why foreign investors had put $40 billion into Indonesia that year – 100 times more than the paltry $400 million Egypt had received in foreign direct investment.

These figures were, so to speak, rounded up, making the point enormously simple to grasp. But they took square aim at Mubarak's *amour propre*. A change of government ensued. The new administration, headed by prime minister Kamal el-Ganzouri, was told by Mubarak to replace dependence on foreign aid and remittances from Egyptians working abroad with foreign investment and foreign exchange earned from exports. 'It is very hard to be in my position and to know that last year we got foreign investment of $400m while in Indonesia – I don't think they have more potential than Egypt – they got $40bn', Ganzouri recited word-perfectly in an interview soon after.[16]

Economic reform did, for a while, make some headway. Limited privatization seeded a sharp rise in domestic private investment. Per capita income rose – almost doubling in five years to nearly $1,500 – but so did wealth disparity and conspicuous consumption while, as the century ended, the proportion of Egyptians living below the poverty line had actually increased from 39 per cent in 1980 to 43 per cent. That wealth gap has now widened further, with international fuel and food price rises raising the spectre of real hunger by 2008.

Closer examination of policy, moreover, bore out the picture of mutation rather than change. Bureaucracies everywhere resist change. Egypt was no different. For nearly half a century, the role of the vast, investment-starved public sector and huge, pitifully paid civil service had been to keep prices low, provide jobs for life, and substitute for imports. Any change from this essentially social function would be wrenching, with the attendant risk of political instability. The violent 1977 bread riots in Egypt – rather like the bread riots in Jordan in 1996 mentioned earlier – had scarred the psyche of the regime. But there was something deeper operating here. Economic reform did not change the nature of power in Egypt, much less open a path towards democratic change as some of its proponents claimed. But it did provide a good X-ray of power.

Among the problems Egypt's reformers debated, for example, was whether the country was capable of producing entrepreneurs from the class of *rentiers* and traders which until then had made a profitable living off the distortions within the system (as indeed had the quiet number of multinationals inside Egypt, very much part of this cosy insider's game). Youssef Boutros Ghali, for instance, took the view that most could not make the transition to open competition and 'should sit back and finance those who can'.[17]

That view, however, assumed a clear political path forward. There would, of course, be nothing of the kind. Western-educated reformers like Boutros Ghali were trying hard to get change. But some of them misunderstood the nature of the regime and were confusing changing the economy with reshuffling the elites.

A litmus test came when the regime balked at selling the four big commercial banks and the state insurance companies. Wariness about eventual competition from outsiders was part of it. But mostly the problem was that state banks lent money on the basis of political connections rather than project and credit analysis, and to the regime's trading and franchise group allies that were incapable of absorbing it productively. The regime, rather than confront the problem of the insiders' game, decided to make more people insiders.

Businessmen made newly assertive by reform and international attention were brought into the regime's policy-making councils. No fewer than 45 businessmen were returned as MPs in the massively rigged 1995 elections, which gave the National Democratic Party, Mubarak's electoral vehicle, 94 per cent of seats in parliament. While many of them entered politics in search of government contracts and patronage, the result was the start of an alliance between business and the military. The military backbone of the regime became even more visible in the spreading fashion of private companies, including retired officers on their boards. Anwar Sadat's *infitah* policy – the half-baked 'opening' to free trade and capitalism that followed the 1973 Arab–Israeli war – tended to put senior officers in control of lucrative public sector franchises. What was going on in this instance was different.

Certainly the regime was widening its reach. But essentially it was doing no more than padding the army and security services backbone of the state with private sector tissue and presenting this as reform. This revealed a total disregard for institutions, or any form of state-building, let alone democratic reform. Mubarak's attempt to expand the base of his regime cast Egypt's tired *rentier* capitalists as the equivalent of tribal notables in a regime like King Hussein's. It was in any case part of a strategy to legitimize the emergence of his son Gamal, a banker, in Egyptian politics.

Mubarak was unabashed by criticism. 'If you want a paved road from here to Hurghada [on the Red Sea]', he said, 'in the flat areas I can do it very quickly. But when I get to the hills I have to change pace – because if I mess that up the whole road is useless'. He complained that 'those sitting in America and Europe cannot understand the reality here'.[18]

But all this not only risked the legitimacy of the economic reform process, making it look like an indolent form of crony capitalism; it made it unlikely to impossible that it could be brought to a successful conclusion. Partly that was because the national security state's overarching preoccupation with stability – which as we have seen entrenched the privileges of the guardians of security to the exclusion of all else – meant the whole debate about reform was deformed. A classic example concerned the status of Egypt's foreign exchange reserves.

As a result of the initial successes of reform, particularly in macroeconomic stabilization, hard currency reserves were rebuilt from almost nothing to over $20 billion. In order to impress on President Mubarak that his policies were succeeding, the reform camp kept exhibiting the healthy reserves as evidence. That turned out to be most unfortunate.

Mubarak, whose eyes usually glazed over whenever the mechanics of economic reform were discussed, lit up at the mere mention of the reserves, according to Egyptian ministers. 'How are my $20bn doing?' soon became the only topic of his conversation with the reformers who had first brought it up. So much so that the whole purpose of having these reserves – to manage the exchange rate as well as collateral against exports – was lost. Mubarak's absolute refusal to see 'my $20bn' dip one dollar below his prestige level led to one of the most absurd and unnecessary devaluation crises of modern times.

In 2000, an artificial shortage of dollars developed, not because of any change in Egypt's fundamental economic position, but because Mubarak was hoarding what he seemed to regard as his personal piggy bank. The reformers were too clever by half in using foreign exchange reserves as the currency of reform inside the regime. Perhaps the president thought that maybe, at last, these slightly foreign individuals with their doctorates from western universities had seen the light and become insiders too. But they were not all blind.

They were, after all, in a good position to realize that no new blood was entering a system that depended on individuals, accountable only to the president, who was dependent on the security services. No individual, political or social force or institution was allowed to emerge that would challenge this set-up.

'In exchange for a fake parliamentary system we have eliminated every layer of real democracy, including elected mayors, elections in the unions, or in the professional organizations like the doctors, the lawyers and the engineers, which were once real forces', said one of the reformers: 'This is possibly the worst time for Egyptian democrats in the past 40 to 50 years.'

* * * * *

The structural impediments to the free flow of information in the Arab national security state that I have described above, which ultimately make Arab rulers the prisoners of the praetorians and keep the Arab ruled under their thumb, are not the whole story. There is, in addition, an aspect of despotic wilfulness that leads just as unerringly to failure in all but the retention of power. There is no better case of this than the late Yassir Arafat. He offers a particularly clear example precisely because he was never able to establish more than a proto-state: there was never more than a half-built labyrinth for him to get lost in.

Arafat, let us be clear, against overwhelming odds, ensured the Palestinians survived as a political force that had to be taken into account in the future of the Middle East. That is not a small achievement. At the height of his power, furthermore, he had full control over less than 3 per cent of the West Bank, with administrative control over another 25 per cent, in surrounded enclaves that Israel's continuing occupation could throttle at will.

Diplomatically, moreover, Arafat and the PLO could make little headway unless the USA was prepared to pressure Israel into honouring its commitments under the 1993–5 Oslo accords. Nevertheless, however weak Arafat's hand was – right up to the abortive Camp David summit of 2000 that we will examine in Chapter VII – his despotic instincts, and a negotiating style characterized by improvisation, a failure to weld together tactic with strategy, and an Olympian disregard for detail, tended to weaken it further.

Edward Said, the late Palestinian–American scholar and polemicist, one of Arafat's most trenchant critics who foresaw that Oslo was unworkable and so one-sided as to amount to a capitulation to Israel, always questioned the political, technical and linguistic competence of the Palestinian peace negotiators. 'They didn't even have a translation' from the English in which they haltingly negotiated the original declaration of principles, he fulminated: 'the only maps that were there were Israeli maps'. Speaking not long after Arafat had banned a collection of his essays, he said the PLO leader was so wrapped up in the pomp of his title as president, he neglected to examine what he would be presiding over. 'They were calling people around the world and saying "Jack" or "Khaled" or something, and asking them: "What does autonomy mean?" It took Arafat one whole year to realize he didn't have a state. He has no stable sense of reality, but he has an incredible sense of survival.' Details mattered little to Arafat, Said argued from long experience, because he always thought that 'somebody – usually the US – can fix it'.[19]

Arafat, his admirers and not only his detractors mostly agree, was profoundly anti-democratic. He obsessively kept all control in his own hands from the earliest days of the PLO. His manoeuvrings in the labyrinth of Arab politics over time tended to magnify his autocratic instincts. All this marked his self-hobbled approach to negotiating with the Israelis.

His instinct to divide and rule, for instance, meant him fielding different negotiating teams at each stage of the peace process – sometimes simultaneously. This explained a number of oddities. Israel, for instance, long believed that Egypt was responsible for Arafat's reluctance to finally settle on Israeli terms. Israeli officials correctly detected that the PLO leader's backbone visibly stiffened following his periodic consultations in Cairo. But that was because Egypt's regional experts gave Arafat the complete picture – illustrated with maps – which his own salami-sliced team could only supply in fragments. On those occasions the Palestinian leader rarely liked what he saw.

Arafat, typically for an Arab proto-despot, deliberately held down the development of potentially rival institutions, such as the elected Palestinian Legislative Council, which, to his discomfort, provided two key negotiators. Fatally, he also had the habit of seizing personal control of negotiations at critical moments, dismissing those experts who had done the detailed bargaining. If this were the action of a leader using the political authority he alone possessed to forge the defining compromise, it would be the work of a statesman. In the vain and wilful hands of an Arafat, it was all too frequently a disaster. Israel's canny negotiators knew how to exploit this.

A senior military intelligence official, subsequently a leading Israeli diplomat, who was present at all the Oslo parleys, told me his team's overriding tactic was simple: to get Arafat alone. Two Palestinian negotiators told me they knew that. But they were powerless to intervene when in August 1995, at the conclusion of the Oslo 'interim' agreement on self-rule, Arafat dismissed his cartographer, Khalil Toufagji. The Israelis swooped in on their man, armed with their maps.

According to Palestinian negotiators, Arafat then signed a map, designed by Israel, and almost identical in its essentials to what Palestinians call the 'Master Plan' and Israelis know as Military Order Number 50. The map shows a network of roads connecting Israel's expanding settlements while slicing up and atomizing Arab territory, both in and around occupied east Jerusalem and around the main West Bank cities turned over to the Palestinians. The map was drawn up in 1982, by Ariel Sharon, arch-hawk and champion of the Israeli settlers, when he was defence minister.

Arafat, his eye always fixed on his next invitation to the White House, patently had no understanding of the role of so-called 'bypass' roads linking up the Jewish settlements and slicing the West Bank into isolated cantons. Geoffrey Aronson, of the Washington-based Foundation for Middle East Peace, argued at the time that the Palestinian leadership, unlike the Israelis, and not subject to any meaningful democratic accountability, had 'almost total lack of interest in or first-hand familiarity with the situation on the ground' in the West Bank. Writing in the August 1998 edition of *Report on Israeli Settlement in the Occupied Territories*, Aronson said that while Sharon (by then Netanyahu's chief negotiator with the Palestinians) was 'well-schooled in the value of an intimate knowledge of the land...Arafat is briefed infrequently on Israel's settlement policy, and his response is generally stunned silence as he looks at maps depicting the dimensions of the enterprise'.

All Israel's maps are well studied. They have not changed for 30 years.

III

The Janus of Islamic Revivalism

There is a famous verse in the Quran, Islam's holy book, which expresses a notion very close to the Christian idea of free will. 'Verily', it says, 'God will not change the state of a people, unless they change the state of their own selves'.

Like much scripture in all religious traditions, the meaning of the verse oscillates between the mundanely literal and the ineffable. Its mixture of clarity and elusiveness, moreover, mirrors the ambiguity behind the Muslim concept of Jihad. Does it mean simply free will, or a sort of Nietzschean, over-powering will? Does it mean the will to overcome one's own weaknesses, or the will to obliterate the enemy? Is it a message of reform or revolution?

Understandably, this malleable text is a favourite of the modern strategists of Islamic revivalism, many of whom explain their endeavour as the primordial need to 'return to ourselves', purged of all alien accretions – if necessary, some advocate, by violence.[1]

Osama bin Laden, the man who has come to embody the phenomenon of modern jihadism, clearly has little time for the doubts and disquisitions of the scholastics. On 11 September 2001 he seared into the mind of the world apocalyptic images of destruction. No less breathtaking was the scale of his ambition: essentially to trigger a clash of civilizations, leading to uprisings across the lands of Islam.

The declarations and edicts issuing from bin Laden and his lieutenants since the 9/11 attacks rarely read anything like a recognizable, much less achievable, programme. Often, they came across as neo-Quranic convolutions marinated in bile, a mixture of blood-lust and bigotry that western minds tend to believe could not possibly transcend an alienated fringe. But to view bin

Laden and his ilk this way is to miss the clarity of their aim and the ingenuity of their tactics.

Hours before the USA and its allies started bombarding al-Qaeda and Taliban redoubts in Afghanistan in October 2001, bin Laden was laying out his stall in a pre-recorded broadcast through Al Jazeera – the Qatar-based satellite television station that now reaches tens of millions of Arabs and Muslims throughout the Islamic world. The time had come, the jihadi leader said, for a worldwide uprising of Muslims to recover their rights and their former glory.

'The world is divided into two sides', bin Laden said, 'the side of faith and the side of the infidels'. He proclaimed that 'now every Muslim has to rise up and defend his Muslim brothers, and wipe out this act of aggression'.

Though patently imminent, no such 'act of aggression' had taken place when he recorded his call to the Muslim masses, presenting himself as the modern champion of their faith and culture. His pre-emptive response, before the USA had had the chance to fire a shot in retaliation for 9/11, was revealing of his tactics. Everything about the attacks on New York and Washington – the sheer scale and effrontery, the pitiless targeting of civilians, their universal visibility – suggested bin Laden was betting on reprisals from the USA which would be similarly indiscriminate, heavy-handed and out in the open for all to see.

It is a time-honoured mechanism: the terrorist dynamic of action, reaction, followed, the instigator hopes, by counter-reaction on a larger scale – in this case pitting Muslims against the rest of the world.

Look at bin Laden's answer to a US interviewer in 1998, after his network blew up the American embassies in Nairobi and Dar es Salaam: 'As I said, every action elicits a similar reaction.'

Ideologically, what this is closest to is the dialectic of late nineteenth century anarchism, or even the tactics of serial insurrectionists like Auguste Blanqui or violent mystics like Georges Sorel, who would influence Mussolini. One might even see it as the jihadi take on Newton's Third Law of Motion. But it is not Islam.[2]

Applied in the twenty-first century, however, it is clear that these jihadi millenarians are firm believers in the thesis of a Clash of Civilizations between Islam and the West, hitherto easy to dismiss as a millennium-old prejudice reasserted at the end of the Cold War by Samuel Huntington, the late Harvard professor, nine centuries after Pope Urban II launched the First Crusade.

It is precisely such a global clash the jihadis were and are trying to precipitate. In it they appear to foresee the restoration of Islam to the power and influence it enjoyed until the end of the eighteenth century. The idea is simple enough. It is to exploit the collapse of American credibility in Arab and Muslim public opinion, and to keep launching actions that will provoke intemperate or ill-judged reactions, which will in turn transform that hostility into militant action across the Islamic world. To succeed, the jihadis need the USA and the West to take the bait.

Before 9/11, there had been a gathering sense of foreboding in the Middle East, mainly linked to the, by then, year-long intifada, the second Palestinian uprising against the Israeli occupation of the West Bank and Gaza. The new US administration of President George W. Bush, partly in response to the failure of his predecessor, Bill Clinton, to get a land-for-peace settlement at the Camp David summit a year earlier, had adopted a 'hands off' approach, letting the conflict fester. This was widely seen as tantamount to giving carte blanche to an Israel now headed by Ariel Sharon – considered a serial war criminal by most Arabs – which was using US-supplied jets and helicopter gunships to pound Palestinian towns and refugee camps, and physically destroy the fledgling institutions of Yassir Arafat's Palestinian Authority.

US-allied Arab leaders, especially those of Egypt and Saudi Arabia, warned Washington with some alarm that this was leading to an uncontrollable build-up of anger in their countries. Their autocratic rule could face threat. But neither that, nor the smouldering resentment at the sufferings of ordinary Iraqis after a decade of sanctions aimed at Saddam Hussein, explained 9/11.

In the first place, the evidence compellingly suggested that the attacks on the twin towers and the Pentagon had been years in the planning. One has only to recall the remarks of Ayman al-Zawahiri, bin Laden's Egyptian lieutenant, to a journalist just after the 1998 cruise missile attacks on Afghanistan in reprisal for that August's bombings of two US embassies in east Africa: 'The war has just started. The Americans should wait for the answer.'

Second, it is now clear that bin Laden's diffuse international confederation had already planned further attacks in 'reaction' to the campaign that was about to be waged against it. Action–Reaction–Action.

Third, the sort of reaction that was expected inside the Middle East prior to 9/11 was that some group would act to raise sharply the cost to the USA of its indiscriminate support of Israel. That was a pattern that had been seen before. After the 1982 Israeli invasion of Lebanon, for instance, and Ariel Sharon's murderous siege of West Beirut, Hizbollah, the Shia Islamist group, first bombed American forces out of Beirut and then fought the Israelis back to south Lebanon, from where they would finally withdraw in 2000 amid mounting casualties.

But this was different. This was 'our Jihad against your Crusade' – and was always going to be, long before Bush ill-advisedly used (and then withdrew) the words 'this Crusade' in telling all nations they could 'either be with us or against us'. One had only to listen carefully to what bin Laden had to say. That message was initially understood in ways that underestimated the Saudi jihadist's global ambition.

True enough, the jihad he declared in 1998 initially had the ostensibly defined goal of driving US forces out of peninsular Arabia, the land of the Prophet and birthplace of Islam, where they had arrived in force after Saddam Hussein's invasion of Kuwait in 1990. In February 1998, bin Laden brought newspaper and television reporters to his camp at Khost in Afghanistan, near where he and his Arab volunteers in 1987 had held off a far superior Soviet strike force, in the battle of Jaji, that amounted to the foundation myth of his reputation as a holy warrior.[3]

He announced the creation of the International Islamic Front for Jihad against Jews and Crusaders, fusing his Arab Afghan veterans from the 1979–89 war against the Soviet occupation of Afghanistan with Islamist radicals from Egypt, Pakistan, Bangladesh and Kashmir. He emphasized as a central grievance US occupation of 'the most sacred lands of Islam, the Arabian peninsula'.

The story of bin Laden's spurned and quixotic offer to the House of Saud after the Iraqi invasion of Kuwait – that he and his Afghanistan war veterans would defend the kingdom against Saddam's depredations so long as the Saudi royal family kept the infidel Crusader armies of the Americans out of the peninsula – is well known. Known too was the intense emotion created in the young Osama by the fact that it was his family's construction firm – by virtue of his father Mohammed bin Laden's close alliance with King Abdulaziz ibn Saud, founder of the modern Saudi state – which had rebuilt, with austere grandeur and measured embellishment, the holy places and great mosques of Mecca and Medina.

It must, therefore, have seemed reasonably predictable he would announce, in terms that could be dismissed at first glance as hysterical, his intention to cleanse the two Muslim sanctuaries of the peninsula of infidel taint and, in a much vaguer way, to help liberate Arab east Jerusalem and free the third holy shrine of Islam – the Haram as-Sharif in the Old City with the Dome of the Rock and the al-Aqsa mosque – from Israeli occupation.

His injunction on all Muslims to 'kill and fight all Americans and their allies, both civilian and military', until US forces 'shattered and broken-winged, depart from all the lands of Islam', must have sounded blood curdling, but part of a tradition of overblown rhetoric that merited attention but not concern. After the African embassy bombings, however, a broader, more ambitious message emerged.

There seems here to be a complex interplay between bin Laden and Zawahiri. The Egyptian was one of the founders of Jihad, the organization that had assassinated Anwar Sadat in 1981. Jihad was a small, vanguardist group that followed the pattern of pan-Arab nationalist organizations in its reliance on cadres from the army, a sort of mirror image of the despotism against which it was fighting. But the most relevant fact about Jihad was that it was a failure.

All the attempts by Arab Islamists to launch national uprisings in the 1990s failed. Veterans from the Afghanistan jihad returned to head insurgencies in Algeria, in Egypt and in Saudi Arabia. They miscalculated the resilience of the region's national security states, and how easily the rulers they aimed to topple would be able to spook their western supporters into backing them almost unconditionally as a preferable alternative to theocrats. Nowhere was that more true than in Egypt, where Jihad and the diffuse network of the Gama'a al-Islamiyya withered under fierce repression.

These setbacks initially provoked a debate among the Arab Afghans and their new allies about whether they should adopt tactics similar to those of the Muslim Brotherhood – widening their circles of influence within society through a ground–up approach leading towards a creeping theocracy – or continue along the path of violence: the long march or the putsch.

Zawahiri, however, unlike the extravagantly tall bin Laden a diminutive, stout figure, seems to have moved, as a result of these national setbacks, to the view that – rather as in judo – the jihadis as the weaker party needed to use their opponents' weight against them. The essence of the idea was to go after the United States, the 'hyperpower' with which most of the post-Cold War world had a love–hate relationship, and virtually all the Arab and Muslim world now loathed.

If the jihadists could not wrest power from the despots in Cairo or Algiers or Riyadh, then they should attack their foreign backers, provoke them into over-reacting, to such an extent that this would stir the masses into action, and shake the ground under the tyrants until they fell. Tactically, the moment was ripe to hit the 'distant enemy'. As Zawahiri wrote in a jihadist primer excerpted in the Arab press shortly after 9/11, if the Americans were adequately provoked, they would almost certainly respond with large-scale reprisals, and 'personally wage the battle against the Muslims', seeding the ground for a 'clear-cut jihad against the infidels'. Action–Reaction–Action.[4]

'Every Muslim must rise to defend his religion', bin Laden said in that first al-Jazeera broadcast after 9/11: 'The wind of faith is blowing and the wind of change is blowing to remove evil from the peninsula of Mohammed, peace be upon him.'

But Zawahiri's tactical perception appears to have coincided with bin Laden's growing belief that infidel superpowers were ultimately paper tigers. After the African embassy bombings elicited a ferocious but largely futile response from the USA, bin Laden recalled how the Afghan Mujahideen, backed by tens of thousands of Arab volunteers, had humiliated the Soviet Union in Afghanistan: 'There is a lesson in this for he who wishes to learn. The Soviet Union entered Afghanistan in the last week of 1979 and, with Allah's help, their flag was folded a few years later and thrown on the rubbish heap, and there was nothing left to call the Soviet Union.'

That victory 'cleared from Muslim minds the myth of superpowers', bin Laden said. 'I am confident that Muslims will be able to end the legend of the so-called superpower that is America', he added, sneering at how American forces 'ran' from Somalia in 1993 after his Arab Afghan forces (he claimed) killed 18 US Rangers.

As previously remarked, the Mujahideen defeat of the Soviet Union in Afghanistan in the 1980s owed much to the backing of Saudi Arabia, Pakistan and, above all, the USA, which cloaked its Cold War aims in their Holy War zeal. Tactically, what turned the tide was Washington's decision to supply the Mujahideen with Stinger, surface-to-air missiles, so deadly to Soviet helicopters that Moscow lost its decisive advantage in the war: control of the air.

But that was not how it looked to Islamists around the world, especially the Arab Afghan volunteers nurtured by Washington's joint venture with jihadis, so many of them recruited, under indulgent western eyes, by bin Laden. For radical Islamists, flush with fervour and the taste of victory against a superpower, Afghanistan was a huge psychological breakthrough, the harbinger of a new Islamic era. It meant that religious zeal, allied to modern techniques and weaponry, could carry all before it.

Just as the significance of Arab defeat in the 1967 Six Day War – as a catalyst in the rise of Islamic fundamentalism as a liberation theology and the irretrievable discredit of secular, pan-Arab nationalism – cannot be overstated, so, to this day, it is fatal to underestimate the significance of the Afghanistan victory against the Soviets to Islamists and many ordinary Muslims in their target audience.

In the Islamist critique, the Israelis won the 1967 war, and subsequent contests, because of their ability to marry the quasi-religious motivation of Zionism with modern technology. This is clearly, and on several grounds, an inadequate understanding of the Israeli 'recipe' for success. It ignores the secular roots of Zionism. It takes no account of the ingredient of democracy, for example, and the legitimacy this confers, not least on institutions. The most important of these institutions, arguably, is Israel's citizens' army, which has no parallel in the Arab context, where the army is an instrument for seizing and holding onto power, not for the defence of the nation. Furthermore, this is a view that places science and technology outside the socio-economic and liberal political context that fosters innovation and scientific advance; they become something that you import. There is a lot more to modernity than Stinger missiles.

In radical Islamism and its violent expression as jihad there is no place for democracy or the modern institutions it creates and legitimizes. In that sense, as I mentioned above, the jihadis are a mirror image of the despots they fight. But that should never lead us to underestimate the importance of the Afghan jihad. For tens of millions of Muslims, for whom Afghanistan was a faraway country of which they knew little, victory against the Soviets – more even than the 1979 Iranian revolution which was, frighteningly for the Sunni, Shia in complexion – was proof that the tide was turning in their favour: that religious fervour and western rocketry were an irresistible combination that could humble an empire.

That is the essence of Osama bin Laden's perception and the core of his self-belief. As he said, three years before 9/11: 'It is our duty to lead people to the light.'

* * * * *

None of this, however, altogether locates the wellspring of bin Ladenist contempt for other faiths – the virulent hatred of Jewish 'Usurers', Crusader 'Nazarenes' and Shia *Rafadah* (Rejectionists) that rocket-fuels contemporary jihadism.

There is no sanction for this in Islam. Muslim belief not only demands respect for all the *Ahl al-Kitab* or Peoples of the Book – the monotheist Jews, Christians and Muslims who trace a common prophetic lineage back to Abraham – but especially reveres Jesus Christ as a prophet.[5]

The story of the Muslim conquest of Jerusalem in 638 is well known. The Caliph 'Umar ibn al-Khattab, second of the *Rashidun* or 'rightly guided', guaranteed to the Christians their religious freedom and holy places, cleaned and ritually purified the remains of the ancient Jewish temple (used under Christian rule as a rubbish dump), and resettled Jews in the old city, from which they had been banished by the Byzantines. Islam, in this seminal and historically verifiable display of pluralism, is an inclusive religion.

Rather than Islam in the formal sense of a set of religious beliefs, the root of bin Laden's Manichean view of the world lies in a sense of Islamic decline. Indeed, in his first broadcast after 9/11, he spoke of '80 years of humiliation [of] our Islamic nation', thereby dating that decline to the post-First World

War collapse of the Ottoman Empire and the end of the Muslim Caliphate. But that perception of decline had been around for a long time before it assumed this deadly form.

Islam, the religious writer Karen Armstrong has memorably reminded us, was a religion of success. Extraordinary success.[6]

Bursting out of Arabia in the seventh Christian century, it established, from Spain to India and beyond, the pre-eminent civilization of succeeding epochs that, for instance, retrieved for a Europe still in the Dark Ages the treasures of Hellenistic thought and science, adding breakthroughs of its own, especially in mathematics and medicine.

But subsequent setbacks came to imply that there was something deeply wrong – not in God's message through the Prophet, but in the way Muslims, rulers and ruled, were interpreting it and following it. That sense was immeasurably magnified because there is no real distinction in Muslim philosophy and theology between religion and state. It follows that no setback can be seen as purely temporal.

As in other religions, moreover, there was from the outset a fierce jostling of rival dynasties and traditions, and a consequent struggle for legitimacy. Three out of the first four Caliphs – regarded in the Sunni tradition as the *Rashidun* or Rightly Guided – were assassinated.

Subsequent regiments of scribes, lawyers, theologians and polemicists combined, often with what Christians would recognize from their own tradition as casuistry, to boost competing claims of legitimacy. Many classic Islamic thinkers, such as the Persian Ibn Sina (eleventh century) and the great Andalusi humanist Ibn Rushd (twelfth century) – known to their contemporaries in Europe as Avicenna and Averroes, the intellectual giants of their time – by contrast conducted philosophical enquiries into the competing claims of purity and power, grappling with an early perception of decadence.

Such decadence was relative. The western claim that Islam had no Reformation, no Renaissance, and therefore no ulterior Enlightenment, is inadequate, part of a Euro-centric narrative. Not until well into this far from linear process would Europe evolve cities of the size and sophistication of Cairo – except, of course, in Muslim al-Andalus. Even after the great Muslim and Arab city, Baghdad, had been sacked by the Mongols in 1258, and the centuries of Abbasid civilization came to an end, Muslims (although not Arabs) were still able to establish three new mega-states – the Ottoman, Moghul and Safavid empires – in the sixteenth century. Islam's influence followed Muslim trade routes north into Russia, south into Africa and east towards China. Much European narrative, furthermore, leaves out the extent to which Europe's revival was built on the universal cultural heritage preserved by Islam, and transmitted through al-Andalus. Few western scholars, moreover, acknowledge the degree to which Europe rebuilt its identity in opposition to and competition with Islam, especially after the Muslims absorbed the Byzantine, or eastern Roman, empire – a rival superpower of the day – with the fall of Constantinople in 1453.[7]

For all the horrors and bigotry characteristic of the times, moreover, never, during that period, did Islam descend into the religious wars endemic in Europe, or the persecution by the Roman Catholic Inquisition of great minds, such as Copernicus and Galileo, or the collective neuroses of witch-burning and pogroms against the Jews. Anti-semitism, historically, is a Christian phenomenon; the Jews prospered in Muslim lands, often as refugees from the Christians, under defined and defended 'protocols of tolerance'.[8]

But even relatively early on, Islam, doctrinally concerned to build a just society and preserve the unity of the Umma, or worldwide community of believers, began to discourage what its clerical establishments saw as divisive speculation in philosophy and theology. This trend, many western and Muslim historians believe, would gradually snuff out the spirit of curiosity and innovation.

By the end of the eighteenth century, when Europe looked as though it might have realigned faith and reason, the Islamic world had slipped behind – at precisely the moment of its collision with an expansionist Europe, an encounter normally dated to Napoleon Bonaparte's short adventure in Egypt in 1798.

Historians supply us with lists of reasons to explain Islamic decline: from the Mongol devastations of the thirteenth century to Europe's colonial depredations in the nineteenth and twentieth centuries; from the paranoid habit of Muslim rulers of importing mercenaries to defend them, to their failure to keep up with Europe in science and, puzzlingly, navigation and naval warfare. They were beaten back in the Mediterranean, especially after the battle of Lepanto in 1572, they lost control of the Arabian Sea and Indian Ocean, and, after being halted twice at the gates of Vienna, in 1529 and 1683, they were stopped in their advance to the Atlantic, which became the springboard for the new, dynamic empires that would overtake them.

Other 'declinist' reasons might include the tendency of the more properly Arab world's merchants and landowners to align with foreigners, or their failure to move forward from trade and rent-farming to manufacturing and industry (in neither case, therefore, did they insist on the historic political prerogatives of the bourgeoisie, as in other regions that gradually set limits to absolute power).

Perhaps the least explored hypothesis about decline is the persistent and in no way resolved tension between the claim to universal loyalty of the Umma, the pan-Islamic Muslim commonwealth, and the claims of national and/or ethno-linguistic loyalties. As already mentioned, I believe there are certain similarities between Islamism (or Islamic revivalism) and the phenomenon of nineteenth-century nationalism in Europe. Both started as a sort of forced march into the future – a physical as well as metaphysical *fuit en avant* or collective leap out of the dark – and then they detoured in extremely sinister and destructive ways. While all these reasons for decline are compelling in different ways, what concerns us here is the perception of decline. For what is clear is that the Islamic world has lived the past two centuries in a state of profound ambivalence towards the West, despised as predatory and corrupt at the same time as it is admired for its cultural, technical and military accomplishment.

It is essential to realize that it was not the spontaneous choice of the Arabs and the Muslims to retreat into Islam. As already remarked, it was only when balance of power politics and subsequent western support for tyranny in the interests of stability and cheap oil thwarted nationalist and democratic attempts at modernization that the Islamist revival acquired momentum.[9]

Obviously, once the European powers thrust into Arab and Muslim lands in the course of the nineteenth and early twentieth centuries – taking Algeria, Tunisia, Egypt, Libya, Syria and the Lebanon, and shrinking the Ottoman hinterland before pointing a dagger at its heartland – the question of modernity, much less democracy, must in many Muslim minds have been displaced by the question of survival.

But there had been no shortage of 'modernist' Islamic thinkers, trying to tease out the lessons of western success and clear the thickets of superstition from Muslim minds. But, while looking forward, they also, like the 'traditionalists', looked backwards to the dawn of Islam – 'returning to our selves'. Even Mustafa Kemal Ataturk, the founder and arch-secularizer of modern Turkey, began by talking of 'cleansing' Islam of centuries of accretions.

Jamal al-Din al-Afghani (1839–97), probably, despite his name, a Persian and very possibly a Shia – who studied philosophy in the Shia holy city of Najaf where the traditions of Ibn Sina were kept alive – came to represent a flowing together of Islamic reform and nationalist assertion that would trickle into almost every political current in the region in the course of the following century. As the great historian Albert Hourani has pointed out, he brought a radical new emphasis on Islam as a civilization rather than Islam as a religion, yet 'only by a return to Islam can the strength and civilization of Muslims be restored'.[10]

Islam needed to reclaim its scientific roots, and harvest the new fruits that had flowered in Europe from stems originally planted by the Muslims. Of course, Islam badly needed a Martin Luther to clean out the stables as well.

But with the unity of the Umma, Islam could once more have a universal mission in the world because, as anyone who studied it could see, it was tolerant, rational and in harmony with the principles uncovered by science throughout the ages, not least by the great Muslim scientists who had not only adorned their own civilization but recovered the civilization of the West.[11]

Under Afghani's disciples, however, the emphasis on reform, and the nature of universalism, gradually changed. Mohammed Abduh (1849–1905), an Egyptian scholar who taught at Al Azhar and in 1899 became the Mufti of Egypt, was above all concerned to show that the road to modernity could be discovered in the roots of Islam. Abduh forsook an initial Islamic puritanism and, under Afghani's influence, read the philosophical works of Ibn Sina. Looking at his European-influenced compatriots, and at the even more westernized Lebanese who were behind many of the new journals and newspapers flourishing across the region, he felt they had painted a veneer of western culture onto an even more superficial knowledge of Islamic culture and thought.

His essential perception was that ostensibly modern concepts could be evolved out of traditional Islamic notions provided they were properly understood and adapted.

Thus, Muslims could identify the concept of *maslaha* – the principle whereby a jurist or judge could select from rival legal traditions to find the best outcome for contemporary public welfare – as the slightly more modern idea of the public good or interest. They would be able to recognize *ijma* – something between the consensus of the learned or scholars and the acceptance of the community – as public opinion. Above all they could authentically claim their own tradition of democracy in the practice of *shura* or consultation.

Abduh's attempt to spring Islam into the vanguard of modernity was partly a job of reinterpreting and unifying Islamic law and adapting it to modern problems, partly a job of revealing the true meaning of old precepts and practices. It both cases it had to involve the exercise of *ijtihad* – literally the exercise of reasoning by analogy, more loosely the exercise of independent but scholarly judgement – to confront the circumstances of modernity unforeseen at the dawn of Islam.[12]

Under Rashid Rida (1865–1935), a Syrian disciple of both Afghani and Abduh, many of the themes – the struggle for a dynamic Islam and the exercise of *ijtihad* – are the same, but the emphasis is on 'returning to ourselves'. The technical skills of modernity, he persistently argues, arise out of the right moral habits and intellectual principles. If the teaching of Islam is properly understood, it will lead to success in this world and the next: 'The Islamic Umma was the heart of the world's civilization so long as it was truly Islamic.' In Rida's *al-Manar* (*The Lighthouse*) periodical, which had an

51

important influence on both Islamic revivalism and pan-Arab nationalism, 'true Islam involves two things, acceptance of the unity of God and consultation [*Shura*] in matters of state, and despotic rulers have tried to make Muslims forget the second by encouraging them to abandon the first'.[13]

Rida inhabited a cultural tradition that was self-questioning but still entire. While, like his intellectual forebears, he retrieved from Islamic traditions practices resembling the principles of democracy and institutions of modernity, increasingly he inclined to look back towards the Islam of the *al-Salaf al-Salih* – the pious forerunners, the elders of the first generations. As Albert Hourani put it, Rida 'belonged to the last generation of those who could be fully educated and yet alive in a self-sufficient Islamic world of thought'.[14]

That sort of focus quickly led to the perception that decay had come about as a result of a surrender to philosophy, speculation and mysticism – rather than the surrender to God, the precise meaning of the word Islam. This meant, essentially, that all developments after the Salafi period and the subsequent establishment of the four orthodox schools of Sunni jurisprudence were deeply suspect. Even more so was anything associated with the mostly Sunni Sufi orders and Shi'ism. Rida eventually tilted towards Wahhabism – the puritanical Saudi reform movement which held that the Shia had introduced other gods and idolatry into Islam – and himself argued that the 'fairy tales' of Shi'ism were introduced by the first Jewish converts to Islam. He also yearned for a new Caliph – with attributes paradoxically nearer to the Shia idea of a priest-king than the decadent Sunni models Muslims had to go on.[15]

Whereas, therefore, the appeal and message of a reformer like Jamal al-Din al-Afghani combined a call to arms against the West with an injunction to learn the secrets of western culture as the prelude to relaunching Islam as a triumphantly universal civilization, the message subtly mutated under his successors – who would seed not only a nationalist sentiment, but a highly defensive modern Islamic revivalism led initially by organizations such as the Muslim Brotherhood. As Edward Mortimer has captured it: 'the emphasis came to be less on cleansing [Islam] from medieval Sufi superstitions or scholastic legalism and more on cleansing it from new heresies, western secular ideas that had crept in under the guise of modernism; less on acquiring (or repossessing) for Islam the sources of western strength, and more on ridding Islam of the seeds of western decadence'.

Rashid Rida does not mark the completion of this process, by any means. But, as Mortimer acutely observes: 'he faces both ways, personifying the transition from the modernist reformism of the late nineteenth century to the tradition-oriented revivalism of today'.[16]

These ideas would mutate further, once detached from the sort of world that gave birth to them: an inclusive and entire world dislocated by the upheaval of modernity and the penetration of imperial power. Such Janus-like modernism easily cleared a path for the Islamic revivalism of this century, especially after nationalism was thwarted and the Arab world proceeded up one blind alley after another, following what Osama bin Laden calls 'earthly flags'.

With the bin Ladenists, the notion of the Umma has been corrupted into fascistic and supremacist ideas analogous to the *Volk*, the *Razza* or the *Raza*, with their primacy over individual human rights and the universal rights of humanity. It is easy to see, moreover, how thinkers such as Rida can lure their disciples down a false path, towards a muscular Islamism that, like fascism, is about men of action, not thinkers – and the vicarious thrill they elicit among orderly conservatives. And, as a recent re-examination of fascism has put it well, 'war is indispensable for the maintenance of fascist muscle tone'. Substitute 'jihad' for war and 'Islamist' for fascist and you have an important element of the attraction of the modern holy warrior.[17]

* * * * *

The Islam and modernity debate, which took place in the lead-up to, during and immediately after the collapse of the Ottoman empire, has emerged again nearly a century later within similar parameters. But there are now two important differences. First, few Muslims invest any hope in the democratic western powers (essentially the USA, Britain and France) that back rulers that oppress them, even if, against the odds, they still admire 'western' values, science and cultural products, as we saw in Chapter I. Second, the West has yet to develop a coherent response to this world-view, beyond a curious mix of bleakness and complacency. A good part of the complacency lies in the embedded belief that the West has resolved most questions relating to religion, culture and modernity. It follows that a 'clash of civilizations' with those who have not – above all in the Islamic world – is bleakly inevitable. The trend towards strident and populist tabloid politics about immigration and the integration of immigrants – which afflicts almost all western countries – is to an extent about this.

But this is a sort of deformed mirror image of what Osama bin Laden and his kind believe. The West needs to be reminded of its own past. We need to carry out a conscious exercise of historical memory, before it is too late. An element of humility, rather than unctuous western cant about Islam as a 'religion of peace', would be a good entry-point to understanding what is going on – and perhaps developing a coherent response.

In the West's view of itself, the wars of religion endemic in Europe came to an end with the treaties of Westphalia in 1648, which ended the Thirty Years War and spurred the emergence of the nation-state, one of the essential building blocks of modernity and a system of states built around the notion of sovereignty. Since then – this canonical view tends to read – war and diplomacy have been about national interest or ideology rather than religion, while Church and State have gradually separated, clearing the way towards representative government.

This is true, but up to a point. For seldom has religion been absent from subsequent, post-Westphalian conflict, in the West, as much as anywhere else. Were we to subject our heritage to the searchlight of history we would find, for instance, that Christians appealed to the authority of scripture on both sides of the debate about slavery. Or that the charging of interest – *haram* under Muslim orthodoxy – was also formally prohibited by Catholic canon law until comparatively recently.

But let us just select a few concrete examples from the past century, which indeed was the century of ideological conflict but a good deal more too.

In that century, it was typical for Cold Warriors to reach, at least rhetorically, for a religious identity in their contest with 'Godless Communism'. This was not just, or even primarily, an American habit. Christian Democracy, to take a clear example, dominated much of western Europe and chunks of Latin America after the Second World War, supported by the Roman Catholic church in conscious, religion-based and militant opposition to Communism.

Fascists also liberally used God on their side: General Francisco Franco characterized his military uprising against the Spanish republic as a Crusade, while his official propaganda painted him in lurid Christian colours as The Sentinel of the Occident. The origins of the swastika are pre-Christian, but some Nazi units wore crosses on their belt-buckles. The military juntas that plagued south and central America from the 1970s, which harboured fascists and vicious anti-semites in their midst, regularly raised Christian banners to justify their actions.

Nor does it stop there. During the Second World War even Stalin famously used the Orthodox Church as a vehicle to mobilize and motivate the people (much as Saddam Hussein, the secular Ba'athist, tried at the end of his reign to co-opt the mosques).

But more modern national and territorial conflicts, too, often have strongly religious overtones.

The 1947 partition of India, for instance, was at one level a conflict between Hindus and Muslims in the subcontinent. The continuing, if now attenuated, conflict between India and Pakistan over Kashmir has become potentially deadlier not just because both sides are now nuclear-armed, but because of the rise of the religious right in both countries – swaggering Islamists in Pakistan and Hindu supremacists in India (built in both cases around organizations originally created in the fetid political atmosphere of the 1920s and 1930s).

Or take the Israeli–Palestinian conflict itself. It is, of course, a territorial and national conflict. But it is at the same time – particularly after Israel captured the old city of Jerusalem in the 1967 Six Day War – a contest between Muslim and Jew for *holy* land, with Jerusalem, a city built on combustible myth, at its heart.

Nor has Europe been immune from this phenomenon.

The end of the Cold War not only unfroze the Soviet Union and its buffer states, it reinvigorated old conflicts with a vivid religious tinge: in Bosnia, Chechnya and Kosovo. This was less the result of a new assertiveness by Islamic revivalists, more like history resuming normal service. The break-up of Yugoslavia, in that respect, was a most instructive experience.

Western European states had ostensibly outgrown their atavism and grouped harmoniously in the European Union. They looked down their noses at these unruly easterners, who appeared to be taking up the story from exactly where they had left it before the Stalinist freeze. Yet it took only a matter of weeks before the westerners started tilting back towards their historic alliances: Germany towards Croatia, France towards Serbia and so on.

Contemporary Europeans, moreover, are not quite so settled in their secularity as they like to suppose. The contemporary debate about the enlargement of the EU centres on whether or not Europe can accommodate Turkey – which, although secular in its political outlook and institutions, is predominantly Muslim. At the same time, the Union has already imported a form of Culture Wars by its existing expansion, especially to include traditionalist Catholic countries such as Poland, whose political parties wish to reopen from the beginning issues such as divorce and abortion that their peers consider largely settled. When Poles, Austrians and others, moreover, insisted on the presence of God in the preamble to any future European constitution, most of Europe resorted to its default posture of holding its nose; there was not so much a debate as a collective sneer. Meanwhile, the French, and, to an extent, the Germans and the English, worry about Muslim girls wearing the Hijab, or Islamic headscarves.

Ever since the Enlightenment, perceptive thinkers in Europe have worried about what would replace the belief in God. Blaise Pascal suggested it would be 'a God-shaped void'. Ernst Bloch pointed to the fatal Marxist mistake of 'cordoning off the soul'. George Orwell, a militant non-believer, nevertheless had the insight that the decline of mass belief would leave a dramatic hole, that 'the major problem of our time is the decay of belief in personal immortality'. Even the literary brawler Norman Mailer maintained 'you cannot found a way of life on a part of man's soul', as he wrote in 1946: 'you cannot found an ethic on economics'. To paint concerns about belief as some sort of Muslim infatuation is fatuous.

In the Culture Wars across the Atlantic in the United States, meanwhile, Christian fundamentalism has already acquired considerable influence – to the point that some scientists even believe the legacy of the Enlightenment could be threatened. That is well beyond the scope of this analysis, but these are examples that the Muslim world cannot fail to notice. Some six months after the US capture of Baghdad, for instance, Lieutenant General William Boykin, deputy undersecretary for defense in charge of pursuing Osama bin Laden, declared that the 'war against terror' was a battle with Satan and that 'we are hated because we are a nation of believers ... a Christian nation'. This is a man who believes George W. Bush was appointed president by God, and that the law of the Bible (Old Testament vintage) should supplant international law, not to mention the Geneva Conventions.[18]

The rhetoric of President Bush himself dripped with religiosity. This, combined with his insistence on dividing the world into those who are 'with us or against us', gave every impression he purported to lead the West in a modern Crusade.

That, of course, was precisely what Osama bin Laden and his followers wanted. Their whole endeavour, as already remarked, is to launch a jihad to counter this supposed crusade and, indeed, the modern jihadi is pretty much the mirror image of the medieval crusader.

The Crusades, in one sense, could be read as a collective attempt to hoist Europe out of the Dark Ages, mainly by asserting religious identity – albeit by the mass slaughter of Jews and Muslims (not to mention heterodox, mostly eastern, Christians). There is little to distinguish that from the thesis of some contemporary jihadis that their mission is to bring the Muslim world out of *Jahiliyyah* (the word for the epoch of ignorance and darkness Muslims ascribe to pre-Islamic Arabia), in part by slaughtering Christians and Jews (not to mention heterodox, mostly Shia, Muslims). As we saw earlier, bin Laden himself states 'it is our duty to lead people to the light'.

Yet bin Ladenism is but one response to the wider sense of failure and crisis in the Muslim world (above all in its Arab core) – the one that takes the form of violent lament for past greatness. A great many Muslims, by contrast, believers among them, seem to partake of the same messy ambivalence towards the problems of religion and modernity as much of the rest of the world.

The job of policy in the early part of this century is to ensure that these Muslims are not driven into the arms of the jihadis – that the West, in other words, does not take bin Laden's bait.

That is not easy. As we have already seen, the moral credit of the West could hardly be lower in the Muslim and Arab world. Similar polls, furthermore, show how more and more people have come to see themselves first as Muslims, rather than, say, Moroccans, Saudi Arabians or Pakistanis. The Islamist extremists are adept at exploiting this identity shift.[19]

They build on doctrine that is common to all Islam: the concern to build a just society and to preserve the unity of the Umma, the worldwide community of believers. That, as we have seen, is already a seductive political combination even before any spark of religious belief is added. Add to it the familiar list of timeless and actual Muslim grievances, the sense of a religion under siege and the lament for lost glory, and what emerges is a liberation theology, forlorn but formidable.

In facing it, it is not helpful for the West to be selectively amnesiac about its own, messy, and still evolving history, or to indulge in democratic triumphalism while supporting despotism out of political and commercial convenience. Nor is there much point to the endless iterations of how all the great religions have essential values in common unless this translates into policies that all sides can agree embody these shared values, in which, as we have seen above, Islamist thinkers include ideas of indigenous democracy.

What that must mean, as already indicated and as we shall see further, is policy changes including the relentless pursuit of a just solution to the Israeli–Palestinian conflict, and the withdrawal of support to Arab (and other Muslim) despots who deny their peoples freedom.

That will be risky and it will be messy. But it could hardly be riskier or messier than the only concrete policy change the USA and a small band of allies have made: the unprovoked invasion of Iraq. The policy changes outlined above would have provided the legitimacy and the local allies needed to crush al-Qaeda and its franchise, which were and are the clear and present danger to the West and to the Muslims. But no: as we shall see in the next chapter, the Bush administration, allied with Tony Blair and precious little else, chose to proliferate, not combat, that threat.[20]

IV

The Time of the Shia

When historians come to examine fully how Iraq was lost they will, of course, alight on the memoirs and the memos, the leaks and the minutes, of those who drove the policy, measuring declaration against execution, ambition against outcome.

They will, without doubt, savour the solipsism of an L. Paul Bremer III, the US viceroy whose 2003 disbandment of the Iraqi army and promiscuous purge of Saddam Hussein's Ba'ath party left 350,000–400,000 men suddenly destitute and bitter, but armed, trained and prey to the Sunni insurgency then taking shape – but whose memoir paints him as a MacArthur of Mesopotamia.[1]

They will be awed by the arrogance and fecklessness of a Donald Rumsfeld, defense secretary and theorist of known unknowns, who summed up the descent into anarchy and looting in the hours after Baghdad fell on 9 April 2003 (when, many who witnessed it are persuaded, quite possibly Iraq was lost) – 'Stuff happens'.

But their research will be greatly assisted by the diligence of the Government Accountability Office (GAO), the investigative arm of the US Congress, which, through more than 140 audits since the war began, has kept on unearthing the bottomless depths of incompetence behind the Bush administration's wilfully misconceived adventure in Iraq.

In late July 2007, for example, the GAO reported that the Pentagon could not account for 110,000 AK-47 assault rifles and 80,000 pistols supposedly supplied to Iraq's allegedly reconstituted security forces – adding to already well-founded suspicions that Iraqi insurgents were using US-supplied arms to attack American and British troops.[2]

Such a discovery might rank as the mother of all known unknowns, were it not that in March that year the GAO also published a dryly damning report on the coalition's failure to secure scores upon scores of arms dumps abandoned by the Iraqi army after the March 2003 invasion – and that by October

2006 it had *still* failed to lock up this giant toolbox that was keeping the daily slaughter going in the overlapping ethnosectarian conflicts that turned Iraq into a charnel house and exacted a steady toll in American lives.[3]

That carnage continues, albeit significantly moderated by the 2007–8 'surge' of troop reinforcements that raised US forces to a peak of 162,000. Though the death toll, among Iraqis as well as occupation forces, fell to around a third of pre-surge levels, the reasons for this abatement were all, as we shall see, temporary and reversible – beginning, of course, with the high improbability that the US government, lawmakers and people would be willing or able to sustain this level of military commitment for very long. Indeed, the surge always looked like one last heave.

More than five years into the war, it was hard to see how any surge could fix an Iraq so traumatized by tyranny and war and then broken by invasion and occupation. By the time of the surge an already indecipherable ethnic and sectarian patchwork had been ripped bloodily to pieces, in a morass of savagery comparable to a mix of Lebanon, Algeria and Afghanistan at the peaks of their bloodletting. Iraq, triumphantly presented as a democratic beacon to the region by its invaders, had reached societal breakdown, as ethnic cleansers poured through its regions like acid, town by village, through neighbourhoods, even street by street. Yes, Saddam Hussein, a vile and cruel tormentor, had gone. But dozens of little Saddams took his place.[4]

By most logical estimates, hundreds of thousands have died, even if the precise figure may never be known. A mass exodus of teachers and doctors, civil servants and entrepreneurs, has haemorrhaged Iraq's future. By mid-2008, according to the United Nations High Commissioner for Refugees, nearly 5 million Iraqis – approaching one in five of the population – had been uprooted by this cataclysm, 2.2 million of them into exile abroad. Instead of bringing freedom to Iraq and the Arabs, the 2003 invasion has scattered Iraqis across the Middle East – as well as creating laboratory conditions for the urban warfare urged on jihadis by Ayman al-Zawahiri, al-Qaeda's strategist.

Politically, no viable institutions have emerged. There was no national narrative. Ministries became sectarian booty and factional bastions. The interior ministry, for instance, purportedly in charge of Iraq's security, according to one analysis had become a feuding federation of warlords headquartering several death squads, partitioned into factional fiefs on each of its 11 floors – with the seventh floor split between armed wings of two US-allied groups.[5]

As we shall examine further, two ostensibly benign by-products of the US invasion of Iraq were: the empowerment of the Shia majority there, giving the sect, a dispossessed minority within Islam, rights they were denied for centuries; and the welcome panic of an ossified Sunni Arab regional order based on a toxic mix of despotism, economic failure and social inequity that incubated extremism. But more than five years on, Shia politicians had shown little willingness to put state above sect, or to do more than take what they saw as their rightful turn in the tyrant's seat. Such was the Sunni jihadi-abetted backlash, moreover, and the intra-Shia fight over the spoils, that the Shia populace had not so much come into its inheritance as entered a new circle of hell.

The Shia-led government of Nouri al-Maliki pursued the narrow sectarian interest of his faction of the Da'wa party and its ally, SCIRI, the most powerful though not the most popular Shia group. The pass that Iraq had reached by mid-2008 made it hard to believe any set of policies – let alone a slow-motion surge unaccompanied by perceptible political advance or national reconciliation – could deliver success, whatever that now meant. Iraq had not just fragmented into three big chunks: a Shia south, Sunni centre and Kurdish north, as mostly outside proponents of a so-called 'soft partition' tended to argue. It had unravelled into a terrifying and blood-spattered patchwork.

Yet some belief was nevertheless invested, again mostly from outside Iraq, in the person of General David Petraeus, the US commander leading the surge. General Petraeus, a post-Vietnam student of counter-insurgency with a PhD from Princeton and a flair for PR, had been lionized for his command of the 101st Airborne Division in 2003–4, and in particular for his 'hearts and minds' campaign in the north, taken up by think tanks and some commentators in the US and British press as a template for what should have been happening in the rest of Iraq as the Sunni insurgency gathered strength, and Shia radicals under Moqtada al-Sadr launched two insurrections against the occupation.

After his withdrawal from the north, however, about two thirds of Mosul's security forces defected to the insurgency and the rest went down like fairground ducks. His forces appear not to have noticed, moreover, that al-Qaeda-inspired jihadis, some of them Saudi Wahhabis, had established a bridgehead in and around Mosul before the war had even started. It might be added that it was while Petraeus was acting as trainer-in-chief of the Iraqi army – barely existent outside rebadged militia and Kurdish pershmerga – that the missing Kalashnikovs reported by the GAO disappeared.[6]

Five years into the quagmire, however, and US commanders found little difficulty in detecting the hand of Tehran everywhere. This usually evidence-free blaming of serial setbacks on Iranian forces and agents was a bad case of denial and a flimsy alibi. In the Iraq affair, the obvious needs continual restatement.

First, the insurgency that came into being after 2003 was overwhelmingly Sunni and Iraqi, built around a new generation of jihadis created by the Anglo-American invasion. Second, to the extent foreign fighters were involved

– particularly as suicide bombers – these came mostly from US-allied and Sunni Saudi Arabia, not Shia Iran. Third, the lethal roadside bombs made with shaped charges that US officials coated with a spurious veneer of technical sophistication to prove Iranian provenance were made mostly by Iraqi army-trained engineers – using high explosives from those arms dumps the occupation forces left so casually unsecured.

It is, of course, the case that Iran has backed a lot of horses in Iraq – maybe even every horse on the Shia side. But had it wished to bring what remains of the country down around US ears it could have done so. So far, it has not. Iran, in its own interest, has preferred a stable, allied and weak Iraq; if it had not, the position of the USA would long ago have become untenable. The plain fact is that Tehran's main clients in Iraq were the same as Washington's: Maliki's Da'wa and the Islamic Supreme Council of Iraq, led by Abdelaziz al-Hakim (which perhaps changed its name from Supreme Council for the Islamic Revolution in Iraq, SCIRI, to prevent the discomfiture of its American patrons).

The mullahs in Tehran and Iran's Revolutionary Guard had a newer and, on the thin evidence, more tentative relationship with the unpredictable Moqtada al-Sadr and his Mahdi army, whose Iraqi and Arab nationalist declaiming is not all music to Persian ears. Sadr, in any event, largely stood down his forces during the surge.

The surge was only one of five factors behind the (no less welcome) relative fall in violence, all of them, as remarked earlier, temporary and reversible.

Caught between the need to crush the Sunni jihadism the invasion transplanted to Iraq and proliferated across the region, and fear of Shia radicalism and the meddling of an emboldened Iran, US forces started financing, equipping and licensing Sunni insurgents who had turned on al-Qaeda in western and central Iraq, sickened by their violence and threatened in their tribal prerogatives. But this recourse to more than 90,000 tribal militiamen – the so-called *Sahwa* or 'Awakening', and former insurgents metamorphosed into 'Sons of Iraq' – could very easily rebound. It fits a US pattern in the region of reliance on strongmen, in this case the only difference being the number of them. It not only started a scramble for patronage that could lead to conflict between Sunnis beyond the fight against al-Qaeda and its attempt to establish an Islamist statelet in Sunni areas. For the majority of Sunni who have no interest in establishing a bin Ladenist emirate in Iraq, much less a new Caliphate, this American tilt towards them – complete with their military reconfiguration – was the most empowering moment since the destruction of Saddam Hussein's regime. In the absence of what they consider to be their rightful share of power – which had always amounted to holding the whip hand in modern Iraq – and unless they become resigned to Shia supremacy (and there was no sign of that), the *Sahwa* could easily turn its guns on the occupation or this or any future Iraqi government. By the autumn of 2008, stand-offs between Sunni militiamen and the Maliki government – which had taken over responsibility for paying them from the USA but instead harassed and arrested them – were becoming frequent.

Commanders with a sense of history, moreover, would surely not be talking up the Sunni militias as 'Kit Carson's Scouts' (a reference to captured Viet Cong, 'turned' by US forces and then used, to little ultimate effect, against the enemy in Vietnam), or the 'oil spots' strategy of trying to seep the bits of Iraq back together again, from the bottom up – as in *les taches d'huile*, tried and failed by the French in Vietnam.[7]

Second, the decision by Moqtada al-Sadr to stand his Mahdi forces aside looked less than permanent. It looked, in fact, like the latest in the many tactical retreats he had learned to make, and responded initially to Shia outrage at fighting between the Sadriyyun and the Badr corps, the armed wing of SCIRI, in Najaf and Kerbala in August 2007, and his need to impose discipline on his increasingly unbridled followers. Furthermore, Moqtada was coming under huge pressure to break his ceasefire as the USA tried to replicate its ostensible success with the Sunni Awakening to raise Shia tribal levies to pick off Sadrist cadres, while the Maliki government, under the guise of suppressing militia rule in Basra and elsewhere in the south, was preferentially targeting its Sadrist rivals, and banning them from future elections unless they disbanded the Mahdi army. Sadr, as we shall see, faced a genuine political dilemma, analogous to the choices that faced Hizbollah in Lebanon, a movement he has sought to emulate: whether to cash in such credit as he had and become a national movement inside the political mainstream, operating by democratic rules, or to trade on resistance as an Islamist vanguard.

Third, Iran, for its part, had been offering a degree of cooperation in stabilizing Iraq. It had been meeting with officials from the USA (as well as countries neighbouring Iraq), even if the two sides frequently read out litanies of grievances at each other instead of discussing plans to restore calm and rebuild Iraq. It was Iranian officials who damped down the spread of fighting across the Shia heartland after Maliki's forces got in over their heads in the improvised Basra 'charge of the knights' in the spring of 2008.[8]

But Tehran's cooperation in Iraq would always have a price, in US and allied recognition of Iran's status as a regional power and its security concerns. The Bush administration would certainly never meet it and, given the last three decades of visceral animosity and distrust between the two sides, and Washington's unconditional support for an Israel that saw in Iran the main challenge to its regional hegemony, it was a moot point whether any future American administration could either. Meanwhile, Iran's Islamic Republic remains the single biggest winner of this war.

Fourth, one chilling reason for the dip in violence was that ethnosectarian cleansing in Baghdad and central Iraq had largely been completed. The perfectly aimed blow by Abu Musab al-Zarqawi and his local al-Qaeda franchise, in destroying the al-Askari shrine in Samarra on 22 February 2006, by targeting the Shia, unleashed two years of inter-communal savagery that saw to that. It is important to remember the contextual and tactical details of this incident, because something like it can easily be repeated. At the time, mainstream insurgents – nationalist or neo-Ba'athist, tribal or Sunni supremacist – had been turning against the murderous Zarqawi and his swaggering henchmen. If even half the reports of shoot-outs between insurgent groups and jihadis were true, al-Qaeda had reason to feel dismay. Its tactical solution was classic.

By destroying a shrine the Shia hold in particular reverence, they aimed to polarize Iraq irrevocably between the idolatrous Shia and the Sunni, stampeding everyone back into their sectarian ghettoes. The Sunni, in this reasoning, would have to hang together or hang separately. In recent memory, this logic was employed by all sides in the Lebanese civil war and the wars of the Yugoslav succession. It works.

The Shia had until then resisted provocations that had killed them by the scores, and then in hundreds, through attacks on their leaders, their pilgrims and their markets, even the destruction of their mosques. But the importance of the golden-domed al-Askari shrine cannot be overstated. It housed the tombs of the tenth and eleventh Shia Imams, direct descendants of the Prophet Mohammed and grandfather and father to the twelfth and last 'hidden Imam', who disappeared around 939 and, in Shia belief, survives supernaturally until his return at the end of time as the Mahdi or Messiah. This attack was on the Shia's very identity and, in an almost literal sense, apocalyptic. So were its consequences.

Although those have died down they could flare up again, especially if large numbers of refugees – disproportionately Sunni – start returning. There is nothing permanent about the blast walls segregating the communities in Baghdad. Another outrage on this scale, such as the assassination of Grand Ayatollah Ali al-Sistani, the most revered Shia spiritual leader, could set this diabolical cycle in motion again. Sectarian warriors know the formula. It is tried and tested.[9]

Fifth, and finally, the numbers of US troops needed to sustain the surge, straining US military might close to its limit and over-reliant on reserve forces such as the National Guard, is intrinsically temporary. One might add that they are not the only force in the region. Iraq's neighbours periodically show signs of weighing whether the moment has come to intervene in Iraq in defence of their perceived interests: Iran behind the Shia, Saudi Arabia and Jordan in defence of the Sunni, and Turkey to prevent the Kurds from establishing their independence.

Public perception of the success of the surge, moreover, especially in the USA, may be connected to the dramatic fall off of media coverage during its course. The Pew Project for Excellence in Journalism and, separately, the Associated Press tracked a tenfold drop in Iraq coverage between 2007 and 2008, in broadcast and front-page newspaper coverage respectively. The significant exception was a spike in September 2007, coincident with the relatively upbeat report on the surge General Petraeus presented to Congress.[10]

The GAO's June 2008 review of the 18-month surge (or New Way Forward in Iraq) painstakingly separated the undoubted and temporary security gains from the equally obvious lack of a strategic framework to restore stability to the country, suggesting – in contrast to a triumphalist Pentagon document issued simultaneously that continued to harp on Iran's meddling in Iraq – that the achievement was little more than a house of cards. The snapshots of Iraq in the rival reports appeared to be talking about two different countries.

The Pentagon claimed 70 per cent of Iraqi forces had reached independent operational readiness, for example, while the GAO put this figure at 10 per cent of units, few of which could operate at all without US military support. The Congressional watchdog blew a gaping hole in the administration's sunny reconstruction narrative, pointing out that Iraq's central ministries, including those in charge of security, had been unable to spend more than 12 per cent of their capital budget. A subsequent report in August 2008 revealed that Iraq was on course to accumulate a $79 billion budget surplus as a result of its (and the occupation's) institutional inability to carry out reconstruction investment. Politically, moreover, all but nothing had advanced in terms of the national reconciliation for which the surge was supposed to create the breathing space. The law to undo the blanket de-Ba'athification decree of Paul Bremer and amnesty the mass of public servants whose jobs under Saddam had required their membership of the Ba'ath party had yet to see a single purged Iraqi readmitted to government service. There was still no agreed formula for sharing oil revenue around the country. There was no progress on the division of power between provinces, regions and the federation (including the question of oil-rich Kirkuk, bitterly contested between Kurds and Arabs), and no clear way forward for the provincial elections due in the autumn of 2008, then postponed to 2009. These were, in any case, all elements of a wishful formula to conciliate the Sunni, which were scattered randomly throughout US policy initiatives and poorly coordinated agencies.[11]

President Bush's earlier assertion, on the fifth anniversary of the war, that the USA was in sight of 'a major strategic victory' in Iraq was a fantasy in keeping with his administration's delusional take on the whole sorry misadventure. There was no strategy.

Strategically, Iraq is a catastrophe. It has confounded two of the main (if undeclared) aims of the war: to deter all but the most determined opponent of US interests by an awesome demonstration of American military force; and by conquering Baghdad to establish hegemony in the Gulf and provide the tools to refashion the whole Middle East in America's democratic image.

What these five years have instead provided is the most public demonstration of the limits to American power – watched live on satellite television throughout the Arab and Muslim worlds like a modern version of the Crusades – which has done incalculable damage to the reputation of the USA (and an exiguous band of allies led by Tony Blair) for statesmanship, for projecting power, for even elementary competence. For many Arabs and Muslims, moreover, this latest, malign, intervention has buried the idea of democracy in the rubble of Iraq.

Having casually overturned the Sunni Arab order in Iraq and established the Shia in power in an Arab heartland country for the first time in a millennium, hugely enhancing the influence of Shia Islamist Iran, the USA and its acolytes have unleashed powers across the Middle East that, so far, nobody can control.

* * * * *

When Saddam Hussein seized absolute power in Iraq in 1979, the first move he made to consolidate his self-promotion from being the power-behind-the-throne was to uncover a Syrian plot. That enabled him and his Ba'ath party subordinates personally and publicly to execute 22 rivals, and cleared the way for a definitive break with the competing Ba'athist regime in Damascus. A year later, he invaded Iran, launching eight years of war against the nascent Islamist revolutionary regime that cost an estimated 1 million lives.

When the Iraqi dictator invaded Kuwait in 1990, Egypt and Syria harnessed the Arabs to the US-led coalition to evict him.

In the spring of 1998, however, as the USA and the UK looked almost certain to unleash heavy bombardments on Iraq for obstructing UN weapons inspectors, it was Syria, Iran and Egypt that raised the loudest voices against military action. Saddam's ministers were received attentively in Damascus, Tehran and Cairo. Even Saudi Arabia, the launch pad for the allies in the Gulf War of 1991, upon which Saddam had rained Scud missiles, was so unhappy at the prospect of a new assault on Iraq that it refused the USA the use of its bases in the kingdom. And in the vanguard of the pro-Iraqi demonstrations that erupted from Turkey to Jordan were the Islamists, for whom the pan-Arab nationalist ideology of the Ba'ath is anathema.

Had Arab leaders, justly famed for their ideological and religious rivalries, their vicious personal animosities, and their vying for regional supremacy, buried their antagonisms? Did they all have some end-of-millennium rush of blood, a vision commanding them to forsake their intra-brotherly intrigues? Most unlikely.

Rather, they were responding collectively to baser and sounder instincts of self-preservation. The realignment then taking place across the Arab world (and including Iran) was a response to the failure and unreliability of US policy in the region, and to fear – especially among USA allies such as Egypt and Saudi Arabia – that American blundering and bad faith could end by undermining their regimes. Western reliance on military force in its attempts to deal with the problems of the region was revealed as politically impotent long before the full-scale invasion of Iraq.

After the Gulf War, and following the collapse of the Soviet Union which had sponsored 'front-line' states such as Syria – notionally in the struggle against Israel but more as pawns on the Cold War chessboard – the peoples of the Middle East believed the victorious US, bestriding the region like a colossus, would fashion an Arab–Israeli settlement, in its own interest as much as anything else. Washington would use its leverage with its Israeli ally – on whom it had used a variety of blandishments to stay out of the Gulf conflict despite Saddam's provocative spray of Scud missiles on Israel's cities – to secure the return of conquered Arab land and a Palestinian state in exchange for Arab recognition of Israel and its right to live in peace. And so it first seemed.

But despite the US-convened Madrid conference in 1991, the 1993–5 Oslo accords between Israel and the Palestinians, and the 1994 peace treaty with Jordan, this did not happen. Israel remained in occupation of most of the West Bank, Gaza and Arab east Jerusalem, and continued to hold Syria's Golan Heights and its enclave in south Lebanon 12 per cent of Lebanese land. After the assassination in late 1995 of Yitzhak Rabin, the Israeli soldier–premier and architect of Oslo, and a series of Islamist suicide bombings in early 1996, Benjamin Netanyahu came to power in Israel, at the head of a right-wing coalition that not only was irredentist in its neo-Biblical belief that all of *Eretz Israel*, the Israel of the Torah and the Old Testament had been granted to the Jews by God, but also held that Israeli security required a solid buffer of occupied Arab land. Just as provocatively (but in this case to a wider Muslim audience), Netanyahu pressed full speed ahead with the Jewish colonization of east Jerusalem – which houses the holiest sanctuaries of Islam after Mecca and Medina – in an attempt to separate the heart of any future Palestinian state from its hinterland in the West Bank.[12]

The US administration of Bill Clinton seemed either powerless or unwilling to press Israel to honour its international commitments. It further muddied the waters by pursuing the 'dual containment' strategy of Islamist Iran and Saddam's Iraq. This signally failed to isolate Iran, which treated and traded with Europe and was courted by Russia. But it also built up the prestige of Saddam Hussein among the Arab masses. Neither the draconian UN sanctions that devastated the living, health and education standards of ordinary Iraqis, while the grip on power of their rulers was strengthened by smuggling, kickbacks, black marketeering and clandestine assets, nor a string of failed military assaults and shambolic plots, had brought him down. The vainglorious Saddam had, in his two decades of absolute power, reduced the median level of Iraqis' income from the respectable levels of a European Union member such as Greece to the sub-Saharan depths of a Mali. Yet many of his people did not blame him, but the United States and the western democracies.

In this topsy-turvy context, and enraged by the failure of the peace process, Arab leaders started putting a brake on the 'normalization' of ties with Israel. By the autumn of 1997 they had boycotted a US-sponsored regional economic summit in Doha – the fourth in a series intended to buttress the now defunct peace process with development architecture – and instead turned up to an Islamic summit in Tehran under Iranian leadership: Iraq's first international outing since the Gulf War. A new regional jigsaw was emerging.

Syria was making up with Iraq, and Iraq was mending fences with Iran. Most striking of all was the more general Arab rapprochement with Tehran. Zbigniew Brzezinski, national security adviser under President Jimmy Carter, summed up the situation after a US stand-off with Iraq in November 1997. 'Our policy of dual containment to isolate two countries has been a smashing success', he said, 'the only problem is that the two countries are the United States and Israel'.[13]

Although this process of realignment was always fragile, it looked very much then as though the Arabs had concluded they had to reach their own regional accommodation, at best reticent to the USA and hostile to Israel. This was the most extraordinary squandering of the political capital America had accumulated since the Gulf War, and Saddam Hussein, no great student of geopolitics but cunning for all that, intended to take full advantage of it.[14]

A Bedouin tale that Crown Prince Abdullah, heir to the ailing King Fahd and then already de facto ruler of Saudi Arabia, is said to have told Madeleine Albright captures the spirit of the moment. A livestock owner, he related, whose flock was losing a lamb every three or four days to a wolf, was persuaded by a friend to buy from him 20 fierce guard dogs to keep the predator at bay. But before long he found he had to slaughter three or four lambs every day to feed the guard dogs. Pausing for effect, Abdullah is then supposed to have gone on: 'at that point, the owner of the flock decided to get rid of the guard dogs and co-exist with the wolf, as that was the least costly, and perhaps the less dangerous course'.

* * * * *

Saddam sensed the moment to break out of his post-Gulf War quarantine. Saddam by name, Saddam by nature. The word in Arabic means 'one who confronts' or 'hits out', and Saddam Hussein had rarely disappointed on that score.

Born into a family of unlettered brigands in 1938, Saddam's Fagin-like stepfather (and Nazi sympathizer) forced him into thievery at an early age. In the turbulent decade following the overthrow of the Hashemite monarchy in Baghdad in 1958, he shot his way up the ladder of the pan-Arab nationalist Ba'ath party, which, by the time it seized power in 1968, had been captured by power-hungry army officers.

When he seized total power in 1979 he consolidated it with henchmen from his home town of Tikrit. Tikrit, north of Baghdad, was described by Gibbon in the eighteenth century as 'an impregnable fortress of independent Arabs'. It was the birthplace of Saladin, the Muslim hero who liberated Jerusalem from the Crusaders. That was the mantle the Iraqi despot sought to don after Egypt withdrew from the confrontation with Israel by making the 1979 Camp David peace, creating a vacancy Saddam sought to fill. There was no limit to his personality cult or his imposture.

The new Sword of the Arabs transubstantiated himself into a descendant of the Prophet Mohammed, and traced a leadership line to Nebuchadnezzar, the Babylonian king who destroyed Jerusalem in 587 of the pre-Christian era. Yet, though he waged permanent war against his own people, fought the

Kurds, the Persians, his former sponsors in the Arab Gulf, the Syrians (through proxies in Lebanon) and, of course, the Anglo-American coalition, it was only as a grandiloquent afterthought in mid-Gulf War that he lobbed token salvoes of missiles in the general direction of Israel.

In his heyday, fighting Iran and courted by the Gulf Arabs and the West as the buffer to the Islamist revolution of Ayatollah Ruhollah Khomeini, he nevertheless did acquire some credibility in the region as an Arab champion – an aura that enabled his backers then to overlook his use of chemical weapons against the Kurds in northern Iraq and the Iranians in the Fao peninsula.

In a rare interview shortly before he invaded Iran in 1980, he said: 'I always tend to differentiate between ... calculated temerity and downright risk.' So long as he could keep tightening the reins of absolute power inside Iraq, not even defeat on the battlefield could teach him his bellicose behaviour was anything other than calculated temerity.[15]

The visible decomposition of the Gulf War coalition was accompanied by disarray in the UN Security Council where, in October 1997, the USA and the UK sought a modest tightening of sanctions after Baghdad started its systematic obstruction of UN weapons inspectors. France, Russia and China, angered by Washington's dual containment policy of mixing up UN-mandated sanctions on Iraq with US unilateral sanctions against Iran – which attempted to extend America's legal reach to sanction European companies investing in Iran – blocked the measure. Saddam saw his chance and kicked out all American inspectors.

As US aircraft carrier groups prowled the Gulf and the Iraqi dictator continued to tweak the imperial tail, the crisis passed, only to re-erupt in February 1998. This time, the Anglo-American military build-up in the Gulf rang alarm bells across the region.

Hosni Mubarak, after consultations with 14 Arab leaders, talks with Madeleine Albright, and sending four alarmed messages to Saddam, said 'we are going to face a hell of a problem' if the air strikes go ahead. The point, he emphasized, 'is not what heads of state think. The point is what public opinion in our countries thinks. You will not find one [Arab] leader who will say publicly: "we support the air strikes".'

Mubarak thought Saddam had sensed, correctly, that popular sentiment in the Arab and Islamic worlds had swung to his side: 'This is not 1991 – I cannot stand against the whole weight of popular opinion.' Washington had imposed sanctions on Libya, Iran and Sudan, but 'done nothing about the Middle East peace process. That is what the people say. And then they see that the USA is preparing to attack Iraq', for ostensibly refusing to yield up all its weapons, while 'at the same time the Israelis have weapons of mass destruction and they say nothing'. The West 'does not understand the psychology of people in this part of the world: there are extremists waiting to act'.[16]

Self-serving though some of this may have been, it reflected genuine fear about the impact of US intervention in the region, and its ability to stir up dormant popular rage. It set the backdrop for Kofi Annan, then UN secretary general, to pull off an eleventh hour compromise with Baghdad that made him the toast of the Middle East.

But it also highlighted that the problem had ceased to be about dealing with Iraq in isolation. US failure to advance Middle East peace, and Washington's muddling of UN sanctions on Iraq with its own sanctions on Iran, helped Saddam emerge from the crisis no longer the regional pariah he was. The status quo ante was no longer available: the regional furniture had been rearranged. Washington and its allies needed to recover credibility by dealing with the now interlocking problems of the region as a whole.

By November 1998, however, for the third time in a year, a new face-off with Saddam set off another round of bluster and melodrama. This particular round of 'cheat and retreat' as the Americans called it ended with allied bombers in the air, literally minutes from their targets, before they were pulled back. But by the following month the two sides came to the clinch with Operation Desert Fox. Having marched their troops up the hill and then down again three times in a year, US (and UK) credibility was at stake, and their patience had snapped. That did not mean their strategy was any clearer.

The US–UK position was apparently simple: Iraq had to be prevented from recreating or deploying non-conventional weapons. But what it failed to explain was how this could be done from the air, especially since the crisis was caused by Baghdad's imputed success in concealing nerve gas and germ warfare agents from UN inspectors on the ground. At that stage, moreover, the 1991–8 inspections had succeeded in uncovering considerably more of Iraq's arsenal than had been destroyed in 40 days of bombing during the Gulf War, or by the salvoes of cruise missiles unleashed on Iraq in 1993 and 1996. Yet, there was a crucial difference: Saddam had failed to honour his agreement with Kofi Annan to allow inspectors 'unfettered access', then halted new field inspections and monitoring of previously uncovered sites. That took the wind out of the Arabs' always somewhat threadbare diplomatic sails. Saddam, as he so often did, had overplayed his hand.

Nonetheless, as the allied missile explosions and scatter-gun Iraqi anti-aircraft fire once more lit up the night sky over Baghdad, Washington and London were still struggling to convey that their strategy for dealing with the Iraqi despot amounted to more than shots in the dark.

As the operation started, President Clinton addressed the nation on television on 16 December: 'If Saddam can cripple the weapons inspection system and get away with it, he would conclude that the international community, led by the United States, has simply lost its will.' Quite so. But beyond demonstrating determination to punish defiance of the Security Council, what credibility did Anglo-American policy towards Iraq really have?

Aerial bombing, as remarked, had about as good a prospect of success as a silver bullet. US reliance on force as one of its two default positions in the region (the other was reliance on strongmen, which had puffed up Saddam as a regional threat) looked sterile.

Throughout this long period of crisis, American and British officials not only made clear that lifting sanctions while Saddam was still in power was, simply, off the table. They gave the impression of hankering back to the end of the Gulf War, when Baghdad, and Saddam, were at their mercy. Yet, they stood aside and watched passively as the Kurds rose in the north and an army-led rebellion in the south turned into a Shia insurrection, drowned in blood by Saddam. The tyrant would soon conduct a viciously careful new audit of wavering and dissent across the country (which would result in the assassination of Mohammed Sadeq al-Sadr, Moqtada's father, in February 1999).

The (then broad) alliance passed up the chance to unseat Saddam, fearing Iraq would disintegrate and destabilize the region. Inside Iraq, the coalition's decision to stand aside as the Shia and Kurds rose up was seen as an inexplicable betrayal. Outside it, the desire to see the back of the Iraqi leader was tempered both by fear someone or something worse might replace him, and by the calculation that his regime was just too strong to be toppled by his opponents.[17]

But American and British policy was shifting. By the end of 1998, President Clinton signed into law the Iraq Liberation Act, a definite, if wishful, move towards regime change as the stated goal, by providing funding for the largely external Iraqi opposition.

This was not a wholly new policy, insofar as the USA, through the CIA, had earlier bankrolled and supported the Iraqi National Congress, an umbrella group led – to use the term loosely – by Ahmad Chalabi in the post-war Kurdish 'safe haven' in north Iraq. That ended in humiliation and rout after Massoud Barzani's Kurdistan Democratic Party (KDP) allied with Saddam to take on his rival Jalal Talabani's Patriotic Union of Kurdistan (PUK), which sought logistical support from Iran. Washington's allies collapsed in bloody disarray, and cruise missile attacks at the time were a petulant irrelevance that did nothing to diminish the scale of the disaster.

Renewed courting of the Iraqi opposition left few in Washington with illusions about the cohesion of the – by the State Department's count – 73 different groups, many of them at each other's throats, much less their chances of survival under Saddam's ruthlessly efficient tyranny. If this motley crew was at all admired inside the Beltway at the time, it was as consummate international lobbyists, which earned them the dismissive sobriquet of the Frequent Flyers Group.

Nonetheless, by Desert Fox the rhetoric had perceptibly shifted too. Clinton told America: 'the hard fact is that so long as Saddam remains in power, he threatens the well-being of his people, the peace of his region and the security of the world. The best way to end that threat once and for all is with a new Iraqi government – a government willing to live in peace with its neighbours, a government that respects the rights of its people.' Tony Blair chimed in dutifully the following day that 'we look forward to the day Iraq has the government it deserves'.

Military briefers in both countries rushed to temper this rhetoric by pointing out that to kill, capture or remove Saddam 'would take many thousands of troops to have any chance of succeeding', as General Sir Charles Guthrie, UK chief of defence staff, put it. Nonetheless, there was a vague hope that Desert Fox would seriously erode, or even implode the regime. 'Change when it does come, often comes suddenly, and at unexpected times', mused Sandy Berger, Clinton's national security adviser: 'Change will come to Iraq at a time and in a manner that we can influence, but cannot predict.'

This thinking will have echoes for later observers of the Bush strategy towards Iraq. In this case it was more of a roll of the dice: hit Iraq hard enough and, you never know, something might turn up – geo-Micawberism parading as high policy.[18]

* * * * *

By the time George W. Bush entered the White House, therefore, the idea of regime change to deal with the still unresolved problem of Saddam Hussein was already a circulating currency. It was openly debated – and had been since Clinton's second term. Indeed, it came up at an early Bush cabinet meeting, but appeared to have little traction until the 11 September 2001 al-Qaeda attacks.

The initial US response to those acts of hyper-terrorism was measured, widely supported and obviously justified. As I remarked in Chapter III,

Osama bin Laden was clearly hoping for a disproportionate response from the USA, a spur to Muslims to rise up against the West and western-allied regimes across the Islamic world. He was disappointed.

Yet, the ostensible ease with which the USA and its allies were able to drive the Taliban out of the cities and al-Qaeda into the lawless frontier areas of Pakistan, and establish the new government of Hamid Karzai with international political and financial support, still left a wounded America deeply unsatisfied. Donald Rumsfeld, secretary of defense, complained there were too few 'quality' targets to hit in Afghanistan. His senior aides, such as Paul Wolfowitz and Douglas Feith, seem to have concluded almost from the moment the jihadi-commandeered airliners hit New York's twin towers that Iraq had to be the target.

Wolfowitz, for example, now Rumsfeld's deputy, had in 1992 authored a bold, post-Cold War strategy at the Pentagon, called Defense Planning Guidance, which argued that America should act decisively and pre-emptively where necessary to prevent the emergence of any rival to its power – among friend or foe. Regionally, that meant preventing the emergence of any hostile power whose resources could help fuel a regional or global challenge to US supremacy. In the Middle East, that meant the USA had to 'remain the predominant outside power in the region and preserve US and western access to the region's oil'.[19]

In 1996, Richard Perle, who worked in the Reagan Pentagon and under George W. Bush was chairman of the Defense Policy Board, along with Douglas Feith, drew up a position paper for Benjamin Netanyahu, Israel's hawkish prime minister, calling on him to tear up the Oslo accords with the Palestinians and work for the overthrow of Saddam Hussein in Iraq. In 1998, both men, under the rubric of the Project for a New American Century (PNAC), wrote to Clinton calling for the military overthrow of Saddam Hussein. The signatories to this petition read like a roll-call of the subsequent neo-conservative agitators for war in Iraq.[20]

After 9/11, with Rumsfeld in the Pentagon bent on revolutionizing warfare, Cheney as the most powerful vice-president in memory, and Bush having decided he was a 'wartime president', the audience for these ideas could hardly have been more receptive. By June 2002, Bush was telling a West Point audience that the old doctrines of deterrence and containment were now obsolete: 'We must take the battle to the enemy, disrupt his plans, and confront the worst threats before they emerge.' The Bush doctrine had emerged.[21]

It is not my purpose here to retell the story, already well documented, about how, on both sides of the Atlantic, the Bush and Blair governments in 2002–3 cherry-picked and customized often dubious intelligence to make a mendacious case for a war that had pretty much been decided on in the spring of 2002, by exaggerating the threat of Iraq's weapons and insisting on a link between Saddam and al-Qaeda for which there was no evidence.

My own position before the war was: that Saddam's WMD capability was 'confined to residual chemical and biological weapons'; that while he had used chemical weapons against the Kurds and Iran, they were not in a position to reply in kind, whereas during the Gulf War and subsequently Saddam was deterred not only from using such weapons but at times from deploying conventional forces in a threatening way; that the idea of his subcontracting to jihadis was bogus, although that might change once the USA started threatening his survival; that the undeterrable creed espoused by bin Laden's band of zealots, an ideology bordering on fascism, was the foremost threat to liberal values and international stability, not Saddam Hussein; and that by going after the wrong target, the USA would further deprive itself of the legitimacy it needed in the Arab and Muslim worlds to crush al-Qaeda, the clear and present danger that attacking Iraq would 'proliferate, not combat'.[22]

But my main concern here is to outline what were the main reasons – as I believed then, and have more reason to believe now – driving this hopelessly misconceived policy.

First, the USA appeared determined to mount such an overwhelming display of military force that it would awe its foes and give the average tyrant great pause, deterring, as I have said, all but the most determined challenge to US interests. It may also have been an attempt to erase the sense of vulnerability Americans felt after 11 September.

Bob Woodward, in the third of his chronicles of Bush at War, *State of Denial*, recounts a conversation between Michael Gerson, Bush's chief speechwriter, and Henry Kissinger. The former secretary of state, asked why he supported the war on Iraq, answered: 'Because Afghanistan wasn't enough ... in the conflict with radical Islam', he said, 'they want to humiliate us. And we need to humiliate them'.[23]

While belief in the efficacy of American military power undoubtedly played its part, a further aspect encouraging the decision to use Iraq as a demonstration model was, simply, that it was doable. Woodward further recounts a report commissioned by Wolfowitz, which concluded that while Egypt and Saudi Arabia, where most of the 9/11 hijackers came from, were the key, 'the problems there are intractable', and Iran 'was similarly difficult to envision dealing with'. Saddam Hussein, by contrast, was weak and vulnerable. While that may have led any dispassionate strategist to conclude that containment had therefore worked in Iraq, this cabal concluded that doability meant inevitability: 'We concluded that a confrontation with Saddam was inevitable. He was a gathering threat – the most menacing, active and unavoidable threat. We agreed that Saddam would have to leave the scene before the problem could be addressed.' Rather than attack the sources of the jihadi problem, in other words, administration strategists sought regime change at the weakest link in the Arab power chain as the lever to transform the entire region.[24]

Nowhere in this expansive vision of an exemplary display of American firepower did anyone explain how it would land a single blow on bin Laden and his ilk. Leaving aside the never convincing and subsequently refuted attempts to connect and conflate the improbable duo of Saddam and Osama, to much of the world, and all of the Islamic world, this looked as though Washington, frustrated by the lack of any quick way to defeat the asymmetric threat of al-Qaeda, was nevertheless determined to stage a show of its unprecedented power in a conventional war.

The second main reason driving the warriors was bound up with the need to re-establish supremacy in the Middle East and, especially, the Gulf. There is scope for disagreement about whether the war was about oil: in the narrow sense of wanting to get access to Iraq's oil reserves, the third largest in the world. Personally, I have always thought the oil aspect of the strategy was far more ambitious. For most of the preceding century, the Gulf had always been under the clear control of an outside power or its local proxy. That role fell to Britain in the first half century, succeeded by the Shah of Iran after the Anglo-American-mounted coup in 1953 against Mohammad Mossadegh after he nationalized Iranian oil. Then, after the fall of the Shah, it fell to Saddam Hussein to act as the de facto policeman and US-backed bulwark against Islamist Iran. The decade following the Gulf War and Saddam's eviction from Kuwait was an anomaly. It made arrangements for controlling the Gulf unsatisfactory: a rogue Baghdad, though defeated, refused to lie down, requiring constant intervention by the USA. From there to the conclusion that control of Baghdad would not only clarify the position in the Gulf but refashion the Middle East in America's democratic image – the seductive fantasy of tyrants falling like ninepins across the region – seems to have been but a short step for the neo-conservatives in Washington.

But the third reason, which could not be dismissed as a fantasy, was the genuine concern about the proliferation of weapons of mass destruction. The conviction – supported by his obstructive behaviour towards UN weapons inspectors – that Saddam Hussein was still trying to develop such weapons, and that these might fall into the hands of terrorists, was the most often and overtly proclaimed purpose of US (and British) policy. If there was any reasoned possibility that any jihadist group around the world might acquire and use such weapons, then that eventuality was so appalling that almost any action to prevent it might seem justified.

As I have stated above, my own conviction, before the war, was that Iraqi WMD capability was 'confined to residual chemical and biological weapons', and that, despite much portentous and lurid rhetoric, and extensive catalogues about what Saddam had done in the past, neither the USA nor the UK could produce clear evidence beyond this. We now know such intelligence as there was to have been flawed, tendentious, politically misused and, in some instances, fabricated and fed into a special unit at the Pentagon and favoured news outlets by Iraqi exiles typified by Ahmad Chalabi. We know now that not one of the nearly 30 assertions about WMD secretary of state Colin Powell made to the UN Security Council in February 2003 – having weeded out what he regarded as the flakiest evidence – turned out to be true. The confidence of what was never more than a case for the prosecution contrasted with the inability of the USA to provide any actionable intelligence to the UN inspectors then on the ground. We know, too, that there were no WMD in Iraq.[25]

Pretty much everyone knew except President Bush, that is, who in his first State of the Union address after the invasion continued to claim that weapons inspectors had 'identified dozens of weapons of mass destruction-related program activities', an assertion that reached the border at which words part company with meaning.[26]

Nevertheless, to repeat, there was nothing intrinsically absurd about the spectre of WMD proliferation. Yet, it is for precisely that reason that the determination to see Iraq as the prime locus of such concern seemed so unconvincing – before, not just after the invasion. The Bush administration's bafflingly cavalier approach to *real* threats from nuclear weapons was, if anything, highlighted by its pursuit of phantom weapons in Iraq.

Pakistan, for example, already had nuclear weapons, and a well-implanted jihadi movement afforded some licence by its military-backed government – whereas Iraq had neither. There was, moreover, already reason to suspect Pakistani involvement in nuclear proliferation, which would later surface in full with the uncovering of the trafficking network run by A.Q. Khan, the 'father' of Pakistan's bomb, in January 2004. But deputy secretary of state Richard Armitage had raised the concern that North Korea might acquire nuclear capability from Pakistan as early as June 2001.[27]

The Bush administration, furthermore, antagonized Pakistan by agreeing to a nuclear treaty with its traditional enemy India. The USA would cooperate with India's nuclear programme, even though New Delhi continued to reject the nuclear Non-Proliferation Treaty – still, despite its flaws, the most successful attempt to halt the spread of nuclear weapons – and would make no pledge not to accelerate its bomb-making capacity or tighten its controls on the export of sensitive technology. This is not academic. India and Pakistan, who have fought three full-scale wars since the partition of the Indian subcontinent in 1947, were twice within hours of war, in January and late May 2002, with the religious right ascendant and rattling their nuclear sabres on both sides of the border. This irresponsible deal would surely communicate to, say, Iran that the best way to get into the nuclear club is by breaking and entering.

North Korea was an even clearer threat. It was known to be trying not only to enrich uranium but to reprocess plutonium, the two routes to atomic weapons. Yet, in 2002, as he prepared to go after his holy grail in Iraq, Bush cancelled the only policy the USA had devised to prevent them: the Agreed Framework hammered out painstakingly by the Clinton administration in 1993–4. Those negotiations only took place, moreover, after Clinton had issued a clear threat of military action unless the Koreans desisted and came to the table – further proof that the approach of deterrence and containment so disdained by the Bush team could work.

The Agreed Framework renewed Pyongyang's commitment to the nuclear Non-Proliferation Treaty, placed inspectors on the ground, and sealed North Korean nuclear facilities, in exchange for fuel supplies, the promise of two light water reactors for electricity, and a US pledge not to invade. Bush's repudiation of the agreement would lead to North Korea – a country with almost no source of hard currency except missile trafficking – restarting its weapons programme. Washington's histrionically muscular stance – featuring Bush's placing Pyongyang within the 'axis of evil' and diatribes about the 'pygmy' dictator Kim Jong-il – led it eventually to rely on China's mediation to get back to something like the Agreed Framework – but only after North Korea had managed to develop a rudimentary bomb.[28]

But perhaps the clearest example showing how the Bush administration was not really engaging in non-proliferation in its approach to Iraq or anywhere else was visible in its disdain for the extraordinary programme designed by Senator Richard Lugar and (now former) Senator Sam Nunn, a post-Cold War initiative passed by Congress in 1992. The Nunn–Lugar programme, known as Cooperative Threat Reduction, was designed to secure nuclear weapons and stocks of enriched uranium and plutonium throughout the former Soviet Union, financed by the USA but in cooperation with Moscow. Its achievements are unassailable.

By the time Bush took office it had secured or destroyed literally thousands of potentially 'loose nukes' that in the context of the disintegration of the Soviet Union could easily have ended up in the wrong hands. Its scorecard after 15 years included the destruction or disabling of 7,300 nuclear warheads, of some 700 intercontinental ballistic missiles and 900 air-to-surface nuclear missiles, as well as more than 500 tons of fissile material. This endeavour, which found and decommissioned real WMD that presented real threats, has been rightly described as America's best investment in peace and international security since the post-Second World War Marshall Plan. Yet, despite rhetorical support, the Bush–Cheney White House and the Rumsfeld Pentagon chipped away at its funding – which in total amounted to less than two months of the escalating cost of occupying Iraq.

It is very hard to believe, therefore, that Iraq was ever really about rogue weapons. It was a demonstration to the world of America's unrivalled military might, a reaffirmation after the trauma of 9/11, to Americans and the world, of the irresistibility of US power. Iraq merely afforded the most opportune arena for this display. Bush invaded Iraq because he could. Unfortunately for Iraq, the Middle East and, of course, the USA and its allies, he could also do it without thought for the consequences.

* * * * *

The cheering crowds the Pentagon's favourite Iraqi exiles promised would greet the Anglo-American forces as liberators were nowhere to be seen as the coalition, harried by Saddam's irregular *fedayeen*, drove up through southern Iraq to take Baghdad, which fell on 9 April 2003. That moment was famously captured by the toppling of the giant bronze statue of Saddam in the capital's Firdos (Paradise) square, its severed head dragged through the streets, like the shattered visage with its lifeless sneer of cold command in Shelley's Ozymandias, all neatly choreographed by an alert American psychological warfare or 'psy-ops' team.

The real Iraqis that materialized on the roads of the south barely a week after the fall of Baghdad told a very different story to the stirring tales of Ahmad Chalabi and his friends. These real Iraqis came by the score and the hundred, then by the thousand, and tens of thousands, until they became millions. They thronged to the shrine city of Kerbala in southern Iraq, many barefoot, heads streaming with blood and backs lacerated by self-inflicted cuts and penitential flagellation. These were the Shia Muslims of Iraq, celebrating, in their way, the downfall of Saddam, their latest and vilest tormentor. They made an unnerving sight.

This march to Kerbala which greeted the perplexed invaders was at its primary level a great swell of religious emotion, a kind of collective transfiguration. Shia rituals had, over the past three decades, been driven underground by the Ba'ath party, the instrument of power of a cluster of Saddam-ite clans drawn from the Sunni Muslims, which in Iraq, unlike in most Arab countries, is the minority form of Islam. Saddam's regime was rightly wary of their politico-religious potency.

The pilgrims were asserting their right to atone ritually for their community's seventh-century betrayal of the Imam Hussein – the Prophet Mohammed's grandson and the emblematic martyr in the Shia canon – whose Christ-like image and black banners were held aloft in this Islamic passion play.

But the mass movement of people was, at the same time, an early and deadly earnest that the Iraqi Shia intended to claim their political entitlement after a century of struggle as a downtrodden majority. Watching from Beirut, Sheikh Hassan Nasrallah, leader of Hizbollah, the radical Lebanese Shia Islamist movement, linked the past and the future when he acclaimed the Kerbala pilgrims as 'inspired by the Imam Hussein's spirit of revolution'.

For the Americans devising policy in Washington and improvising government in Baghdad – who if they understood the difference between Shia and Sunni at all tended to see Shia politics as a blur of men in turbans beholden to the theocrats of Tehran – this was all alien and threatening. Donald Rumsfeld was soon warning that the USA would not allow anyone 'to transform Iraq in Iran's image'. Yet such statements revealed, as much as anything else, puzzlement about Iraq in general and the Shia – about 60 per cent of its 26 million people – in particular.

For more than a decade after the 1991 Gulf War, US spy satellites and patrolling allied warplanes had watched daily almost everything that moved in Iraq. But for knowledge about actual Iraqis, Washington had been listening to what it wanted to hear from the disproportionately secular and gilded exiles championed by the neo-conservatives in and around the Bush administration. US planners thus sent their troops into battle with an image of a country that resembled Iraq in every respect except the fears and hopes of its people, especially the Shia.

The Anglo-American alliance was thus surprised when the Shia failed to rise against Saddam as its forces stormed through their heartland on their way up to Baghdad. A stream of pre-scripted claims of Shia insurrection poured from the allied propaganda machine as the campaign advanced. Eventually, the penny dropped. After the Gulf War, the administration of George H.W. Bush had carelessly incited a Shia rising, initiated by embittered Iraqi troops fleeing Kuwait, that at one stage took control of most of the south. Combined with a simultaneous uprising by the Kurds in the north, it came tantalizingly close to overthrowing Saddam: at its height, the regime had lost control of 14 out of

Iraq's 18 provinces; by its end, Saddam's army had bullets left for only two days' fighting. While allied planes flew overhead, Saddam crushed the intifada, massacring untold tens of thousands, and the USA did not lift a finger.[29]

'The people could not, and cannot, forget what happened', said Sheikh Ali al-Ruba'i, representative of Grand Ayatollah Mohammed Ishaq Fayadh, one of Iraq's most senior clerics – referring to what the Shia regarded as the Anglo-American betrayal rather than Saddam's savage reprisals. He was speaking barely three months after the fall of Baghdad in the shrine city of Najaf, near where thousands of bodies were still being unearthed from mass graves: 'Only if the American forces now keep their promises might this yet be forgotten'. Sayyed Riad al-Hakim, son and spokesman of another grand ayatollah, Mohammed Sae'd al-Hakim, concurred: 'People heard [Tony] Blair's claim that "this time it's for real"', he said, 'but the masses ask us about the quality of American promises'.[30]

While Washington and London eventually took on board that the Shia were still locked in the trauma of their betrayal, they seemed taken aback at the speed with which Shia clerics and politico-religious leaders of undecipherable hues moved to establish their authority among Iraqis. From the cities of the south to the slums of Baghdad, the Shia establishment that survived the tyrant's massive purges stepped into the vacuum left by the collapse of Saddam's regime, providing not only welfare and basic services, but a semblance of the law and order the occupiers conspicuously failed to enforce. This religious authority worked as a restraint. Yet the unmistakable gathering of Shia strength, and Anglo-American nervousness about it, was already beginning to highlight what an extraordinary gamble the whole Iraq enterprise was. Irrespective of the shrill debate then raging about whether this adventure would nudge Iraq towards democracy or tip it into anarchy, one certainty was already hard and visible on the ground: Iraq's new rulers had transformed the balance of power in the region.

There was little doubt that the invasion and occupation could have as big an effect on the Middle East as Israel's crushing defeat of the Arab armies in the 1967 Six Day War – or perhaps even the very creation of the state of Israel in 1948. The USA was now a power in the Gulf and the Levant in the most blunt and front-line way. Neither the Americans nor the Arabs seemed to have a clear idea what this intrusion meant, but they all knew it spelt the end of the status quo.

The violent push into Iraq had set in motion tectonic shifts. The USA had not just overthrown a rogue regime: it had overturned a Sunni regime in the Arab heartland. Put another way, by opening the path to power for Iraq's Shia majority, Bush and the Washington neo-cons had undermined the nearly millennium-old dominance of Sunni Islam in Iraq and the Arab world, an unbroken run of power since the Fatimids, a heterodox Shia dynasty, collapsed in Cairo in 1171 and gave way to Saladin. Change does not come much bigger than that – but did it bear any relation to the aims of the intruders?

The reality of this upheaval seemed more apparent to Iraqis and Arabs than to the occupiers. Indeed, it looked as though the Americans had transformed the calculus in the Middle East as the British were said to have acquired an empire – in a fit of absent-mindedness.

Sunni leaders throughout the region, horrified by this challenge to their hegemony, as well as Shia leaders who oscillated between a bold new assertiveness and cautious disbelief, did not seem to know what to make of what the Americans were up to. Up until this radical departure, Washington had resolutely stood by Sunni rulers who defended the status quo, while taking fright at Shia leaders, who were inclined to raise the banners of social justice and the dispossessed.

'America is not even committed to its own ideas', said Grand Ayatollah Mohammed Hussein Fadlallah, the Najaf-born spiritual guide of Lebanon's Hizbollah until he fell out with Tehran in the early 1990s: 'its Arab allies are all tyrants, it has no use for anyone else'.[31]

The Shia remembered, as so many in the West did not, that the USA and European as well as Arab countries were prepared to back Saddam Hussein in his 1980–8 war against Iran to stop the Persian Shi'ite Islamist revolution of Ayatollah Ruhollah Khomeini reaching the Arab world. After Iraq's army collapsed in the 1991 Gulf War, Washington's two main Arab allies, Egypt and Saudi Arabia, persuaded the USA not to march on Baghdad and finish the regime off, arguing for imperative need to preserve 'the territorial integrity of Iraq'. Everyone genuflected to this goal, ostensibly to prevent the establishment of an Iranian satellite state in southern Iraq – ignoring the fact that the Iraqi Shia had fought against their Iranian coreligionists for eight years. What Riyadh and Cairo really wanted was to conserve Sunni hegemony in the Arab world; allowing Saddam to stay in power was a price well worth paying to achieve it.

The Sunni autocrats of Saudi Arabia and Egypt, moreover, had persuaded succeeding administrations in Washington that democracy was too risky in the Arab world, since it would only serve Iran and fundamentalism because of its inevitable outcome of 'one man, one vote, one time'. That the Shia (in Iran, south Iraq, eastern Saudi Arabia and, to an extent, in Kuwait) were sitting on about half of the world's storehouse of oil – one of God's little jokes – was not entirely irrelevant either.

Yet, as we have seen, it was out of the rot of the Sunni order that 9/11 was hatched – inspired, planned and executed largely by Saudis and Egyptians.

The Shia had no stake in this order and their attitudes were correspondingly different. Whether or not they were about to emerge as democrats, Shia leaders after the fall of Saddam definitely scented power, and not just in Iraq. All over the region they visibly had a new spring in their step.

One month after the fall of Baghdad, Mohammad Khatami, Iran's already embattled reformist president, visited the Lebanese capital Beirut, the first leader of the Islamic revolution to do so. Tens of thousands lined the route from the airport, through the teeming Shia southern suburbs to his hotel; some 50,000 Shia, the largest group in Lebanon's mosaic of 17 sects, filled a stadium to wave Iraqi and Iranian flags and Hizbollah banners at him. Nothing that big had happened since the late Pope John Paul had visited the country in 1997. Khatami cautioned against giving the USA or its Israeli allies any pretext to extend military action beyond Iraq, a warning – prescient as it would turn out – to Hizbollah to curb its militancy. In fluent Arabic he called for a 'popular government' in Baghdad, based on one man-one vote, denouncing any 'alien regime' as immoral. Less noticed was how he described Saddam's fall as a 'valuable opportunity' – for reform in the region and justice for the Shia.

Justice was what 450 Shia notables demanded in Saudi Arabia that same week. They presented a four-page petition to then Crown Prince Abdullah, succinctly titled 'Partners in the Nation' – something Saudi Shia have never been. Regarded as heretics by the ultra-puritan Wahhabi strain of Sunni Islam that legitimizes al-Saud rule, the Shia have been excluded from public life, denied their religious rights and politically hounded. Now, remarked Najib al-Khonaizi, a Saudi Shia writer, the upending of the regime in Iraq had blown the lid off the simmering tensions between Shia and Sunni in the Gulf and across the region.

It is an irony some Shii savour that their new horizons in the Arab world were opened not by the Persians, but by a Wahhabi fanatic whose loathing of their 'infidel' sect ranked with his hatred of the Americans: Osama bin Laden. It was 9/11 that led to a chain of 'wins' for the Shia, who played no part in the attacks. They 'won' in Afghanistan through the fall of the Taliban, which had persecuted the Hazara, the country's Shia minority. They 'won' again in Iraq, through the destruction of an oppressive Sunni regime. Even Iran, although still part of Bush's 'axis of evil' and under mounting western pressure to close down its nuclear programme, has emerged as a clear net winner. The Afghanistan and Iraq wars have, in a sense, allowed the USA to almost encircle Iran. But they have also rid Tehran of two mortal enemies – the Taliban and Saddam – as well as immeasurably enhancing Shia influence in the region. On the same day President Khatami was being feted in Beirut, for instance,

Ayatollah Mohammed Bakr al-Hakim, head of the Persian-accented Supreme Council for the Islamic Revolution in Iraq (SCIRI), was returning in triumph from exile in Tehran to the holy city of Najaf.

Yet Shia Islam is no monolith. Shia clerics have often been more enquiring in theology, philosophy and science than their Sunni counterparts, some of whom have taken refuge in flat-earth theory, repressive state orthodoxy or bin Laden's Manichean bigotry. In both Iran and Iraq, moreover, imperfect evidence suggests that, given the chance, clerical as well as popular majorities would come out against theocracy or the clergy having a constitutional role in government. A real liberation of Iraq would, among other things, highlight the historical divide between the Persian and Arab Shia. It did not take long, for example, for signs to emerge that influence was leaking away from the Iranian ayatollahs' stronghold of Qom to Najaf, historically, along with Kerbala, the spiritual centre of gravity of the Shia. The Supreme Council, for instance, was quick to change its allegiance from Iran's Supreme Leader, Ayatollah Ali Khamenei, to Ayatollah Sistani.

In the early months after the fall of Saddam, however, the new balance of power was still sketchy, little more than the play of shadow and light across the country and the region, before the steady drip of blood began. But even then, and against the backdrop of a mounting Sunni insurgency, it was safe to say that the outcome of this fascinating gamble to refashion the Middle East would ultimately depend on whether the USA would prove able to work with the Shia. Because if it lost its nerve and started to work against them, there was little doubt it would bring the revolutionary strain in their faith to the fore.

* * * * *

Shia Islam is a religion in which the themes of betrayal and dispossession run deep. The Imam Ali, whose tomb in Najaf gives the shrine city its emotional pull and pre-eminence, was – in most accounts – struck down by one of his own followers in 661. He had been the first to embrace the Islamic faith revealed to his cousin, the Prophet Mohammed, whose daughter Fatima he married. But, upon the Prophet's death, he was passed over three times as his successor, until he became the fourth Caliph, leader of all Muslims, in 656.

But when his successors lost the caliphate to the rival Umayyad dynasty, Ali became posthumously the first Shia Imam. His son Hussein, the Prophet's grandson, was slain at Kerbala in 680 – his small band of followers massively outnumbered in a suicidal contest that earned him the legend 'Prince of

Martyrs' – and betrayed by the people of Kufa who promised support but failed to rally to his cause. Kerbala turned the jostle for position and clash of values of early Islam into a permanent schism, in which the Shia – from *Shi'at Ali*, or partisans of Ali – were and remain the minority.

In their view, leadership of the community of believers was wrenched from the Prophet's house by impostors more concerned with worldly power than the will of God. This theme of usurpation emerges in another name the Shia sometimes give themselves: the *Ahl al-Beit*, or People of the (Prophet's) House. All of the 12 Shia Imams were direct descendants of Mohammed, but none except Ali led the whole Islamic commonwealth.

In the ninth or early tenth century, amid persecution by the Umayyad, then Abbasid dynasties, centred in Damascus and then Baghdad, the quasi-apostolic succession of the Shia imams ended. The 12th Imam was, by tradition, hidden as a child in about 873, then 'disappeared' around 939. As already remarked, in popular Shia belief the Hidden Imam (*Na'ib al-Amm*) survives supernaturally, a harbinger of justice who will return at the end of time as the Mahdi, or Messiah.

This doctrine, redolent of some of the Christian and Gnostic belief then common in the Middle East, is profoundly repellent to the orthodox Sunni. So too are the rituals associated with the Imam Hussein – comparable to the central event of the crucifixion in Christianity – and indeed the whole Shia iconography, which for the Sunni strays into idol-worship. The triptych of Ali, Hussein and his half-brother Abbas, and their mother Fatima, is all too reminiscent of the Holy Trinity and the Holy Family (though all Muslims revere Jesus Christ and his mother Mary). Any Christian (but especially a Catholic) who enters a Shia house, from Isfahan to Najaf, or from Karachi to the Lebanese Bekaa, will feel a shock of recognition at the religious images.

Despite this highly emotive iconography, the themes of martyrdom and betrayal, the esoteric messianism and the theoretical obeisance to an Imam – in Sunni practice a mere prayer-leader, for the Shia a sort of priest-king – Shia thinking has at times tended to be more dynamic than Sunni orthodoxy. That may in part be due to the Shia being a disadvantaged and episodically repressed minority.

Well before the Shia stagnated into a minority, their clerics embraced the need to update and continually reinterpret their doctrine in the light of modern developments. The Sunni establishment, by contrast, from the tenth and eleventh centuries began to discourage philosophical speculation and theological innovation as divisive and potentially heretical. Over succeeding centuries two very different approaches emerged, central to which was the problem of the concept of *Ijtihad*, mentioned in the previous chapter. This device – literally meaning reasoning by analogy but, more generally, independent reasoning by qualified scholars – is the means through which the Muslim 'learned' or *Ulema* adapt the revealed word of God in the Quran and the doings and sayings of the Prophet (*Hadith*) to evolving circumstance. The Sunni *Ulema* declared 'the gates of *Ijtihad*' closed nearly a millennium ago, once the four recognized schools of orthodox Islamic jurisprudence took shape (and the last significant Shia dynasty, the Fatimids, was dissolved). Though riven by the same debates, senior Shia clerics – significantly referred to as *Mujtahid*, from the same Arabic root as *Ijtihad* – continued to assert the indispensable validity of *Ijtihad* and the need for considered independent reasoning to confront the challenges of modernity. That is what puts many of them in the same philosophical tradition as the Islamic modernizers examined in the last chapter (or even the Saudi Islamist reformers we shall meet in the next chapter).

A second and profound difference is structural. The Sunni *Ulema*, though clearly not without moral autonomy, have for the most part become embedded in the state, which appoints, finances and ultimately polices them, at the same time as they confer legitimacy on the regime. Shia *mujtahids*, by contrast, are supported by followers who selected them as 'sources of emulation' (*Marja' at-Taqlid*). In addition to the *Zakat* – alms for the poor that all Muslims are supposed to pay – the Shia pay the *Khums*, a tithe originating in the share of booty set aside for the Prophet's house, now in theory for the upkeep of his descendants, the black-turbaned Sayyeds. This gives the Shia clergy independent financial clout and patronage. Thus, where the Sunni clergy tends to be uniform and conformist, if not always monolithic, the markedly distinct Shia approach tends to create multiple centres of competing influence. That leads (even in Iran) to perpetual debate, with lively differences that are political as well as religious. The epicentre of that debate, since the upheaval triggered by the fall of Saddam, became the Iraqi shrine city of Najaf.

* * * * *

To step into the alleys around the Shrine to Imam Ali after the fall of Saddam was to step back in time. The old houses, leaning giddily across the narrow paths, where leading clerics received petitioners and followers, have changed little since the Middle Ages. Blistered donkeys jostled with destitute widows. The infirm came to seek alms. It would be easy to dismiss it all as the wreckage of a civilization, all the more poignant in Iraq, endowed with oil riches in modern times and blessed throughout the ages with two great rivers, the Euphrates and the Tigris, for its people to live between.

But Najaf was in ferment. And, although haltingly articulated, circulating in its narrow streets was something between a feeling and a conviction that the time of the Shia might at last have come.

The banners and portraits of the Shia martyrs to Saddam's tyranny hung everywhere. The bookstalls were crowded, with Iranian and Azeri, Afghan and Pakistani customers, as well as Iraqis. In the main square, facing Ali's tomb, brightly tiled in turquoise blue and daffodil yellow in the Shia manner, a bewildering variety of new newspapers lined the pavements, men in turbans staring out of them. Animated throngs of mullahs came and went, crowding into the houses of the leading clerics.

In one cramped room inside the house of Grand Ayatollah Fayadh, some 30 men crouched around a sheikh in one corner. An assistant with a wad of dinars was taking money in as his master signed religious guidance edicts, and giving it out as the sheikh read petitions and granted requests for alms. In an adjoining reception room, Sheikh al-Ruba'i explained that there was heavy demand for fatwas or religious edicts that sanctioned working for the occupation forces, from Shii who feared being branded as collaborators. 'If it's in the service of the community, it's OK', he said. More ominously, even in those early days, he said that the *Hawza* – Najaf's supreme religious authority, made up of Fayadh, who is of Afghan origin, Grand Ayatollah al-Hakim, Grand Ayatollah Bashir Hussein al-Najafi (born in pre-partition India) and Grand Ayatollah Ali al-Sistani, its Iranian-born leader – was under mounting pressure to declare a jihad against the occupiers. 'Every day people accuse the *Hawza* of being aloof from reality', he said, 'we are under a lot of pressure'. Pausing frequently to underline his distaste for 'extremism', Sheikh al-Ruba'i said the *Hawza* would only sanction rebellion if 'Islamic bodies and institutions' came under threat, and would not respond to the promptings of hotheads.

In a nearby house, Mohammed Bahr al-'Ulum, a reformist ayatollah who would become a leader of Iraq's first (occupation-appointed) governing council, is more to the point about the reasoning behind Shia restraint. He traced the exclusion of the Shia from office and national wealth to the British – the colonial power that bolted Iraq together in the 1920s from three fragments of Ottoman imperial debris – and Shia 'stupidity' in rising against them. He recounted how Sunni tribal sheikhs from west and central Iraq had been sending envoys to the south to press the Shia into resistance. With a quizzical look resembling the late actor Alec Guinness at an oblique angle, the snowy-bearded ayatollah savoured the Shia sheikhs' reply: 'We are with you, but in these past 20 years all your young men were with [Saddam's] *Fedayeen* and

Republican Guard, killing all our young men; now we only have old men, women and children, so give us another 20 years to join you.'

But Bahr al-'Ulum was no sectarian. 'I never want to see any form of exclusion again', he said animatedly, shuffling his heavy robes. The solution, he said, which the *Hawza* fully endorsed, was for a broad-based democratic government that – while it clearly would reflect the Shia numerical majority – would guarantee the rights of all religious and ethnic groups, 'minority rights as well as majority rights'. Like a wide spectrum of Najaf clerics, he foresaw a strong advisory role for the religious authorities, especially as 'a safety valve against extremism'. But nothing like the full prospectus of the Islamic revolution.

The *Hawza* of Sistani has emphatically dismissed the notion that Khomeinist theocracy – the *Wilayat al-Faqih* or rule of the supreme jurisprudent – could be transplanted to Iraq. From the so-called 'quietist' school of Shi'ism, they mostly see this idea as an aberration from Shia tradition and practice, discredited and declining even in Iran, where influential clerics such as Jalaleddin Taheri of Isfahan, or the grand ayatollahs Hossein Ali Montazeri (once Khomeini's designated heir) or Youssef Sanei in Qom – fed up seeing their faith dragged through the dirt of power politics – have denounced clerical dictatorship as a façade for vested interests built up after the 1979 Islamic revolution.

The position of Sistani, who for long periods is about as visible as the Hidden Imam, sometimes has to be teased out from fatwas or senior representatives of the *Hawza*. But he clearly takes his political inspiration not from Iran's Islamic revolution of 1979, but from its constitutional revolution of 1906. The clergy took part in that widespread revolt against the absolutism and corruption of the Qajar dynasty, aimed at establishing a directly elected parliament, representative government, and the rule of law. While jealous of their socio-religious prerogatives, for the most part the clerics sought a new contract between rulers and ruled – not to become the new rulers. That is a crucial difference between the Najafi concept of the *Marja'* and the Khomeinist model of the *Wilayat al-Faqih*.

One might add that in the debate over Islam's place in Iraq's new constitution in 2005, Sistani did not, as widely suggested at the time, come out in favour of an Islamic order based on *Shari'a* law. He supported, and won, acceptance in the new charter that Islam was the religion of the state, which guaranteed full freedom of religious belief and practice to all its citizens. While Article II states that Islam is a 'basic' (in some translations, 'fundamental') source of legislation, no law can be enacted that contradicts 'the established provisions of Islam', but equally no law can be established that infringes 'the principles of democracy', or the 'rights and basic freedoms' enumerated in the rest of the constitution. While there is ample scope for clash and collision in these provisions, so there is in most constitutions (as American cultural warriors have every reason to appreciate). This was no pure blueprint for secular liberalism. But nor was it a warrant for theocracy. Indeed, in some respects, it resembled the 1989 Jordanian National Charter (discussed in Chapter II), which placed Islam as but one source of legislative legitimacy.

Even the SCIRI leader, Mohammed Baqr al-Hakim, widely seen as a cat's paw for Tehran conservatives but whose movement transferred its allegiance from Iran's Supreme Leader, Ali Khamenei, to Sistani and the *Hawza* soon after returning to Iraq, took an early opportunity to formally eschew Islamic government. 'We do not want a dictatorship, no one-man or one-party rule', he said in an interview with *Der Spiegel* in June 2003: 'Iraq will be a democratic state in whose government all groupings in society will be represented – and it will be a state that respects and serves the values of Islam and all other religions.'

It was nevertheless clear from the outset that deep divisions bubbled beneath the surface of Shia politics, boiling over even before the war ended, with the mob murder near the Imam Ali shrine of Sayyed Abdel Majid al-Kho'i, the pro-western son of a former *Hawza* leader who had just returned from 12 years of exile. Few clerics would openly discuss what happened in this confused and ugly incident. But it suggested the beginnings of a vicious turf battle, between internal forces and returning exiles, and between Iraqi Shia leaders of Arab and Persian origin. Most fingers pointed at Moqtada al-Sadr – at whose bolted door the badly wounded al-Kho'i sought and was apparently denied sanctuary.[32]

Moqtada was the son of a leading cleric, Mohammed Sadeq al-Sadr, assassinated by Saddam in 1999, and the cousin and son-in-law of Mohammed Baqr al-Sadr, the *Hawza* leader executed in 1980. Many Shia clerical dynasties lost scores of members to the Ba'ath's death squads and hangmen, but images of these two prominent Sadr martyrs – neither of whom sought the refuge of exile from Saddam – held pride of place in homes and offices, and on windows and walls across southern Iraq, once the war ended. Indeed, Saddam City, the sprawling Shia slum adjoining the capital, was renamed Sadr City within hours of the fall of Baghdad.

The white-bearded clerics of the *Hawza* disdainfully pointed out that the youth Moqtada had no clerical standing. For all that, he was laying claim to a dual inheritance. Baqr al-Sadr, along with the Hakim, had nearly 50 years ago founded the shadowy Da'wa party – an intermittently potent force decimated by repression again and again, which nevertheless managed to launch seven assassination attempts on Saddam. During the 13 years of devastating post-Gulf War sanctions, however, his father, Sadeq al-Sadr, wove together a powerful network of welfare and resistance that – as the Iraqi scholar Faleh A. Jabar summarized it – 'managed to reconnect the Najaf clerical world with urban milieux and rural tribal domains'.[33]

After the invasion, this was a potentially very powerful, if still inchoate alliance that Moqtada – who at that time looked to a Khomeinist ayatollah based in Qom, Kazem al-Haeri, as his 'source of emulation' and the spiritual guide of the Sadriyyun – was seeking to use as a power-base and counterweight to the *Hawza*. One result of Moqtada's aggressiveness, however, was to push both the Supreme Council of the Hakims and the Da'wa into the *Hawza*-influenced mainstream. According to his aide and spokesman, Sheikh Adnan al-Shahmani, Moqtada completely disavowed the Iranian model of clerical rule. He was an Iraqi and Arab nationalist and, in any case, 'it would be impossible to have the same system here'. Sadr, furthermore, Shahmani swore, 'has no ambition to be in government'. None of this could disguise, however, that in that blistering summer after the invasion, all these groups had already started fighting for essentially the same Sadr inheritance. Held in periodic check only by the assault on the Shia by Sunni jihadis, that fighting continues.

*   *   *   *   *

The day before he died in a car bomb explosion outside the Imam Ali shrine in Najaf, Ayatollah Baqr al-Hakim warned that somebody was trying to start a civil war in Iraq. In an interview with *al-Ahram*, the leading Egyptian newspaper, he said: 'there are circles working to create a conflict between Shii, just as there are circles that are seeking to spark inter-Arab conflict [in Iraq]'.[34]

The blast that killed the SCIRI leader and an estimated 100 worshippers outside the shrine was so great that when his coffin was laid to rest, attended by hundreds of thousands of mourners, it contained only the ayatollah's watch, pen and wedding ring.

The massacre occurred in a month that had seen unidentified bombers destroy the Jordanian embassy, blow up the headquarters of the United Nations, killing special envoy Sergio Vieira de Mello, and raze the offices of Baghdad's police chief. All four attacks would later be claimed by Abu Musab al-Zarqawi. The attacks not only blew a hole in the credibility of the occupation, they served as a devastating warning to pro-western Arab governments, America's allies that might seek to come to its aid in Iraq, and Iraqis willing to work with the occupation forces. The war of attrition was on – and it was aimed every bit as much at the Shia as at the occupiers.

That war, given the recent history of Iraq and the invasion's violent over-turning of the balance of power, was inevitable. But it thrived in the political vacuum created by the occupation. The USA mismanaged victory, and not only in its failure to prevent lawlessness and its gifts to the insurgency in disbanding the army and outlawing all Ba'athists. The USA acted as though it believed that since it had won the war it could do what it liked with the peace. Bremer, for instance, planned to nominate an advisory council of hand-picked Iraqis to write a new constitution, alongside 'caucuses' of notables from which a transitional Iraqi administration would emerge. The overarching point is that while democracy, in the absence of WMD, was rapidly becoming the post facto justification for the invasion, the invaders lost their democratic nerve.

The Coalition Provisional Authority always hesitated before surrendering any sort of control to Iraqis lest the wrong sort came to the fore, preferring neat diagrams of socio-political engineering that bore no relation to the begrimed reality of Iraq. When Najaf, for instance, held local elections in June 2003, the CPA cancelled the results. Instead of a broad-based provisional government, it superimposed on the country's ethnic and sectarian patchwork a mosaic of squabbling exile groups with little or no standing inside Iraq. Instead of acting on Sistani's call for an elected constituent assembly, drawing members proportionally from Iraq's 18 provinces in a way that might have connected up the largely émigré governing council with emerging internal political forces and given the transition popular legitimacy, the USA preferred protégés even though they would obviously come to be seen widely as quislings. A legitimate provisional government tied to a constituent process could also have won wide international backing under the auspices of the UN – and surely would not have blundered so obdurately as the American 'coalition of the capable' did. The majority of Iraqis might just have been persuaded they at last owned their country and were part of a national project to rebuild it, in a framework of both external and internal legitimacy. 'America does not want to acknowledge it is incapable of controlling the situation and rebuilding Iraq', said Akram Zubeidi, a spokesman for Sistani, that August.

Sistani's fatwas and statements serially vetoed Bremer at each of his stumbles towards a sovereignty that would visibly have been under even greater American tutelage. The grand ayatollah emerged as the most influential political force in Iraq, a paradox given his interpretation of Shi'ism was that the clergy should steer clear of government. In the unreality of the Green Zone in Baghdad – the imperial fortress from which the CPA and its Iraqi adjuncts purported to govern Iraq – it took an awfully long time for the occupiers to realize that one of the main keys to controlling Iraq was held in Najaf by Sistani and the *Hawza*.

Eventually, the USA could no longer thwart elections. But by the time they took place, through 2005, it was too late. By then, as Charles Tripp, the historian of Iraq, has pointed out, real power lay elsewhere, not in the formal institutions of representative life. Washington's attempt to insert favoured exiles into new, US-conceived forms of power, after it had blown apart the last vestiges of the centralized Iraqi state, forced it to court and work with local forces with muscle and intelligence on the ground. Iraqis, too, had no alternative but to retreat into these local, communal networks. When they did get to vote they voted local, by sect. They could see all too well what was happening and needed the protection of local power and militias, not just against the occupation but to shield them from the murderous onslaught of the jihadis, especially al-Qaeda and the *takfiri* fanatics who regarded all Shia and many Sunni who disagreed with them as apostates to be slaughtered.[35]

After the February 2006 bombing of the al-Askari shrine in Samarra, Shia death squads showed they were the equal of their Sunni counterparts in industrial-scale slaughter, even if it had been no part of Shia objectives to start a civil war, but rather to take majority power in Iraq. In the orgy of sectarian score-settling that followed the bombing, Sistani and the *Hawza* lost all control. But the shortcomings of Shia politics had come into view long before then.

Given what was (literally) an opportunity in a millennium to raise their people to state power, Iraq's Shia politicians failed to rise above factionalism, to embrace the national interest, and to develop representative forces practising an inclusive politics of legitimacy. To be fair, the Shia community withstood stoically the post-invasion massacres and provocations that local Sunni supremacists and imported jihadis committed to goad them into civil war. But, to be equally fair, their leaders proved incapable of governing, even allowing for the constricting parameters of a US protectorate. The experience suggests a structural weakness in Shia politics. It is not just the legacy of repression and exile, of dispossession and poverty, although that is clearly important. It is that such wealth and institutions the Shia as a community have been able to build up have been around its religious leaders but not its political formations, which are anaemic and invertebrate by comparison.

Uncomfortably, both for the Shia and the occupation, the partial exception here has been Moqtada al-Sadr.

The USA has floundered its way through a prodigal list of favourites in its futile attempts to run Iraq, from Ahmad Chalabi, the silky weaver of neo-con dreams, to Nouri al-Maliki, a prime minister immobile in a web of sectarian nightmares. Moqtada al-Sadr, it is fair to say, was definitely not one of them. But is he the spider at the centre of the web as painted, in lurid but broadbrush strokes, by the Anglo-American occupation (a *Newsweek* cover, of

4 December 2006, headlined 'The Most Dangerous Man in Iraq', made Moqtada look like Dracula rising from his coffin)? Or is he the emerging pan-Iraqi champion, and icon of Arab resistance, painted surreally by his followers? The answer is important. Because, vicious paradox though it may be, it is this unruly scion of a politico-religious tradition the West barely understands who is positioning himself to inherit power once the bungled occupation of Iraq is over.

For this, Moqtada owes some thanks to Saddam Hussein, but a great deal more to those who toppled his dictatorship.

As we have seen, within hours of the fall of Baghdad, Saddam City became Sadr City, festooned with the portraits of Moqtada's martyred father-in-law and father, dominating tableaux of insurrectionary workers, students, farmers and mullahs that could have been designed by Eisenstein. Given that the exiles on whom the Americans depended for their read-out on Iraq seemed convinced that the networks built by Sadr's father, Mohammed Sadeq al-Sadr (Sadr II), had died with him in 1999, the USA was presumably unaware of the potent force that was re-awakening. At that time, furthermore, Moqtada was regarded as little more than an unlettered hooligan, his Mahdi Army, set up to oppose the occupation and the émigrés, little more than messianic posturing.

In October 2003, an extensive poll by the reputable Iraqi Centre for Research and Strategic Studies (ICRSS) showed that while Iraqis profoundly distrusted the Americans and the exiles, only 1 per cent said they supported Moqtada. All that changed when the ineffable Bremer closed his newspaper and issued a 'kill or capture' warrant for Moqtada's arrest in connection with the (earlier described) murder of Abdel Majid al-Kho'i. This was another of the many own-goals of the occupation.

Moqtada responded with two militarily hopeless but politically deadly insurrections in April and August 2004. His popular support, an ICRSS poll revealed that May, rocketed to 68 per cent, second only to Sistani. In what seemed at the time an almost preternatural apotheosis, he had become a hero not only to the Shia but to some of the minority Sunni prosecuting a lethal insurgency in central Iraq (Sadr sent relief convoys to the besieged Sunni city of Fallujah in the Euphrates valley, in a brief but ultimately abortive effort to forge a united front against the occupation).

Nevertheless, precisely because of his military weakness and his revered forebears, he had become the worst possible kind of enemy to face within a region and a religious tradition steeped in the cult of martyrdom. Even when he was under American siege during the second uprising in the Wadi as-Salaam (Valley of Peace) in Najaf – a vast cemetery overlaying an underground warren of crypts – it was moot whether that would be the last resting place of a maverick militia leader or the graveyard for Washington's plans to set Iraq on the path to stable governance.

The Anglo-American forces thought, reasonably enough, they could easily overrun his ragtag militia. This was a fundamental misunderstanding. The tactics of the Sadriyyun are more political than military, combining fast escalations with tactical withdrawals. There was no chance of the coalition beating them by purely military means: the Mahdi volunteers 'win' by being seen to stand and fight, losing hundreds of martyrs to US tanks, rockets and shells. It would be easier fighting ghosts. Sadr has always been a lot shrewder than he looks.

His claim to the politico-religious inheritance of the Sadrs, and the underground resistance to Saddam led by the Islamist Da'wa party, has been burnished by his own resistance – both to the occupation and the *takfiri* intrusion led by the Iraqi franchise of al-Qaeda. His lack of theological standing, moreover, while it may scandalize the *Hawza*, is of little consequence for those of his followers who distrust the quietism of the Najaf clerical hierarchy.

Even though the December 2005 elections produced a Shia-led coalition built around Maliki's Da'wa and the Islamic Supreme Council of Iraq, the single biggest winner – in a parliament where two thirds of MPs are Islamist – was Moqtada.

As already remarked, his father, Sadr II, built a very powerful network, that wove together the slums of Baghdad and the Shia tribes of the south. Mainstream commentators on the Iraqi Shia tend to dismiss this movement as an 'underclass', but that is to miss the point. Contemporary Sadrism, as Patrick Cockburn has highlighted, was a response to the disintegration of Iraqi society as a result of the post-Gulf War economic blockade, which led to the destruction of the possessing classes of the Shia and the mass impoverishment of the community as a whole.[36]

That is why the (often deadly) rivalry between the Supreme Council of the Hakims (and the *Hawza*) and the Mahdi Army is not just between exiles and those who stayed and faced Saddam, not just between Arab and Persian, or between quietism and militancy. It is not even just Badr versus Sadr – a militia shoot-out. It is at the same time a *class struggle* within the Shia community, of the popular masses led by Moqtada against the clerical and merchant elites of Baghdad and the holy cities: 'This struggle, more than the sectarian conflict or confrontation between Anbari Sheikhs [the Sunni Sahwa] and al-Qaeda in Iraq fighters, is likely to shape the country's future.'[37]

The vast web that Moqtada inherited from his father, woven through the mosques and largely invisible to the Ba'athists let alone the occupation, makes him Sadr III – not a king but definitely a kingmaker. US policy had turned a hooligan into a hero. By serially postponing and obstructing democracy until the situation was too far gone, the occupation had indeed brought the revolutionary current in Shi'ism to the surface.

Rather than recognize this, US commanders keep on trying to tie Moqtada and the Sadriyyun to Iran's Revolutionary Guard. This, again, largely misses the point. Sadr proudly acknowledges ties to Hizbollah in Lebanon, a radical, disciplined and, above all, successful movement, on which he is trying to model the Mahdi Army. Hizbollah lost 84 men in the August 2004 siege of Najaf, for example, while Moqtada himself can even be seen imitating the characteristic tics and gestures of Hizbollah chief Hassan Nasrallah – such as pushing back his turban from the right side of his forehead.[38]

But, as already remarked, Tehran's main clients in Iraq are the same as Washington's. It is the US-allied Supreme Council's Badr Corps that was trained, financed, armed and, at one stage, commanded by Iranian Revolutionary Guards. It is part of Moqtada's appeal, in his guise as Iraqi and Arab nationalist, that he is able to dismiss these rivals for his inheritance and their *Hawza* sponsors as Persians, which also goes down well with some Sunni. It is an important difference because whereas the Hakims want power in Baghdad, consolidated by an oil-rich mini-state in the Shia south, Moqtada wants to be *the* Shia leader of a united Iraq.

With power, however, comes responsibility, even in Iraq, where so far it has been treated as sectarian booty. There will come a time when Moqtada will have to demonstrate whether he really can win credibility among the Sunni – or whether he is just the centre of a spider's web.

The opportunity is there. The Maliki government has abandoned any pretence of governing on behalf of all Iraqis. There was no more squalidly eloquent example of this than the execution of Saddam Hussein at the end of 2006 – a public lynching disseminated around the world courtesy of a mobile phone camera and the internet, on the Eid al-Adha, the feast of the sacrifice, the holiest Muslim feast day, in the most virulent insult to Sunnis in Iraq and throughout the Islamic world. Instead of the triumph of the rule of law over tyranny, this was a spectacle conceived as an act of vengeance designed to dramatize Shia hegemony.

As the summer of 2008 drew to its end, there was little sign that this sort of virulence, unleashed by the invasion, could be brought under control, rather than temporarily contained; channelled by a common national project rather than flushed into violently sectarian tributaries. It was impossible to discern any plot or overall narrative in Iraq's affairs, only fathomless sub-plot, as militias and bandits – some rebadged as police or Iraqi army – and insurgents and jihadis vied ruthlessly for control over their fragments of the country.

A new wave of violence was cranking up, anticipating the end of the surge – and as the election of Barack Obama as US president raised the question of withdrawal. At the end of this book we shall examine the options: for the Iraqis and the Americans. But it did not look as though there were any good options left. The invasion was always unlikely to create any and the remedial options as the occupation blundered along had been squandered.

Iraq could become a shell state, like post-Soviet Afghanistan, prey to warlords and militias, and the seedbed of rival Taliban: on the Sunni side, a lethal hybrid of extreme Islamism and irreducible nationalism; on the Shia side, a fusion of Shia puritanism with tribal tradition – to create two spectres that could haunt the Islamic world and its relations with the West for generations. Alternatively, one side – the majority Shia – could resolve their leadership struggle and impose their writ on the country. Or – the least bad outcome – Iraq could emerge exhausted into a loose confederation, with a weak central government with agreed tasks such as the allocation of oil revenue.

For that to happen the USA needed to stay long enough to avert a new bloodbath, but leave soon enough to make Iraq's high-wire faction leaders – their safety net removed – reach some sort of modus vivendi.

That outcome would be eased by some sort of rapprochement between Shia Iran and Sunni Saudi Arabia (which is possible), and if Washington buried the past and sought a diplomatic grand bargain with Tehran. That might, conceivably, be made possible by President Obama, if he recognizes that solving not just Iraq but many of the conflicts of the Middle East requires Iranian cooperation.

V

Arabia Infelix

The endgame approaching in Iraq was far from the only drama playing out in the Arab world. While the Iraqi debacle unfolded, a hardy perennial of Arab political repertory was being restaged to its south, in Saudi Arabia. Shortly after the fall of Baghdad a wave of attacks by al-Qaeda's followers in the kingdom began, aimed at creating conditions for the overthrow of the House of Saud. Could the al-Saud, the absolutist monarchy that rules Saudi Arabia with theocratic zeal, the custodians of the birthplace of Islam as well as a US ally sitting on a quarter of the world's proven oil reserves, survive? The short answer was: Yes – in the short term.

This chapter will attempt a longer-term answer. It will argue that this crisis, although currently contained, is of a different order to the series of threatening challenges this extraordinarily resilient and resourceful dynasty has dealt with since the modern Saudi state was established. This crisis is not so much about facing down a (so far) not very competent proto-insurgency as about the future direction of the Saudi state and the sources of legitimacy of the al-Saud. It is a challenge they need to surmount and not just survive, if they are to secure not just their own future but make Saudi Arabia an anchor of the stability and progress of the Gulf and the region.

The preponderance of Saudis among the hijackers of 9/11, in planning the October 2000 attack on the *USS Cole* in Aden, and the steady flow of Saudi jihadis as suicide bombers for the Sunni insurgency in Iraq, had awoken widespread anger in the USA at perceived Saudi complicity in Islamist fanaticism. At government-to-government level, however, this was far outweighed by fear that the ruling House of Saud – for the most part a dependable ally that had provided secure oil shipments, generally at reasonable prices – could be swept away by the forces of bin Ladenism. The Bush administration's stated enthusiasm for the stirrings of Arab democracy and the transformation of the Middle East was decidedly muted when it came to dealing with its oil-rich but theocratic Sunni ally.

Conventional wisdom, moreover, which Saudi rulers did nothing to discourage, held that democratic experiment could only favour radical Islamists. The partial, men-only, municipal elections held for 178 local councils in the spring of 2005 – which delivered an almost clean sweep for Islamists backed by religious networks – served the monarchy as a useful demonstration to its American friends. Was it not so much safer to persist with a wholly appointed and consultative *Majlis as-Shura*?

Nevertheless, the kingdom, named after the al-Saud family, is in trouble.

That is not so much because the local franchise of al-Qaeda turned its guns on Saudi Arabia shortly after the fall of Baghdad in 2003. That threat, to reiterate, is manageable in the short term. The House of Saud, moreover, has a remarkable record of resilience.

It is because the House of Saud's legitimacy has traditionally been conferred by its alliance with the House of ibn Abdul Wahhab – the eighteenth-century religious reformer who gave his name to Wahhabism, the totalitarian strain of Islam practised in and exported from Saudi Arabia. This fusion of temporal and religious power is the bedrock of the Saudi state. The problem is that Wahhabism, in its essentials, is also the creed espoused by bin Laden, while the Saudi ruling family is also dependent for survival on its more than 60-year-old alliance with the USA.

If the al-Saud take no action to resolve this dilemma, it is unlikely that the world will watch with equanimity. It is a deep-rooted problem that cannot be left to rot behind the brittle façade of the kingdom's modernity.

The Saudi al-Qaeda, by the end of 2005, appeared to have been contained, after a wave of suicide attacks that rocked the kingdom. The campaign began in May 2003, with a triple car-bomb explosion at a westerners' residential compound in Riyadh. Within a year, however, Saudi police seemed to have found ways of disrupting the bombers; in April 2004 alone they claimed to have foiled five major attacks. But as a result, Saudi jihadis started fielding small cells of gunmen, and directing them against expatriate oil industry executives and workers, Saudi security forces, US military contractors, foreign journalists, and, indeed, any random target that looked western.

The opening of an Islamist offensive in the birthplace of Islam was enough to suggest, at the very least, that the House of Saud was facing a serious problem. That was all the more so since only recently had it publicly allowed that it had a problem at all.

In the 18 months between 11 September 2001 and the Riyadh compound attacks, the al-Saud had struggled to come to grips with the fact –

acknowledged everywhere except Saudi Arabia – that 15 of the 19 hijackers who immolated nearly 3,000 people in New York and Washington were Saudis, and that their inspiration was an erstwhile merchant prince of the kingdom, Osama bin Laden.

Even a year after 9/11, Prince Nayef, the powerful interior minister and a possible future claimant to the Saudi throne, was telling a Kuwaiti newspaper that the attack on New York's World Trade Center was a Zionist plot. When five western oil executives were killed at Yanbu, the Red Sea petrochemical port, on 1 May 2004, Prince Abdullah (then crown prince and de facto ruler because King Fahd had been incapacitated by a stroke in 1995, and now the king since Fahd's death in July 2005) said he was '95 per cent certain' Zionists were behind it. What other explanation could there be, this *cui bono* reasoning went, when such attacks turned international opinion against Muslims?

It is conceivable that these two masters of the Saudi kingdom sincerely believed this. We are, however, on more solid ground in saying that once bin Laden's al-Qaeda swivelled round its gunsights and trained them towards the heart of the kingdom, the al-Saud began discovering other possible culprits.

The turning point came with the 29 May 2004 attack at al-Khobar in Eastern Province. This is the region that contains the largest oil deposits in the world and is, in addition, the homeland of Saudi Arabia's persecuted Shia minority. That assault was deadly in its sinister intent.

Islamist gunmen attacked two foreign oil company office blocks and an expatriate enclave, killing three Saudi and 19 foreign civilians as well as nine Saudi policemen. They sought out Christian, Hindu and Buddhist 'infidels' to murder, setting Muslim hostages free. As in Yanbu that same month, they were able to mount the spectacle of dragging the body of a westerner for more than a mile, spitting slogans as they went, without hindrance. Even though the attack turned into a siege, with Saudi security forces ringing the compound and commandos landing on the roof of the building where the gunmen held over 40 hostages, three of the attackers were able to, or allowed to, escape.

One week later, in Suwaidi in south Riyadh, a slum-like warren of densely packed alleys that is home to half a million Saudis, as well as 15 of the 26 militants on the kingdom's most-wanted list of that year, gunmen attacked a BBC crew, killing cameraman Simon Cumbers and seriously wounding security correspondent Frank Gardner. Two days after that, an American employee of Vinell, the US military contractor that trains the Saudi National Guard, a praetorian force of Bedouins headed by King Abdullah, was stalked and shot dead outside his Riyadh home.

But the real chill of fear descended upon the expatriate community the following month, when Paul Johnson, an American technician working on

Apache helicopters, was kidnapped and subsequently beheaded on camera, his head sawn off for an Islamist webcast. The way the gunmen at al-Khobar had searched out non-Muslims to murder had badly rattled the gilded *gastar-beiter* of the gated compounds. Until then, most foreigners working in the kingdom were stoic about the possibility of suicide attacks, reasoning they were statistically more likely to die in, say, a traffic accident. But the obscene slaughtering of Paul Johnson, on top of the gruesome murders at al-Khobar, marked a psychological turning-point: there is nothing abstract about being beheaded.[1]

Throughout this period, the exultant chatter on the Islamist websites used by al-Qaeda followers was deafening. More ominously, Abdulaziz al-Muqrin, then leader of the self-styled Qaeda Organization in the Arabian Peninsula, made clear their tactics were to stampede western and other 'infidels' out of the kingdom, and to destabilize world oil markets by targeting soft but neuralgic parts of the Saudi oil industry. Ultimately, the goal was to overthrow the House of Saud, and he called for an uprising against the 'apostate' monarchy.[2]

There was and is no such uprising in prospect. But the extremists have undeniably been able to expose the weak grip on security of an otherwise impeccably authoritarian government. That really frightens people. 'We know what the worst fears of the average Saudi are', said an adviser to the then Crown Prince Abdullah after the al-Khobar siege: 'He fears, above all, chaos.'[3]

While, as we shall see, there is an element of self-interest in this observation, the undeniable sense at that time of a state of siege had pitched the government's in any case weakly articulated reform programme into abeyance. Like nearly all Arab rulers, the House of Saud tends to see the future as an antithetical choice between reform or stability (you can have one or the other), rather than a fork in the road between reform and revolt and eventual ruin.

Campaigners for reform, meanwhile, always at risk of being flung into the regime's dungeons, felt totally undermined by the terrorist offensive. As Mohsen al-Awajy, a leading Islamist reformer jailed during the 1990s, put it: 'Since the Riyadh bombings [of May 2003], consideration of almost all our demands for reform has been suspended – the situation makes it unwise for us to put pressure on the Saudi government.'[4]

True though that was, the ruling family had finally to acknowledge publicly that al-Qaeda, a diffuse phenomenon incubated in good part by the fanatical Wahhabi strain of Islam the al-Saud have imposed as the kingdom's sole creed, was its problem too.

Even as the slaughter at al-Khobar was continuing, the then Crown Prince and now King of Saudi Arabia, Abdullah, vowed to crush 'this corrupt and deviant group' in Saudi society. In an echo of President George W. Bush's you're 'either with us or against us' declaration after 9/11, he warned that 'those who keep silent about the terrorists will be regarded as belonging to them'.

In a regime where members of his own family and leaders of the clerical establishment share the same hostility towards the West, and towards the great majority of Muslims who do not subscribe to Wahhabi extremism, this was – at least at face value – a huge statement.

If taken to its logical conclusion, it would require the House of Saud to re-examine its relationship with the Wahhabi clerical establishment – the historic compact that is the foundation stone of the Saudi state.

* * * * *

This is, in fact, the third time the House of Saud has set up a state in penin-sular Arabia. The formula in its third and enduring attempt was to harness the fighting skills of the Bedouin tribes and power them at full throttle with uncompromising religious zealotry. But that was not how it started.

The epic begins in the mid-eighteenth century, when an Emir from the Nejd in central Arabia, Sheikh Mohammed ibn Saud, took in an itinerant preacher by the name of Sheikh Mohammed ibn Abdul Wahhab. In 1744 (some sources say 1747), the compact between the two houses was sealed by the marriage of al-Saud's son and ibn Abdul Wahhab's daughter.

This fusion of temporal and religious power lasts to this day. It is the bedrock of the Saudi kingdom. Its essential promise is to banish chaos and darkness – an echo of the pre-Islamic *jahiliyya* or epoch of ignorance that God sought to end through his revelation to the Prophet Mohammed – and substitute order, human and divine.

The al-Saud are thought by some to hail originally from the nomadic Durra tribe, by others from remnants of the Bani Hanifa. Either way, by the eigh-teenth century they had become oasis settlers, Hadari rather than Bedouin, without any significant tribal confederation through which to press their ambitions. Their alliance with ibn Abdul Wahhab furnished them with an imputed religious legitimacy through which they sought to raise themselves above rival tribal emirates, such as those led by the al-Rasheed from the pow-erful Shammar tribal confederation or the Bani Khaled of Hasa in the east. The 'detribalization' of the settlers, coupled with their population growth, obliged them to find an alternative formula to build up their political and mil-itary strength to resist the predatory tribes, who would exact tribute from the

Hadari or, in its stead, booty from raids on their settlements. The very weakness of the emerging entity's tribal affiliations and identity, furthermore, left the new polity theoretically open to everyone.[5]

But the magic ingredients in the alliance of the houses of Saud and ibn Abdul Wahhab were religious reform and Jihad – a holy war to reclaim the peninsula of the Prophet Mohammed and the birthplace of Islam for true believers.

Abdul Wahhab espoused probably the most literalist, rigorous, antique and exclusivist interpretation of Sunni Muslim orthodoxy ever attempted as a form of governance, in which politics and religion were identical. It harked back more than a thousand years to the rule of the *Rashidun* – the first four, 'rightly-guided' Caliphs who succeeded the Prophet at the head of the Islamic commonwealth – and to the *al-Salaf al-Salih*, the pious ancestors and followers of the Prophet, from which derives the term Salafi, the preferred term fundamentalists use.

The Wahhab-Saud forces came to be known as Wahhabis but describe themselves as *Muwa'hidun* – literally, Unitarians, to emphasize their extreme interpretation of monotheism. They also refer to themselves as the *Ahl al-Tawhid*, people of the oneness (of God), who therefore regard any apparent deviation from monotheism, particularly evident to them in the practices of the Christians and the Shia – as infidel or apostate. They chose as their principal enemy the Ottoman Sultanate and residual Caliphate, which they saw as a decadent promoter of shrine and saint worship, permissive of abhorrent 'polytheist' religious observance by Jews and Christians, and, worse still, tolerant of the 'idolatrous' and 'rejectionist' (*Rafadah*) Shia Muslims, for whom they reserved the lowest circle of hell.

In short, this, in the strict sense of the word, *totalitarian* creed anathematized *all* other beliefs as illicit. It defined literally everyone else as 'the Other'. In the process it drew up as broad a definition of 'non-believers' as has ever been devised. Wahhabism thus provides limitless sanction for Jihad (making it hard for jihadis or their victims to understand how, as the al-Saud insist, al-Qaeda is in any way 'deviant' from this orthodoxy).

Merely in the context of Arabia the claims of this creed were huge – one reason ibn Abdul Wahhab was expelled from other regions of the peninsula before finding refuge with the obscure but ambitious al-Saud. The Wahhabi claim is to have found Arabia in a tribal stew of idolatry and chaos, war and pillage, ignorance and vice. In effect, the Wahhab-Saud forces claim to have ended the second Arabian *jahiliyya* or age of ignorance. That would put them, if true, on a par with the Prophet himself – a vast boast indeed.

Any westerner, moreover, could hardly fail to note the similarity between these Saudi claims and the self-justifying protestations of the European colonialists who, invariably, conquered and occupied other peoples only for the purpose of redeeming and civilizing them. Saudi–Wahhabi propaganda is a mirror image of the Orientalist discourse about the Hobbesian fate from which the West saved the East. It is a self-serving myth to justify the hegemony of the al-Saud and the Nejd over a regionally and religiously diverse nation, which was unified by force, we should recall, only after 52 battles in the course of a 30-year war of conquest. In military terms, at least, this was an enterprise of Prussian proportions – with the difference that *Tawhid* came to mean not just the 'oneness' of God, but the oneness of Arabia under Saudi hegemony.[6]

Had the early Wahhabis limited their campaign to the Nejd and central Arabia – in which neither the Ottomans nor anyone but rival emirates at the time had any interest – the first Saudi state would quite possibly have survived. Instead, over 60 years they spread the Jihad far and wide, conquering the holy cities of Mecca and Medina, even marauding into what is today Iraq to sack the Shia shrine city of Kerbala in 1801.[7]

From the Sublime Porte in Istanbul the Wahhabis were seen as a challenge to the legitimacy of the Ottomans – whose obligation it was as inheritors of the Caliphate to secure the Hajj pilgrimage route to Mecca for Muslims world-wide – and as brigands and Bedouin upstarts wreaking mayhem in Ottoman lands. The Ottomans sent an Egyptian viceroy, Ibrahim Pasha, into Arabia with an expeditionary force. By 1818 he razed the beautiful adobe capital of the al-Saud at Diriyyah, and buried their putative kingdom.

They bounced back within decades, however, building a second emirate, this time centred on Riyadh. But they were undermined by bloody rivalries within the family, and their undiminished lust for conquest and zeal for conversion soon brought them into renewed conflict with the Ottomans, who successfully backed a takeover by the al-Rasheed, forcing the al-Saud to take sanctuary in the emirate of Kuwait.

As the twentieth century dawned, the power of the Ottomans faded and the intrigues of their subjects multiplied. Abdul Aziz, a young scion of the House of Saud, saw his chance. In 1902, with 40 companions, he seized the Musmak adobe palace in central Riyadh, routed the al-Rasheed and rallied the central Arabian tribes to the Saudi cause. This stirring tale of daring and resolve, embellished by the years, became a powerful foundation myth for the third Saudi kingdom.

Abdul Aziz, later known to the West as King Ibn Saud, first expanded north of Riyadh to Qassim, the geographical heart of the Nejd and the beating heart of Wahhabism. There he found the forces for his Jihad: the ferocious *Ikhwan* or Brothers, a combination of Bedouin warriors and Wahhabi missionaries who would carry all before them.

With the post-First World War collapse of the Ottoman empire, Abdul Aziz took Hai'l and the northern heartland of the al-Rasheed – the British would set the boundary of his expansion northwards by drawing the border of Iraq – then the eastern province of Hasa from the Turks. By 1926 the *Ikhwan* had conquered the Hijaz from the Hashemites, the last serious rivals in the peninsula to the al-Saud, and taken Mecca and Medina. By 1932, having largely secured the south bordering Yemen, King Abdul Aziz declared the kingdom of Saudi Arabia.

A kingdom he had united by the sword was further bound together by Abdul Aziz's policy of marrying widely and frequently. Along with his 52 battles he sired 43 sons, both subordinating the defeated Arabian nobility and creating blood-bonds of loyalty with the leading tribes. The fanatical zealots of the *Ikhwan*, however, recognized no state or tribal boundaries in the jihad they aimed to continue. The first Saudi state had arisen out of a conflict between oasis settlers and nomadic Bedouin who observed no frontiers. Now, in the third and definitive attempt to create a kingdom, Abdul Aziz was forced to choose between a settled state within internationally recognized borders and an uneasy alliance with the strike force that helped bring him to power. He did not hesitate. Helped by British-supplied modern armament, he destroyed the *Ikhwan* in battle at al-Sabala in 1929.

The House of Saud's religious cover for this was provided by the House of ibn Abdul Wahhab. Indeed, Ibn Saud had taken care to renew the historic compact between the two houses by marrying a descendant of ibn Abdul Wahhab immediately after he captured Riyadh in 1902. And so the bonds between the two houses were strengthened. The Wahhabi clerical establishment was given decisive social control, not only over religion and public comportment but over education and justice. Above all, it enjoyed the power derived from conferring legitimacy on the Saudi rulers, who had now named the land of the Prophet after themselves.

The politico-religious symbiosis of the House of Ibn Saud and the House of al-Sheikh, as it is now known, built the world's first modern Muslim fundamentalist state.

* * * * *

In 1945, President Franklin D. Roosevelt, on his way home from the Yalta summit with Churchill and Stalin, met King Abdul Aziz ibn Saud aboard the *USS Quincy*, anchored in the Great Bitter Lake midway up the Suez Canal.

Having settled the dispositions of post-war Europe, Roosevelt laid a foundation stone of the post-war Middle East. The USA, in essence, would guarantee the security and integrity of Ibn Saud's kingdom, while the Saudis would guarantee the free flow of oil at reasonable prices. That bargain is still more or less intact.[8]

Since that historic meeting, Saudi Arabia has emerged as the world's largest oil exporter. But the state created by Ibn Saud has remained essentially static, while its subjects have been dragged headlong into modernity. It is a modernity that rests on the shakiest foundations.

The underlying notion seems to be that you can buy in technology, innovation and selected slices of education from the West, yet completely insulate yourself from the values and culture that help inform and create these advances. It is, in short, a modernity imported like an air conditioner, not only divorced from the underlying culture that produced it but in conflict with the culture it inhabits. It is a recipe for cultural schizophrenia.

Within loudspeaker distance of a fire-and-brimstone mosque in Riyadh, for example, a shimmering mall housed a Harvey Nichols emporium with an outlet for La Senza, the lingerie chain. It was identical, in all respects except the slightly gaudier range, to a similar shop anywhere else. But there was one fundamental difference. Because women may not mix with men outside their family and are kept in a mixture of seclusion and segregation, it follows that they cannot work in a lingerie boutique – which was therefore staffed entirely by men.

Saudi businesswomen – who operate with signal success but in a more or less separate environment to men – have been raising their voices with growing frequency to call for a boycott of these kinds of arrangement, which are beyond satire.[9]

A similar absurdity arises from the ban on women driving. In practice, that has required the import of more than 1 million foreigners to serve as drivers. In other words, a driving prohibition supposedly intended to keep women from temptation by denying them any independence leads to them being thrown into daily contact with male strangers. Only a society that has a living memory of the social conventions of slavery could be capable of countenancing such a paradox.

But probably it is in the field of education that this schizophrenia is most vividly and wrenchingly lived out.

On the one hand, Saudi Arabia has an educated middle class, almost 1 million of whom have studied abroad – often to a very high level. The kingdom has also educated its girls for nearly two generations. Saudis, moreover, often have an intellectual depth to them that is less easily found in many

Arab countries, where political and commercial pressures have debased and ground down the currency of ideas to convenient and remunerative cliché and myth. 'There is something curiously un-callused about the Saudis', a veteran diplomat in the kingdom observes, 'an innocence perhaps born of their relative isolation'.[10]

But then turn to school textbooks, drawn up under the authority of the Wahhabi establishment. These drill into impressionable young Saudi minds the religious duty to hate all Christians and Jews as infidels, and to combat all Shii as heretics. A theology text for 14-year-olds, for instance, states that 'it is the duty of a Muslim to be loyal to the believers and be the enemy of the infidels. One of the duties of proclaiming the oneness of God is to have nothing to do with his idolatrous and polytheist enemies.' The history textbooks typically emphasize the al-Saud hegemonic myth mentioned earlier, burying any attempt to weave regional specificity or religious breadth into national identity under a suffocating narrative of Nejdi supremacy and Saudi redemption.[11]

The theological extremism follows the theses of Ibn Taymiyya, a forerunner of Wahhabi thinking who died in 1328, and who asserted the discretionary power of Muslim scholars to 'correct' their rulers. He also preached a passionate and, as we saw in Chapter III, un-Islamic loathing of non-Muslims, even suggesting it was permissible to kill Muslims if that was the only way to reach the target of the infidels – a sentiment fully shared by bin Ladenists. Some of his writings, followed by ibn Abdul Wahhab in his own foundation text, 'The Elucidation of Doubts', are stridently Takfiri, giving licence to modern jihadis who anathematize all their opponents as 'apostates' deserving death.[12]

'It is really not very difficult to understand how we got to where we are', exclaimed one reformist intellectual, asking rhetorically if there was any difference between the sectarian bigotry of Osama bin Laden and the intolerant outpourings of the Wahhabi establishment.[13]

The critical difference, of course, is that while the House of al-Sheikh (or Abdul Wahhab) props up the House of Saud, al-Qaeda wants to bring it down. Can it succeed? The short answer is No – at least in the short term. Saudi Arabia is not the Iran of the Pahlavis, even if there are superficial similarities.

First, the blood-ties established by King Abdul Aziz with the leading tribes continue to be a powerful and cohesive binding force. That is part of the reason why the then Crown Prince Abdullah, a half-brother to the late King Fahd, was the designated successor to the throne rather than his rivals in the so-called Sudairi Seven – full brothers of the king, born of Ibn Saud's favourite wife. Abdullah is said to have the loyalty of the tribes – exerted partly through his control, since 1963, of the National Guard, a praetorian guard rooted strongly in the Bedouin.

Second, the Saudi King's preferred title is the Custodian of the *Haramien* – the two holy mosque cities of pilgrimage – Mecca and Medina. This role is the nearest modern equivalent to the Caliphate in Islam. Unlike the neo-imperial fantasies of the Shah of Iran, that confers real legitimacy.

Third, as already remarked, this is the House of Saud's third go at building a state. They are, above all, haunted by the spectre of division and chaos. 'Whenever there has been a downfall of the House of Saud, it has been as a result of divisions within the family, and in one case because we were invaded by a much bigger power [the Ottomans]', said one ranking prince: 'There is thus an understanding that [family] unity is vital.'[14]

Over the past half century, moreover, the al-Saud have demonstrated an extraordinary resilience to frequent political emergency and massive social dislocation. They have managed the sudden access to great wealth from ownership of a quarter of the world's oil reserves – as well as a giddying switchback of even more sudden spikes and collapses in the price of oil. The kingdom more or less copes with the import into its closed society of foreign labour equivalent to one third of its population – not to mention millions of annual pilgrims to Mecca, some of whom are organized partisans of international Islamist causes.

The House of Saud has also confronted great political challenge. It managed to resist the radical pan-Arabism of Gamal Abdel Nasser, when Nasserism appeared to be sweeping all before it from Syria to Yemen, in an Arab 'cold war' subplot to the Cold War between the West and the Soviet Union. It successfully resisted Ayatollah Khomeini's attempts to export Iran's Islamist revolution to the Arabian peninsula. The family came through the trauma of deposing the incompetent and spendthrift King Saud in 1964, and the assassination of his successor, King Faisal, by a disgruntled nephew in 1975. It also managed to survive the 1979 seizure of the great mosque at Mecca by Islamist fanatics – a huge blow to the ruler's prestige as keeper of the holy places. And it was confident (and perhaps, frightened) enough to risk allowing more than half a million foreign troops on its soil – the birthplace of Islam – during the 1990–1 Gulf crisis. 'If you were a political scientist reviewing all that has happened to us over this time', observed one young prince, 'you would surely reach the conclusion that we are no longer here'.[15]

Many have bet against the House of Saud, forecasting its demise in a paper trail of books, articles, pamphlets and diplomatic dispatches stretching back decades. But here it still is. The immediate threat to its survival, moreover, should not be exaggerated. During the worst of the al-Qaeda violence in Saudi Arabia, as many people were being killed in a week in Iraq, or a month in Gaza, as died in the year in the kingdom since the triple suicide bombings of May 2003. In comparison with the national Islamist insurgencies of the 1990s, furthermore, Saudi Arabia's was nearer in gravity to Egypt's than Algeria's – and they were both defeated.

Even so, the government had shown a patchy ability to get a grip on security, amid widely discussed fears that al-Qaeda cells might land a deadly blow on major oil installations or, probably more achievable, try to assassinate a senior prince in the hope of triggering a wider crackdown and broadening the conflict. 'If anyone wants to kill a member of the royal family, it is not very difficult', said one of its members: 'Tradition obliges us to keep an open house to anyone who wants to approach us.'[16]

One Saudi diplomat and veteran adviser to King Abdullah, a recent study of the Algerian civil war on his desk, said the regime was well aware of the trap. The government 'does not want to overreact – we must avoid widening the circle of sympathy for these people'.[17]

Quite how numerous 'these people' are has always been a matter of conjecture. Saudi officials have said the kingdom sent some 20,000 volunteers to the jihad against the Soviet Union in Afghanistan – significant numbers of them recruited by Osama bin Laden. That statement was made in May 1996, following the November 1995 bombing of a National Guard facility in central Riyadh that killed five US trainers. Initially the government went into its normal state of denial, making vague accusations against Iran and/or Iraq, even though the attack followed a year-long crackdown on radical Islamists of the *al-Sahwa al-Islamiyya* (Islamic Awakening), and local residents near the scene of the bombing were inclined to attribute it to 'Arab Afghans'. Indeed, four Afghanistan volunteers were duly and publicly beheaded for the attack the following spring, and the unusual government statement was by way of assurance that the overwhelming majority of their comrades had been successfully reintegrated into Saudi society.[18]

But the Arab Afghans had within a decade given way to a second generation of fighters, inspired rather than centrally directed by al-Qaeda. 'These are not the Mujahideen who fought against the Soviets in Afghanistan. These are people who set their face against Saudi society before they left [to fight in Bosnia, Chechnya and then Iraq]', said Jamal Khashoggi, a Saudi journalist then acting as an adviser to Prince Turki al-Faisal, the long-time former intelligence chief who became Saudi ambassador to London and then Washington.[19]

Abdulaziz al-Muqrin was a case in point. Until he died in a shoot-out not long after the beheading of Paul Johnson, Muqrin had been behind most of the mayhem in the kingdom, gloating in website statements over the 'slaughter' of 'infidels and Crusaders' at al-Khobar and Yanbu. According to Mohsen al-Awajy, the Islamist reformist who at that time had been trying to mediate between the government and the insurgents, Muqrin fought in Bosnia and took part in the failed assassination attempt on President Hosni Mubarak of Egypt in Addis Ababa in 1995. Extradited to Saudi Arabia, Muqrin was subjected to 'intolerable torture', said Awajy: 'After his release, he acted as a revenger, not a *mujahid*. He is very simple-minded, with no political brain. He has the gun, but no mind to control this gun. He is a killer.'

They are 'a minority within the minority' of Islamist insurgents, Awajy reckoned, who believe they can overthrow the al-Saud by fomenting anarchy and demonstrating their inability to deliver security or spread prosperity. He nevertheless cautioned that they were deadly and dangerous: 'They have already decided to die and want to kill as many people as they can before they do so. Let us recall that it only took 19 individuals to change the face of the planet on September 11.'[20]

Many Saudi security experts nevertheless believed that the second generation of insurgents were close to buckling. 'They have not only lost a lot of people: they have lost infrastructure, their safe houses, and the weapons, explosives and cash they must have built up over years', argued Khashoggi: 'People are no longer protecting them or taking them in.'

Such views appeared to be borne out by the subsequent record. The security services foiled a major attack on a neuralgic oil complex at Abqaiq in 2006. In June 2008 the authorities announced the detention of 520 terrorist suspects since the beginning of that year, accused of planning bomb attacks on oil installations, some of them acting under the orders of Ayman al-Zawahiri, the al-Qaeda number two, some of them returnee volunteers from Iraq. To be set against that, the kingdom – which for decades had headed off discontent at home by encouraging Saudi youth to go to fight for Muslim causes abroad – was continuing to produce jihadis in impressive numbers.

Saudi Arabia provides almost laboratory conditions to incubate thousands of bin Ladens and Muqrins. That is its strategic dilemma.

The backdrop could hardly be less propitious. American support for the al-Saud, previously unconditional, could no longer be guaranteed after 9/11, and the periodic outbreaks of anti-Saudi hostility in the US Congress and the media it brought in its wake. Yet that alliance was one of the main reasons bin Laden and his kind see the Saudi rulers as apostates. It remains a reliable recruiting sergeant, especially when the Saudi public for which they both compete was being radicalized daily by US policy in Iraq and Israel–Palestine, and the seemingly unstoppable rise of Shia Iran. As previously remarked, the live daily broadcasts via satellite television of the Iraqi, Palestinian and (in 2006) Lebanese conflicts, commented on and analysed in a plethora of websites, made a compelling case to Saudis, as well as other Arabs and Muslims, that Washington was indeed leading a war against Islam.

Saudi diplomacy did start responding to this new and dangerous situation, stepping into the political vacuum it saw American power creating across the region. From 1998 and the Anglo-American skirmishes with Saddam Hussein and gradual turn towards a policy of regime change in Iraq, as we saw in passing in the previous chapter, Riyadh started exploring the possibility of coexistence with its neighbours – including Iran. By 2002, as Ariel Sharon was retaking the West Bank by force, Abdullah got the Arab League summit in Beirut to endorse a comprehensive peace plan, offering Israel full recognition in exchange for the return of all Arab land captured in the 1967 Arab–Israeli war and a Palestinian state. From 2004 onwards, and with just as little success, Riyadh tried to mediate between Syria and Lebanon – where Rafiq al-Hariri, a Saudi protégé, would be assassinated the following year – as well as between the internal Lebanese factions. When Fatah, the nationalist linchpin of the PLO, and Hamas, the Islamist group that won the 2006 Palestinian election, came to blows, it was the Saudis, through the Mecca agreement of 'national unity' between the two factions, who mended the fences (although those, too, were soon kicked over after Hamas seized control of Gaza in June 2007).

Inside the kingdom, such opinion polls as there are regularly show the main preoccupation to be jobs. Per capita incomes, before the 2007–8 escalation in oil prices, had fallen to about a third of the level of 20 years ago. Nearly two thirds of the indigenous population is under 25, yet the oil-dominated economy creates few jobs to employ them, while a bloated royal family with no clear definition of where a privy purse ends and a public budget begins continues to squander fabulous public wealth. Military spending, for example, is about three times the average for a developing country, and is used as a mechanism for distributing power and wealth within the top ranks of the House of Saud – more than 5,000 princes strong.

Meanwhile, mosques and classrooms continue to spew out Wahhabi fanaticism, and Saudi Arabia had for decades been exporting these ideas, by endowing mosques, schools and religious foundations; as we saw in Chapter II, just during the reign of King Fahd, Riyadh claimed to have established 1,359 mosques abroad, along with 202 colleges, 210 Islamic centres and more than 2,000 schools. In addition, it episodically supported pan-Islamist movements such as the Muslim Brotherhood and, as already remarked, sponsored jihad abroad from Afghanistan to Bosnia. As we saw in Chapter IV, if the jihadis were able to establish a base in Iraq, that was in part because Wahhabi proselytizers built bridgeheads in cities such as Mosul in the final years of Saddam Hussein's rule.

At the same time, the Saudi leadership often appears paralysed, by the choices it faces, the need to build consensus and unity across disparate factions within the family, and the constant jostle for position within it. With the death of ibn Saud in 1953, internal rivalries and a patrimonial approach to government by the leading princes became a constant feature of al-Saud rule, shaping every contour of the emerging Saudi state. As Steffen Hertog has observed, 'Saudi bureaucracy building often seems not to be a case of "form follows function" but of "form follows family"' – in particular the huge Sudairi clan of the al-Saud. Saudi Arabia remained an absolute monarchy, but it would no longer be ruled by an absolute monarch.[21]

Succession battles highlight these features of Saudi rule. While the then Crown Prince Abdullah was nominally in charge after King Fahd's stroke in 1995, his (Sudairi) brothers constrained his freedom of manoeuvre. Abdullah loyalists disputed this. 'I know of nothing the crown prince has really wanted to do that he has been unable to do', one senior adviser once told me elliptically. But the way a former courtier of the late King Faisal explained it, the crown prince's rivals, particularly Prince Sultan, the defence minister (now crown prince), and Prince Nayef, the interior minister, needed to keep the stricken king in place for the last decade of his reign precisely to thwart Abdullah: 'In any normal country, Christian or Muslim, when the ruler is incapacitated he is replaced. But none of the brothers is willing to see King Fahd leave the scene. Because if Prince Abdullah succeeds, will he make Sultan crown prince? And if so, will he keep defence? And if so, will he really stay in charge of the army? And so it goes on, right down the line. This is not a kingdom; it's a big sheikhdom.'[22]

One Saudi diplomat preferred another comparison: 'The problem of the succession is, and will continue to be with the current line-up, like the gerontocracy of the Politburo in the Soviet Union after Brezhnev, whereas what we need is a 50-year-old prince who is open to the world. From where, when, or how we don't know – we need a miracle.' King Abdullah, still the repository of reformist hope, was 83 in mid-2008; his imputed successor, Crown Prince Sultan, was 80. And there was no sign that the four main factions inside the al-Saud were willing to skip a generation and choose from among the 60-plus grandsons of Ibn Saud.

Before ascending the throne, and in response to numerous and voluminous petitions from Islamist reformists and liberals demanding change, Abdullah in 2003 launched a 'national dialogue'. Although it has proceeded in fits and starts, it nevertheless marked a moment of real Glasnost by Saudi standards. It held out some prospect of more open government, tighter financial controls on the royal family's share of national wealth, greater rights for women, and – a very distant prospect – the gradual introduction of elections. Abdullah at least appeared to recognize the threat to his dynasty of political and social stagnation, and to acknowledge the need for a more modern and open society. His brothers did not appear to see things that way at all.

No sooner was the national dialogue under way than Prince Nayef summoned a number of dissidents to his office where, according to one reformer present, they were told: 'What we won by the sword, we will keep by the sword.' Prince Sultan said publicly, in March 2004, that the kingdom was not ready for an elected parliament, because voters might choose 'illiterates'. Sheikh Saleh bin Abdulaziz al-Sheikh, then minister of Islamic Affairs and a pillar of the Wahhabi establishment, rejected even the term 'reform' as pregnant with liberalism and licentiousness.

As king, nevertheless, Abdullah has introduced some incremental change. He has started an overhaul of education, rewriting textbooks, changing teaching methods and vetting teachers. He has demanded the active cooperation of the clerical establishment in curtailing the flow of Saudi volunteers to Iraq. He has instituted de-radicalization programmes for groups of jihadi prisoners willing to reintegrate into Saudi society. Suggestively, although without confronting the Wahhabi hierarchy, the King has built tentative bridges to the Shia, personally convened or taken part in inter-confessional forums with Christians and Jews, and tried to foster a more pluralist conception of Islam within the kingdom.[23]

As part of preparations for membership of the World Trade Organization (WTO) – which reformers hope will provide momentum for change without ideological confrontation – he has started to modernize the centrally planned economy and to decentralize it, beginning some privatization, but especially through the creation of new economic zones and poles of industrial development, to create desperately needed jobs.

It should be underlined that the Saudi regime, though it has in important respects built a *rentier* state in which oil revenue has freed its rulers from the political bindings of its society, has also had some important successes in institution building. Naturally, with a Basic Law that majors on the state's responsibility to provide a decent livelihood for its subjects, rather than their freedoms and rights as citizens, it has built up flabby bureaucracies with big fiscal obligations to vast and unproductive clienteles that immobilize large swathes of that state. Yet it has, at the same time, created some effective modern institutions – in the words of the German scholar of Saudi Arabia, Steffen Hertog, 'technocratic enclaves' – such as the Saudi Arabian Monetary Agency (SAMA), the quasi central bank founded by Ibn Saud with American (and

Lebanese) expertise in 1952, SABIC, the world-class petrochemicals company set up in 1976 with a mix of state and private capital, and, of course, Saudi Aramco, gradually bought from its mainly American owners between 1972 and 1980, in a way that created a national oil company with foreign cooperation rather than confrontation, with professional training of its personnel abroad. Saudi Aramco is arguably the best national oil company in the world, and it emerged even though factions within the regime were trying to build up a more classically clientilist national oil company, Petromin, alongside it.[24]

It is therefore not unreasonable to hope that other institutions and companies of this calibre could emerge, especially in the new atmosphere of competition inside the Gulf, between Saudi Arabia and the dynamic and innovative emirates bordering it to the east: Dubai, Abu Dhabi and Qatar. There are some in the Saudi elite, furthermore, who see in institutions such as Saudi Aramco and SAMA modern sources of legitimacy that could eventually outweigh the clerical establishment.

But, as we saw in Chapter II and the case of Egypt and its theoretically compelling economic reform strategy, such ideas can be taken only so far before they hit the wall of political reality – in Egypt's case, the discretionary power of the military/Mukhabarat state; in Saudi Arabia's, the politico-religious compact between the houses of Saud and ibn Abdul Wahhab.

Of course, economic reform is an intrinsic good in countries that so desperately need to modernize and to create jobs for their citizens. Indeed, using something like WTO membership to introduce, for example, insurance companies in Saudi Arabia, regarded by some leading clerics as an offence against God's plans, is tactically astute. But none of this will get to grips with the irreducibly political (and in the Saudi case, politico-religious) nature of the problem.

The al-Saud need to curb decisively the corrosive power of the religious establishment and lead the kingdom towards a form of modernity that its religious heritage can sustain. That surely means that the most visibly feasible way forward is to enlist Islamist progressives – the most potent source of ideas for renewal.

That is a risk they may not be willing or able to take. As one senior prince, a modernizer who fears opening the door to Islamist reformers, puts it with a certain melancholy: 'we liberals sit around a bottle of Scotch and complain to each other, and then, the next morning, do nothing. Yet if we don't get real progress, economically, socially and politically, we are going to be in a terrible mess in five to ten years.'

Yet while both the clerical establishment and al-Qaeda revile such 'whisky liberals', they see as their principal adversary the Islamist reformers who advocate far-reaching change – but work within essentially the same politico-religious idiom as they do. That is precisely what makes them such a potent threat: Saudis, and Islamists elsewhere in the Arab and Muslim worlds, understand their language and can see where they are coming from.

This loosely connected group, that sometimes describes itself simply as *Islahiyyun* or 'reformers', partly emerged from the ranks of the earlier *al-Sahwa al-Islamiyya*, the Islamist awakening that posed a different sort of radical challenge to the regime – the same discourse of post-Afghan jihad zealotry that the bin Ladenists would take so much further. Many Saudi Islamists, seeing how change was blocked across the Arab world from Algeria to Egypt in the post-Afghan euphoria, went back to the sources to think things through from first principles. That led to some devastating critiques of ibn Abdul Wahhab, but, above all, the rediscovery of the thinking of Islamic revivalists of more than a century ago. The ideas of, for example, Mohammed Abduh (see Chapter III), of *maslaha*, akin to the modern idea of the public good or interest, of *shura*, or consultation, and above all of *ijtihad* (see Chapters III and IV), or independent reasoning to marry Islamic belief and teaching with modern challenges, resurfaced almost as a newly minted currency of ideas in Saudi Arabia. The idea of civil society was reborn, with Muslim credentials the Wahhabi establishment justly feared.[25]

These ideas got unusually wide airing. Encouraged by the then Crown Prince Abdullah, the newspaper *al Watan* (the nation, or homeland), set up in 1998, became a forum for their debate. Every bit as important, the internet threw up its own widely disseminated discussion groups, such as the *Muntada al-Wasatiyya*, set up by Mohsen al-Awajy (*Wasatiyya* means 'centrists', the suggestively Islamist equivalent of the Marxist revisionist sense of the term).

There are three seminal departures pioneered by the emergence of this – still embryonic – force. First, they have presented collective demands, breaking with the tradition of individual petition at the *majlis*, or court of the prince. The turning point was the 2003 petition, called 'A vision for the present and future of the homeland', signed by leading Islamist reformers and liberals – although the former were and are the real force. Second, as this pluralism implies, the document is founded on the principles of confessional and political diversity in Saudi Arabia. But, third, for the first time, reformers both liberal and Islamist broke the taboo about speaking out against Wahhabism, implying that its heritage and ideology was the deathly hand holding back the emergence of Saudi Arabia as a successful modern state its citizens would easily support.

In this respect, the 2003 Saudi 'Vision' document is as suggestive of a path forward as the 1989 Jordanian National Charter mentioned in Chapter II, or the still unrealized Iraqi constitution of 2005 (Chapter IV). They all draw on and revisit the sources of renewal of states and peoples that are and will remain Islamic, and in important ways, Islamist.

The idiom, however strange to western or liberal ears, is a large part of the story, because it furnishes those who use it to articulate reform with a recognizable immediacy, an authenticity and a legitimacy that shields them from the usual charges of foreign influence and intrusion. Sheikh Abdulaziz al-Qassim, a former (defenestrated) Saudi judge and reformer, is a particularly authoritative version of the genre. 'Al Qaeda and the clergy are essentially doing the same thing in different ways – putting pressure on the House of Saud for being less devout than it should be. This paralyzes reform', he maintains: 'The only way out of this is to dilute the link with Wahhabi fanaticism. The only way forward is to win the legitimacy of society itself – through political reform that does not depend on the approval of the clergy. If you make society part of reform you can overcome the clergy – it is the only way.'[26]

The demands of the Islamist reformers include free elections, freedom of expression and association, an independent judiciary, a fairer distribution of wealth, and a clearer foreign policy arrived at through open debate – in short, a constitutional monarchy, although not a bicycling monarchy. 'We are limiting our demands to very specific issues, and reiterating the al-Saud's right to stay at the top of the tree', says Mohsen al-Awajy: 'They think it's for tactical reasons but the fact is there is no real alternative.'

Just how fundamental it is that liberals and Islamists take on Wahhabism – leading even the ruling family occasionally to clash with the clerics, for example over the Saudi pipeline of jihadi volunteers to Iraq – cannot be overstated. But it is the Islamist reformers, numerically and ideologically, who are the real force here. They can maintain credibly that they intend no separation between mosque and state, but a redefinition of the relationship between the al-Saud and the al-Sheikh.

'Saudi Arabia has to be an Islamic state; it is the birthplace of Islam. The question is *which* Islam?', is the judgement of Jamal Khashoggi, who before his interlude in the Saudi embassies in London and Washington with Prince Turki al-Faisal was fired as the editor of *al Watan* for publishing articles questioning the theological legacy of Ibn Taymiyya – but [at the time of writing] was back at the head of this newspaper as a vibrant but cautious conduit of these ideas. 'The alliance should be between the state and Islam, not between the House of Saud and the House of al-Sheikh', he concluded, before he was reinstated by the hand of King Abdullah.

Awajy, who lost his job as a university professor and has not been reinstated, argues that 'the contract between the two houses is no longer in the interests of the Saudi people; if we tolerated it in the past it does not mean we will in the future. Real reform cannot take place within the Wahhabi doctrine.'

The Wahhabi establishment has pumped the poison of bigotry into the Saudi mainstream throughout the existence of the kingdom. After 9/11, it became impossible to ignore that its ideas and al-Qaeda's were pretty much the same. It is hard to imagine how the House of Saud will survive much beyond the short term unless they break decisively with these ideas. Or, as one Saudi reformer put it: 'if this clerical establishment is incapable of imagining the solutions we need to modern problems, then the answer is clear – we have to find another establishment'.

VI

Getting Away with Murder?

It is midnight one Saturday in downtown Beirut and the Buddha Bar is heaving. A cavernous copy of its Parisian namesake, with a 20ft-high Buddha statue as its presiding spirit, the bar was just one incarnation of the Lebanese craving for imported novelty and gift for fun.

The son of a Maronite Christian warlord, assassinated during the 1975–90 Lebanese civil war by a vast bomb, allegedly at Syria's instigation, thrust his way through the throng to the bar with the aid of a bodyguard out of central casting: black T-shirt, tailored leather jacket, wrap-around shades and designer stubble.

At the bar itself the eye is necessarily drawn to a towering gold icon for Johnnie Walker whisky. 'Almost everything that takes place in this city happens under the eyes of Johnnie Walker', drawled one regular patron. Beirut, it would appear, was back in business, restored to its pre-war position as the playground of the Arab world.

The city's downtown area, reduced to rubble by 16 years of inter-communal slaughter conducted with heavy weapons, has been rebuilt. Though a few shell-shattered hulks, such as the old Holiday Inn, still scarred the skyline, the core of the city was now resplendent with restored or faux-Ottoman buildings, gleaming sandstone, limestone and marble, recreated churches and mosques, and streets of bars, cafes and restaurants, the sweet smoke of hubble-bubble pipes wafting between them.

Behind this splendid façade, however, a politically unreconstructed Lebanon was lurching towards crisis, weighed down by huge reconstruction debts and trapped in a looming confrontation between western powers and Syria, the aspirant regional power which had not just dominated but micro-managed the country's affairs since the war it helped bring to an end. The glittering Beirutis, rubbing along resentfully with a grasping Syrian secret police regime, recalled nothing so much as a famous poem about pre-war Beirut by the exiled Syrian poet Adonis. Sardonically entitled *The Golden Age*, the verses bathetically descend to 'the age of the golden boot'.

Nor had Beirut anything like recaptured its pre-war pre-eminence. Before the fighting started in 1975, Beirut had been the region's unchallenged entrepôt. Reaching back almost into pre-history, to the Phoenicians and beyond, the coastal settlements of the Levant were an entrepreneurial bridge between the civilizations emerging along the Nile and between the banks of the Tigris and the Euphrates. It has been well said that the flag of modern Lebanon should contain a dollar sign instead of a cedar tree, for it is by vocation a merchant republic.

Before its descent into tribal war, its gifted bankers recycled petrodollars seeking a remunerative home in the West, while its canny middlemen reeled in westerners seeking to sell prized technology or arms to the East. Beyond the tiresome clichés about the 'lost Paris of the Orient' it was an authentic East–West interface, facilitated by a mixed Muslim–Christian culture, laid out in an intricate Byzantine mosaic of its 17 different religious sects.

As well as being the financial and services hub of the region, Beirut was its media and publishing capital, and an education centre too. It was freewheeling, with some more or less democratic habits, and was thus a magnet for the émigrés and exiles spat out by the Arab autocracies surrounding it – and thereby for the Israeli state to its south that needed to monitor and sought to seduce them. These elements also combined to make it a den of regional intrigue, a listening post as well as playground – somewhere between Bogart's *Casablanca* and Batista's *Havana* by way of Noriega's *Panama*.

In a delightful memoir of the celebrated St George Hotel's bar – 'the centre of the centre of the Middle East' – the Palestinian writer Said Aburish recaptured how spies such as Kim Philby or Archie and Kermit Roosevelt sat drinking cheek-by-jowl with regional potentates, oilmen, arms-dealers and reporters (from one of whom, *New York Times* correspondent Sam Pope Brewer, Philby stole his wife Eleanor), while plots were hatched and coups planned. The Buddha Bar had a long way to catch up.[1]

Glittering though this Beirut Redux now looked, it was a shadow of its former self. Then, the city and its preoccupations were regional and international. Now, even though its people typically speak several languages and are widely travelled, it was pretentious and provincial. It was international mostly in the sense that it risked becoming the meat in the sandwich between an obtuse and unreformable Ba'athist regime in Syria and a regionally aggressive USA, which on this occasion was being egged on by France, the main hold-out in President George W. Bush's war of choice against Saddam Hussein's Ba'athist tyranny in Iraq. Less amnesiac Lebanese feared the country would be pulled back once more into sectarian chaos.

✳ ✳ ✳ ✳ ✳

The Lebanese emerged from the long years of bloodletting somewhat sur-prised to find they still had a country.

The 1975–90 civil war had seen cities and villages razed, 145,000 killed and perhaps double that number wounded, 17,400 'disappeared', 3,614 car bombs, and a generalized sectarian retreat into homogeneous communities. But despite it all, there was a palpable will among ordinary Lebanese of nearly all persuasions to find a new way forward, a way of living together. They had yet to find it.[2]

One of the reasons for that was Syria, and what one Lebanese political leader characterized as its creeping *Anschluss* to absorb a country no pan-Syrian or, for that matter, pan-Arab nationalist had ever accepted as a stand-alone entity. Another reason was the craven corruption of much of the Lebanese political class, and its pandering to outside powers to back narrow, sectarian interests. Many of these leaders, and the flotsam in their wake, had interlocked with the Syrian nomenklatura in the shared pillage of what should otherwise have been a much more vibrant economy and open society. The new 'age of the golden boot' was an age of parasites and plunderers.[3]

But Lebanon has always been something of a geopolitical oddity, some-thing that has a lot to do with its topography. In a region that abounds with scores of religious sects spawned by millennia of doctrinal controversy, Mount Lebanon has for centuries offered a secure fastness for the most heterodox among them.

The Maronite Christians, aligned with the Roman Catholic Church and originally from Syria's Orontes valley, fled to the mountains an age ago to escape Byzantine (Christian) persecution – not, as subsequent myth-making had it, Muslim oppression. The Druze – whose precise religious beliefs are known only to their elders and initiates, but who appear to derive from the defeated heterodox Shi'ism of the Fatimid dynasty a millennium ago – also found refuge in Mount Lebanon. These were the original core communities of the mountain, to be joined by Sunni and Shia Muslims in the narrow coastal plains and the valleys, and in the course of time by Greek Christians, Orthodox and Catholic, Armenian Christians, Chaldeans, Syriacs, et al.

The Sunni prospered under the (Sunni) Ottomans who, nevertheless, ruled the Lebanon by proxy through a mountain emirate of almost interchangeable Maronite and Druze notables. The Shia, originally inhabitants of the mountain as well as the valley, were gradually driven south. The Maronites and the Druze, however, were structurally tribal and highly fissiparous. The earliest known document referring to the Maronites is a papal bull from 1216, absolving the losers in a civil war provoked by the allegiance of part of the community to the Franks, or Crusaders. The Druze were also known to hedge their bets. In the mid-thirteenth century, the Druze Buhturid dynasty had forces fighting on both sides when the Mamluks drove the Mongols out of Syria at the battle of Ayn Jalut near Lake Tiberias.[4]

The pivotal modern change came as a result of the Maronite–Druze civil war of the mid-nineteenth century. In a pattern the Lebanese seem unable to avoid repeating, that conflict sucked in outside (in this case) European powers led by the French who, in 1920, carved out 'Greater Lebanon' from post-Ottoman Syria. An ostensibly 'Christian' triumph, this redrawing of the map added to Mount Lebanon territory and peoples that were not Christian. In time, that would necessitate the National Pact of 1943 to launch Lebanon's independence. The Pact prescribed an inter-communal power structure extrapolated from the last ever population census, taken in 1932. It gave a proportional majority and political predominance to the Christians, led by their biggest community, the Maronites, on the arithmetically assisted assumption of a 6:5 population balance in their favour – probably not true even in 1943.

It was a bluff, but a magnificent bluff. It enabled the Lebanese to revel in their heterogeneity – and profit from it – for three golden decades. The dark side of Lebanon – the huge wealth disparities or the reality of a Shia underclass, the lack of a public health system and rudimentary state education system, the corruption and feudal pattern of sectarian politics, or the denial of basic rights to Palestinians and the misery of their refugee camps – was drowned out by the clink of champagne glasses.

What brought this much-embellished period of Lebanese history to an end is as much disputed as the fanciful history each sect has manufactured to enhance its own antecedents. But the seeds of conflict – within as well as between each community – were visibly there long before a shot was fired.

In the then-ruling Maronites' view, the arrival in Lebanon of the Palestine Liberation Organization – ejected from Jordan after losing the 1970–1

'Black September' war against the late King Hussein – tipped the delicate confessional balance unacceptably in favour of the Muslims. Just as it had in Jordan, the PLO did indeed behave with all the arrogance of a state-within-the-state, and invited Israel's retribution by using south Lebanon as a base from which to confront its enemy. But Israel had begun targeting Lebanon before the PLO established its headquarters there – for example, by destroying the fleet of Middle East Airlines at Beirut airport in 1968. Lebanese Muslims, moreover, and especially the Shia, had long been pressing for a fairer share of power, and the PLO only joined the Muslim–Druze alliance after Maronite militias had launched their armed attempt to reaffirm Christian hegemony.

A Syria then led by Hafez al-Assad, the so-called Sphinx of Damascus, entered the fray as a result. His aims were to prevent what by 1976 looked like inevitable Christian defeat; to abort the emergence of a Palestinian stronghold on Syria's borders; and to reassert its pan-Arab credentials while pursuing pan-Syrian goals legitimized by an invitation to intervene from the (Maronite) Lebanese presidency, subsequent endorsement of its role by the Arab League, and eventual international resignation that no one else seemed able to stabilize Lebanon. Even Hafez al-Assad had his uses to the West as a strongman.

The conflict moved from the cities to the mountains, from the hotel towers to the refugee camps, and then back again. The kaleidoscope of sectarian alliances kept shifting and re-combining, amid fathomless sub-plots of intra-sect and factional vendettas. In a lethal cocktail of egotism, many Lebanese managed simultaneously to be ultra-fanatics and craven turncoats. The Maronites were especially addicted to slaughtering each other: a leitmotif of this horrendous war was the savagery with which some of these Christian dynasties sought to wipe out each other's entire families.

Viewed from a wider scope, Saudis and Syrians, Iraqis and Libyans, Iranians and Israelis used Beirut as their address of choice to communicate with each other by car bomb. Lebanon became their preferred arena for proxy war. Soon enough, alarmed western powers led by the USA and France blundered in, with the forlorn ambition of re-establishing a semblance of order. Soon enough, with only the dimmest notion of the dynamics of this conflict and its rules of engagement, the multi-national forces came to be regarded as just another militia, and got truck bombed out.[5]

The idea of Lebanon went up in smoke.

The long war and Israel's opportunist invasion in 1982 – when the then Israeli defence minister Ariel Sharon all but razed West Beirut as he sought to crush the PLO – shattered the country into cantonized fragments. When the shooting eventually stopped, Syria was left holding most of the pieces.

* * * * *

The Lebanese republic was supposed to be relaunched by a new national entente – the 1989 Taif accord. This readjusted the confessional balance to give Muslims and Christians parity in parliament, where a Shia speaker presides, and to transfer some executive power from a presidency still held by the Maronites to a Sunni Muslim prime minister. Most militias were disbanded and partially folded into a new national army while, under the terms of the accord, Syria was to redeploy its troops to its border with Lebanon within two years, and then leave.

In practice, Israel's continuing occupation of 12 per cent of Lebanese territory north of the Israeli frontier, which skirted the Syrian Golan Heights Israel occupied during the 1967 Arab–Israeli war, gave Syria an alibi to stay. Syria's participation in the US-led Gulf War coalition to evict Saddam Hussein's Iraqi occupation force from Kuwait, and subsequent entry into ultimately sterile peace negotiations with Israel, pushed the Syrian occupation of Lebanon far down anybody's list of regional priorities. It was simply not an issue with the Americans.

The then lord of Damascus, Hafez al-Assad, seized the opportunity to license Hizbollah, the Shia Islamist movement that became the most effective irregular army in the world, as the spearhead of resistance to the Israelis. For Syria, the liberation of south Lebanon was always secondary to its use of Hizbollah to remind Israel that although Damascus had failed to recapture the Golan in the 1973 Arab–Israeli war, it still intended to cause the Israelis pain until they returned the Heights.[6]

Lebanon thus became a pawn in a new proxy war. Neither Israel nor Syria wanted to risk a direct, all-out conflict. Both were happy enough to fight to the last Lebanese. The Lebanese, as they struggled to emerge from the ruins of their tribal war, paid a high price, including two major Israeli incursions in 1993 and 1996. The Syrian Ba'athist nomenklatura, meanwhile, busily set about recreating Lebanon in its own image, the better to loot it. Damascus reconsecrated the pre-war sectarian system in a manner designed to highlight its own role as indispensable arbiter and bulwark against a relapse into conflict. Its post-war occupation force, at one time 40,000 strong, cast a pall over the country. But its real instrument of rule, as elsewhere in the Arab world, was the Mukhabarat: its own intelligence services and their loyal Lebanese surrogates.

They cultivated political clients and former warlords who slipped effortlessly out of their militia fatigues into the new power structure. They used divide-and-rule tactics to prevent, above all, the emergence of any cross-confessional, democratic national force. Samir Franjieh, a left-of-centre opposition leader from a leading Maronite clan, put it this way: 'the state should be based on all rights for individuals and all guarantees for [the 17] communities. What we have now is all rights vested in the communities but usurped by their leaders.' So long as Syria could manipulate these leaders, all of whom required its licence to operate, it could dominate Lebanon.[7]

The arrival in 1992 of Rafiq al-Hariri, a billionaire construction magnate who spread into banking and media, raised hopes that at last a Lebanese champion would articulate a national project to revive the country. Hariri, a Sunni who made his money in Saudi Arabia and helped negotiate an end to the war, was to be prime minister for ten of the first 14 post-war years. He resigned in October 2004 after Syria forced him, his cabinet and parliament to change the constitution so that the ineffectual but pliant President Emile Lahoud could stay on another three years.

That resignation was the proximate beginning of a defining political crisis in the modern Arab world. This crisis was in its way almost as important as the Iraq drama playing out bloodily to Lebanon's east. It would establish the extent to which Arab despots – in this case the rulers of Syria – could continue in the eyes of many to get away with murder.

* * * * *

Rafiq Hariri's advent raised great expectations. Fouad Siniora, the finance minister who was to succeed him as prime minister, recalled arriving in the post-war ruins of a Beirut starved of electricity, amid a swirl of rumours that Hariri had moored ships in the port with the power generating capacity to light up the whole city. Some Lebanese appeared to confuse the billionaire and philanthropist with Aladdin's genie.[8]

But when Hariri did arrive, the currency stabilized and Lebanon's credit was restored. As prime minister he was able to call on an international network of friends, not just in the Gulf but among European leaders such as Jacques Chirac, or, with James Wolfensohn, in international financial institutions such as the World Bank. He was adept at mobilizing the Lebanese diaspora – and his own banks – to buy up a stream of international bond issues for reconstruction. The rebirth of Beirut was his work.

During the war, 'infrastructure' had come to mean little more than holding the high ground, a few power generators and each militia having its own port.

Now, there was a plan to recreate central Beirut, and Solidere, a company part-owned by Hariri, would do it. The core idea was to make the city the uncontested capital market of a broader Middle East that would need huge sums to develop and reconstruct.

Politically, Hariri struggled to establish himself as the *primus inter pares* of the troika of 'presidents' set up by the Taif Accord – not just the president and prime minister but a powerful speaker of parliament, Nabih Berri, former chief of Amal, the Shia militia, who was Syria's principal political agent in Lebanon. Showing scant regard for inter-confessional rivalries, Hariri preferred to operate as the chief executive of a business. He liked to get things done and would willingly distribute money to oil things along. Critics said he was treating Lebanon like a company in which he was making himself chief shareholder. Admirers underlined that, unlike most Arab leaders, he was putting his own money into the country rather than using public office to loot the treasury. His goal, he once confided, was a Lebanon independent of but in step with Syria. In pursuing it, Hariri had two important advantages. First, Syria needed his unique international reach not just to sell the Lebanese reconstruction story, but to augment its own meagre diplomatic and financial resources. Second, his exasperation with Lebanon's political class was so widely shared by the Lebanese it became a source of genuine, cross-community popularity.[9]

At the height of his influence, however, he made little attempt to use this following to remould the confessional system into a new national consensus. While Hariri rebuilt much of Lebanon, he left it politically unreconstructed.

Hariri and his friends complained that Syria meddled from the first, leaving them with little margin for manoeuvre. 'The Syrians interfered from day one', he said: 'They installed as speaker of parliament Nabih Berri. He's their representative and he proceeded to get the government by the neck.'[10]

The prime minister's critics were harsher. Michel Mouawad, son of Rene Mouawad, the popular president assassinated in a bombing widely attributed to Syria as the war drew to an end in 1989, said: 'The Syrians employ Hariri as a marketing director. He's good, he really is, but the problem is their system is no longer marketable.'[11]

Nor had reconstruction been an unqualified success. The cost was huge, saddling Lebanon with a $36 billion debt, equivalent to almost twice its gross domestic product. The lifeblood of remittances repatriated from Lebanese abroad, perhaps three to four times as numerous as the 4 million who lived in the country, had started to dry up. With its banks, mostly smallish family affairs, grown fat and lazy on government borrowing, Beirut, moreover, was losing ground to rival financial centres such as Dubai. Its stock market remained tiny, dominated by the banks and Solidere. The regional media business, discomfited by Mukhabarat oversight, as well as the lack of basic infrastructure (such as broadband internet connections), was heading for Dubai and Qatar. Lebanon was even beginning to lose its niche in areas such as education and health services to these Gulf city-states, whose dynamism, ironically, was partly powered by an inflow of Lebanese émigrés. A lot of the energy pulsing through Beirut, by contrast, was the energy of dissipation.

Lebanon's descent into a miasma of clientilism under Syrian tutelage, the parcelling out of post-war institutions as booty for the warlords, and the paralysis of government caused by the president, prime minister and speaker jostling for position as though they were Roman triumvirs, were all part of the reason. 'What we have here', observed Samir Franjieh in 1998, midway through the reconstruction process, 'is like [post-Soviet] Russia: liberalism, without democracy, which gives you as its end-result the Mafia'.[12]

'Twelve years after the start of reconstruction you come to the realization you've rebuilt some of the infrastructure – by no means all and by no means in all regions – at a very high cost', said Nasser Saidi, a former economy minister and central banker: 'Very little effort went into the building of institutions or into learning the lessons of the war and making people accountable for what they did. Maybe there were too many people to punish, but that doesn't mean you should reward them by putting them in power. It's obvious we could have built something better without them. It's not just the high debt and so on, it's that there's no participation in political life.'[13]

Each community, by contrast, had carved out a share of the state. The Council of the South to develop southern Lebanon and the national electricity company, for instance, became fiefs of Amal, the Shia militia-turned-gravy-train led by Nabih Berri, Syria's foremost ally. Amal was not only the preferred Syrian proxy but the biggest snout in this trough. The two functions were intimately connected. Amal, for example, levied surtaxes of up to $200 for each container coming through the port of Beirut – which in the first 15 years after the war imported more than $6 billion of goods a year. It shared this racket – worth some $350 million – with its patrons in Syria's intelligence services and their allies in the Lebanese security services. Enough crumbs fell from this well-set table to keep in circulation many hired guns left over from the war.[14]

By late 1998, coincident with General Emile Lahoud's assumption of Lebanon's presidency, Hariri had concluded this situation was no longer sustainable. But he also judged that he had a green light from Syria to confront its worst aspects. He misread the signals, and thereby began sowing the seeds of what would become the Syrian–Lebanese crisis of 2004–5, detonated by his own assassination.

* * * * *

The emergence of General Emile Lahoud as president in 1998 was seen as an opportunity for the political and national renewal that had eluded post-war Lebanon. The main losers of that war, the hitherto dominant Maronites, had boycotted the two intervening general elections. Pining after discredited leaders who were either dead, jailed or in exile, they repeated the same mistake as Lebanon's Sunni Muslims in the 1920s, by opting out of a political process they could no longer control. The hopes vested in the Maronite general Lahoud were based not so much on his not wholly evident merits as the expectation he would make the alienated Maronites feel they had a stake in that process. Cardinal Nasrallah Sfeir, the Maronite Patriarch who had by default assumed political leadership of his community, foresaw the 1998 presidential 'election' as 'an occasion either to revive the country or to destroy it'.[15]

Lahoud's main achievement was to preside over the reconstitution of a 60,000-strong national army, absorbing remnants of the civil war militias and making of it arguably the most successful example of non-sectarian institution-building – important as a Christian-led vehicle of national unity rather than a fighting force it would never be.

Hariri was at first cautiously hopeful about Lahoud. 'I need to see a president whose programme is similar to mine so that we are aiming at the same goals', he said: 'He has to cooperate with me if there is to be change. I need a partner, not a follower.' He said the Syrians 'recognize the situation cannot continue as it has been and are ready to see a change – provided it does not change Lebanese behaviour towards Syria or towards the peace process'. This reference to Middle East peace was ultra-sensitive but, in a sense, academic. Lebanon's last attempt to reach a peace with Israel separately from Syria was doomed to failure, provoking the 1982 assassination, by a vast bomb, of Bashir Gemayel, the Maronite warlord and president-elect. There was no extant politician intending to repeat it. Syria had seen to that.[16]

But by late 1998 the deadlock over Middle East peace had derailed Syria's already faltering attempts to restructure its economy, making it dependent on Lebanon's more open and vibrant economy. Bankers and government officials in Beirut reckoned that Syrians working, investing and racketeering in Lebanon were by then repatriating $2.5–3 billion a year. That made Lebanon Syria's biggest single earner. Hariri was acutely aware of this and believed Damascus would take steps to avoid killing the goose that was laying such golden eggs. Anti-Syrian riots the previous year, by Shia and Sunni Muslims rather than the usual, Christian, suspects, had alarmed Damascus.[17]

'We had a serious sit-down', Hariri said, with, among others, Syrian president Hafez al-Assad, vice-president Abd al-Halim Khaddam and Ghazi Kenaan, the military intelligence chief who had been Damascus' viceroy in Lebanon since 1982. He was confident he had their backing to end the post-war reign of the warlords, to name his own cabinet, and in particular to side-line Nabih Berri. 'Berri will be screwed', Hariri predicted privately: 'I have said clearly I am not prepared to continue doing things this way. Everyone knows what's coming, and they can only avoid it by not electing me.' Which, of course, is precisely what 'they' did: Hariri was dumped.[18]

Syria, it turned out, had other worries. While Hafez al-Assad remained its undisputed master, his health was failing. Hizbollah's successful resistance to the Israeli occupation made it foreseeable that Israel would withdraw from its 'Security Zone', which, far from providing security, was sending home in body-bags a politically costly stream of Israeli casualties. Damascus anticipated international pressure to rein in Hizbollah and pull out Syrian troops from Lebanon once Israel withdrew. Risking any prior upheaval there must have looked premature to cautious men like Hafez al-Assad. 'Assad likes to walk along well-lit paths', cautioned a former US official who saw the Syrian president regularly during that period.[19]

Six months later, ruefully reflecting on his misjudgement of Syria, Hariri noted that 'the country has divided into a Lahoud camp and a Hariri camp', reconstruction had stopped, and the intelligence services had been given free rein to intimidate the judiciary, the last check on their discretionary power. He nonetheless believed this situation could not last more than another six months because, examined objectively, this was damaging to Syria's overall interests. 'The Syrians don't have any interest in seeing all this happening', he said.[20]

Rafiq Hariri was indeed recalled as prime minister, his bloc in parliament greatly strengthened, in November 2000. By then, however, his antagonistic relationship with President Lahoud and the political paralysis in the country had grown exponentially, relieved only by a stop-gap, international financial bail-out for Lebanon that Hariri managed to engineer in the autumn of 2002. Conditionality clauses in this package, requiring the privatization of utilities and new budget and spending targets, were there because Hariri wanted them to help him push through reforms. But nothing happened. In freewheeling Lebanon, as elsewhere in the Arab world, politics is everything.

Yet Hariri would make the same mistake again in the summer of 2004. He again came to believe Syria, in its own objective interest, would give him a mandate for change. Only, on this occasion, the president he believed was Hafez's son, Bashar al-Assad.

* * * * *

When Bashar al-Assad succeeded his father in the summer of 2000, there was a glimmer of hope that the Syrian regime – a prototypical Arab national security state built on hollow nationalist slogans and a dysfunctional command economy spiced by crony capitalism – might reform itself. There was indeed a 'Damascus spring', lit up by disputatious political 'salons' Bashar himself encouraged. But it was brief, and ended with several of the leading participants in jail. Western governments, especially France and the UK, tried to encourage the young Assad, thrust unexpectedly into the political front line after the death in a car crash of his brother Basel. They, and the USA, believed he needed help to break free from his father's Old Guard. He did eventually break free, pushing aside regime veterans such as Khaddam and army chief of staff Hikmat Shihabi – both of them heavyweight Sunni Muslim ballast for the minority Alawite rule camouflaged by the Ba'ath party. But the purpose seemed to be to consolidate power for a family circle interested more in enrichment than in statecraft.

Yes, after 9/11, the young Assad was invaluable to the USA in supplying dossiers on Islamist activists compiled by its tentacular Mukhabarat. But being itself a secret police state, it tended to see all other systems the same way and assumed that being in the good graces of the Central Intelligence Agency was its 'get-out-of-jail-free-card', as one former US official put it.[21]

Despite repeated warnings from the USA, in the year leading up to the Iraq war, companies the USA said were fronted by individuals connected to Bashar, his brother Maher al-Assad, their brother-in-law, Asef Shawkat, and their cousin, Rami Makhlouf, continued to sell weapons including east European tank engines and transporters to Saddam Hussein. Syria was at the same time illegally receiving Iraqi oil at a discount of between $14 and $20 a barrel.[22]

There was in this an element of need as well as greed. Syria had long depended on windfalls to keep its rickety economy and bloated security apparat afloat. Until the end of the 1970s the oil-rich Gulf rulers bankrolled it as a 'frontline' state in the conflict with Israel. In the 1980s it got free oil from Iran in exchange for siding with the Islamic Revolution in its 1980–8 war with Iraq, Syria's Ba'athist rival, and it continued to receive arms it would never pay for from the Soviet Union. In the late 1980s Syria found some oil of its own in the north. By then, of course, it had its fingers deep in the Lebanon honeypot, as well as the diplomatic shield fashioned out of its support for the 1991 Gulf war coalition against Iraq and subsequent entry into the Middle East peace process. But there was something more nakedly commercial about these transactions with Iraq – with which Syria had maintained the most vicious Ba'athist rivalry for some three decades – even if Damascus was anticipating that America would get a very bloody nose in Iraq.

Elementary common sense and, indeed, US intelligence predictions suggested Syria would cease such blatant arms contraband as the Iraq war neared. Not a bit of it. As one American official pithily recalled: 'the dumb bastards redoubled their shipments; they were going to get every last dinar out of Iraq before we went in. At its heart and soul, it's a mafia regime', he said: 'It's hard to know where state interests end and personal interests begin. But we started seeing that mafia interests began trumping state interests every time.'[23]

The Lebanese, of course, already knew that. They had already seen how, since Bashar took over, those in charge in Damascus – including Ghazi Kenaan, the military intelligence chief who ran Lebanon for 20 years – had become more interested in the increasingly twisted economics of the country. 'This is no more than a giant racket', expostulated one Lebanese politician: 'Under Hafez al-Assad, Syria saw Lebanon as political patrimony to be used in the larger Middle East game. But these people are no longer interested even in the politics, any more than Al Capone was.'[24]

There was a certain whiff of class animus in all this, of patrician scorn towards new money grubbily acquired and contempt towards ostentation because, although the civil war had no decisive outcome, it certainly engendered social mobility. 'One reading of the war is that it was a social revolution', said Samir Franjieh: 'It was not strictly speaking about poverty, but about relative poverty and relative wealth – it was an attempt to settle the question of rank and standing in society.'

'The problem is that these people, for all their millions, know they lack legitimacy and the Syrians – who are themselves Alawite outsiders from the mountains – know that and find it easy to play on their sense of insecurity', said an opposition politician.[25]

'There is no normal economic relationship between Syria and Lebanon', complained Walid Jumblatt, the hitherto Syrian-allied lord of the Druze who by late 2004 had become leader of the opposition: 'It's their mafias and local clients overmilking our cow.' Bashar al-Assad, Jumblatt said, had divested himself of all wiser counsellors such as Khaddam and Shihabi: 'Now it's purely clan rule, naked Alawite rule, and they can't give up one bit of Lebanon.'[26]

Jumblatt was speaking at Mukhtara, his ancestral palace in the Chouf mountains, transformed into an armed camp after the car bomb attack of 1 October 2004 on his close ally Marwan Hamade, another former economy minister who had just pulled out of the government in protest at Syria's decision to extend President Lahoud's term. Hariri resigned as prime minister three days after that attack and was in the process of allying with Jumblatt's Druze and the Christian opposition.

Jumblatt's father, Kamal, who in another Lebanese high wire act combined the role of feudal lord with leadership of the Progressive Socialist Party, had led the Muslim–Left alliance in the early stages of the civil war. He was assassinated in 1977, as the Syrian army began tightening its grip on the Lebanon. Yet Walid, a mercurial and cerebral man who became a warlord by default, was still sucked into the Syrian orbit. Such was the realpolitik of survival. Now, however, by denouncing the Syria–Lebanon set-up as police states run by clans and mafias, the son risked the fate of the father.

That September of 2004, Damascus accused Hariri and Jumblatt of inciting France to ally with the USA in pushing Resolution 1559 through the UN Security Council. This called on Syria to end its meddling in Lebanese politics, withdraw its remaining 14,000 troops, and for the disarmament of remaining militias, meaning, essentially, Hizbollah. The resolution was a frontal challenge to Syrian hegemony in Lebanon.

Jumblatt said he had 'originally proposed [to the Syrians] they keep their troops here as long as Israel occupied any part of the country, but that they stop interfering in Lebanese affairs. But they just can't do it. Now they're accusing me of colluding with Hariri to provoke the French into 1559. According to them, Marwan Hamade actually wrote [the resolution] in Sardinia [Hariri's holiday retreat].'

'I appear to be Public Enemy Number One, and we have gone backwards 28 years [to his father, Kamal Jumblatt's assassination, almost certainly at Syrian hands]. Now they're like Bush – you're either with us or against us.'[27]

Jumblatt's and Hamade's real crime, however, had been to foster cross-community unity. Three years previously the Druze leader had received the Maronite patriarch, Cardinal Nasrallah Sfeir, in the Chouf, in a historic reconciliation between the two communities that devolved into an alliance between Jumblatt's parliamentary bloc and the mainstream Christian opposition. That was threatening enough, from the Syrians' point of view. But they got really spooked once Hamade became the linkman in the then emerging alliance between Hariri's powerful Sunni bloc and the opposition. As Nayla Mouawad, the MP and widow of the president who died for doing much the same thing, put it: 'The great taboo for the Syrians is to have any bridge between the communities.'[28] As Jumblatt himself explained: 'Hariri is the key factor here because he's a Sunni. The Druze and the Christians are not enough without the Muslims. We would be able to resist a bit, maybe, but we're still too weak.'

Hariri was at the time philosophical about the threats from Damascus. He was aware a showdown was coming, but disdainful of Syrian tactics. 'They are in deep trouble and do not know what they're doing', he said: 'They think it's France ... they accused me of being behind all of it – imagine, the reaction of the whole international community – I'm flattered.' But he confirmed accounts by his allies of a dramatic meeting – a mere 12 minutes long – in Damascus with Bashar al-Assad on 26 August, one week before the Security Council adopted resolution 1559. The young Syrian president informed him that Lahoud would have his presidential term extended. Bashar told him he would break Beirut over his and Jumblatt's head rather than leave it.

'We destroyed the country once and we can do it again – we will never allow ourselves to be pushed out', was the precise threat.[29]

* * * * *

Syria's methods in Lebanon were crude. But its diplomacy was a fiasco. In November 2002, Syria, then a rotating member of the UN Security Council, gave its assent to the unanimously endorsed resolution 1441, requiring Saddam Hussein's regime to bring Iraq into full compliance with a string of previous UN edicts requiring him to disarm. While the precise meaning of 1441 would soon enough divide the western allies, it was an opportunity for Damascus to build bridges to the Americans and reinforce links with the Europeans – to prepare a soft landing for its political system.

As we saw earlier, the Syrian regime appeared to think it had curried enough favour with Washington by supplying intelligence on Islamist activists after 9/11. The Assad coterie was, in any case, busily making a killing selling weapons to Saddam according to the US State Department. After the fall of Saddam gave way to a gathering Sunni insurgency against the occupation, however, Damascus stood accused by Washington of allowing Saddam loyalists to use Syrian territory to plan attacks on its forces and as a transit route for jihadi volunteers. 'We are concerned that Syria is allowing its territory to become part of the Iraqi battlefield', a senior US official said menacingly in the autumn of 2005: 'That's a choice the Syrians have made and we think that's an unwise choice.' The neo-conservative cabals that helped crank up support for the Iraq war had already been baying for Bashar al-Assad's blood for at least a year.[30]

As Hariri saw it then, the Syrian Ba'athists were courting the same fate as their estranged Iraqi cousins. 'They can't see the American train coming down the track', he said: 'They think it's like in the desert, a mirage. But they are walking down the same track as Saddam Hussein. And Lebanon will be their Kuwait.'[31]

But what ranked as an almost gratuitous act of political and diplomatic vandalism was the way Syria burnt its bridges with France and Jacques Chirac. This relationship, facilitated by Hariri, was Damascus' only real window on the world. Yet the Syrian leadership not only rebuffed insistent French suggestions it withdraw from Lebanon, and rejected warnings against reimposing President Lahoud, in addition President Assad ignored letters from Chirac.[32]

In that fateful autumn of 2004, almost everyone with any purchase in Damascus tried to stop the Syrian regime from galloping over the precipice. The Saudis and the Egyptians tried. The Emir of Qatar attempted to mediate between Syria and Hariri for ten days. Iyad Allawi, then the interim prime minister of Iraq, warned Bashar he was running out of time to save his regime. Even Iran – always a tactical rather than, as Damascus fondly supposed, strategic ally of Syria's – tried to persuade Assad to give up its insistence on keeping Lahoud.

The Lahoud fixation was, indeed, puzzling. Bashar himself had that very summer let it be known, to a Hariri emissary and an Arab journalist, that there were several alternatives to Lahoud as president with whom he would be comfortable. The explanation for the sudden and vehement *volte-face* will eventually emerge in full. But in one account, his brother Maher al-Assad, a commander of the Republican Guard, and brother-in-law Asef Shawkat, who would soon become chief of military intelligence, intervened. They told Bashar that while there were indeed other presidential candidates politically in line with Syria, changing Lahoud could severely complicate, even unravel, the regime's business interests in Lebanon.[33]

During the 26 August Damascus meeting at which Assad threatened Hariri, the Syrian president told the Lebanese prime minister his decision very bluntly: 'I am personally interested in this matter. It is not about Emile Lahoud but about Bashar Assad.' According to Saad, Hariri's son, Bashar said: 'President Lahoud is me.'[34]

The Syrian regime tried to offset the consequences of this ruthlessness through a sort of diplomacy-by-numbers. The Damascus view of international relations was trapped in the Cold War. Its reflex reaction was to look backwards, to figure out what had worked in the past. It had little idea how 9/11 had changed international and regional politics. Thus, when challenged by France for meddling in Lebanon and America for meddling in Iraq, Syria's instinctive reaction was to float the idea of reviving peace talks with Israel. According to one intermediary between Syria and the USA, as international pressure grew on Damascus the Assad family circle reassured itself that America had found itself another Vietnam next door in Iraq. 'They think it's Vietnam, they think they're [the US] as good as defeated', he said. While there were undoubtedly some resemblances, this seriously misread America's mounting frustration at Syrian complicity in the Iraq insurgency. Syria did, however, achieve the diplomatic feat of pushing France and the USA together. Paris and Washington had convergent interests in this affair that easily enabled them to put to one side their differences over Iraq. Like many of his predecessors, President Chirac was, in the French foreign ministry cliché, the desk officer for Lebanon at the Quai d'Orsay, genuinely interested in the fate of Lebanon and his friend, Rafiq Hariri. President Bush was interested in Syria's impact on Iraq, Israel and Lebanon – in that order.

As 2004 drew to a close, keen observers of Syria suspected that Damascus might withdraw its remaining 14,000 troops – and then foment unrest to demonstrate just how indispensable Syria's stabilizing presence had been. Sheikh Naim Qassem, number two in the leadership of the Syria-aligned Hizbollah, wondered aloud about this: 'Are they [the Americans] ready for the consequences of a [Syrian] withdrawal? If they corner Syria, maybe it will make them a present [by leaving Lebanon].'[35]

That underestimated the degree of international, and regional, consensus about ending the Syrian occupation of Lebanon, and the extent of American and French hostility to its behaviour. By the end of 2004, the Syria-in-Lebanon story looked as though it had reached a turning point, for a still ambitious and hopeful Beirut as well as a nervous but reckless Damascus. As Beirut publisher Jamil Mroue put it: 'The situation is like a huge boil: it's ugly and it's livid but it's only when it bursts that you'll know whether it's benign or malignant. Either way, it's the end of an era.'[36]

✳   ✳   ✳   ✳   ✳

What eventually burst, on 14 February 2005, was 1,000kg of military grade high explosive in a van aimed at Rafiq Hariri's six-vehicle convoy as it passed the St George Hotel, the scene of so many intrigues in Lebanon's past. Hariri was killed instantly and 22 others died, including members of his entourage. Basel Fleihan, a close confidant and former economy minister who had returned from a glittering future abroad to help him rebuild the country, died weeks after, agonizing with burns over 95 per cent of his body. It was a Valentine's Day massacre worthy of any mafia.

Of course, the Lebanese finger pointed immediately towards Syria. And, of course, Damascus repeated the standard *cui bono* argument, a basic building-block of conspiracy theorizing in the region: how could it possibly be them, if they were the ones who would most obviously be blamed for it? Assassinations, moreover, had been common currency in the region, freely spent by Damascus, and more often than not had worked – at least in the short term. This time, however, something snapped.

The Lebanese temper, tried to the limit by Syrian thuggery and pillage, definitely snapped. US and French patience had clearly snapped. Arab rulers, not easily shocked, were unnerved by the audacity of this regicide. Syria was given a last chance to comply with resolution 1559 and withdraw, while with the new resolution 1595, the Security Council readily endorsed President Chirac's call for an international investigation into Hariri's murder.

Mass protests on the streets of Beirut brought down the pro-Syrian government of Omar Karami after two weeks of agitation carefully calibrated with the opposition in parliament. Syria, kept unaware of its isolation by clients such as President Lahoud, seized on a vast demonstration by Hizbollah on 8 March as a chance to reinstate Karami. But Hizbollah did not lift a finger to save Damascus' client government. The party was for the first time brandishing the Lebanese flag – an emblem of the opposition's so-called Cedar Revolution – as well as its own militant banners. Its leaders were in contact with the opposition. Hizbollah was positioning itself for a leading role in the post-Syrian future. An even bigger rally by the opposition on 14 March gave Bashar no option but to pull his troops out, which Syria did by 26 April, ending 29 years of occupation. His only other option would have been to commit mass murder, live on satellite television. Instead, Syrian intelligence and its local satraps continued their campaign of bombings and assassinations.

Nevertheless, the UN probe into Hariri's assassination began with exemplary determination. The International Independent Investigation Commission (UNIIIC), set up by UN Security Council resolution 1595, was headed by Detlev Mehlis, a tenacious and forensic German investigator. In the teeth of what looked to be Syrian intimidation – car bombs in June and July of 2005 killed the combative Lebanese–Palestinian journalist Samir Qassir and narrowly missed killing Elias Murr, the formerly pro-Syrian interior minister who had become defence minister in an opposition-led government – Mehlis gathered evidence. 'People concluded that this was a real fight and we had a chance of winning: they started to talk', as one local analyst put it.[37]

A series of raids conducted by the UNIIIC, backed by reinvigorated Lebanese judicial authorities, led to the arrest of the four main Lebanese security chiefs, including General Jamil as-Sayyed, head of the *Sureté Générale*, and General Mustafa Hamdan, head of the Presidential Guard, Lahoud's security brigade. The spectacle of four generals in an Arab country's security services being held over the assassination of a politician was not just unusual.

It was unique. It electrified the Arab world, introducing into people's minds the profoundly subversive idea that Arab despots, for so long untouchable within a political culture of unbridled power and legal impunity, could be held to account. The Mehlis report, which appeared on 21 October 2005, mesmerized public opinion.

The confidential version of the report – which found its way into the public domain with perhaps intentional ease – said a witness had alleged Maher al-Assad, Asef Shawkat, Jamil as-Sayyed and Mustafa Hamdan were plotting Hariri's murder approximately two weeks after the Security Council adopted resolution 1559. A taped conversation between General Rustom Ghazaleh, Ghazi Kenaan's successor as Syrian viceroy in Lebanon, and a 'prominent Lebanese official' described as Mr X seemed to illustrate how Syria and its clients routinely discussed how to make and unmake Lebanese governments. In this case, X offered to order Hariri to resign.[38]

Another UNIIIC witness in the confidential version of the Mehlis report describes a conversation with General Hamdan in October of 2004, in which the presidential guard chief, after describing Hariri as pro-Israeli, allegedly says: 'We are going to send him on a trip; bye, bye Hariri.'[39]

Mehlis managed to pin down the role of an Islamist group called al-Ahbash, widely thought to have had a long mercenary relationship with Syria. The UNIIIC used special software programs to look painstakingly through Lebanese telephone records. These recorded 97 calls from Ahmad Abdel-Al, an al-Ahbash leader, to General Hamdan, including four in the hours after the 14 February blast, and, most sensationally, a call by his brother, Mahmoud Abdel-Al, to President Lahoud's mobile phone just minutes before the attack on Hariri's convoy. The investigators also traced otherwise anonymous prepaid phone cards at the heart of the plot, including pre-assassination surveillance of Hariri's movements. Lebanon, and the rest of the Arab world, was amazed by this virtuoso reconstruction of a web of incriminating phone calls. But the Syrian regime, with its prehistoric grasp of technology, seemed stunned. The Mehlis report concluded 'there is probable cause to believe that the decision to assassinate former prime minister Rafiq Hariri could not have been taken without the approval of top-ranked Syrian security officials and could not have been further organized without the collusion of their counterparts in the Lebanese security services'.[40]

By the time it realized it had been backed into a corner, it was too late for Damascus to react effectively. On 12 October, Ghazi Kenaan, the former master of Lebanon, called a Lebanese radio station, defended his record in the country, then according to the official Syrian report went to his office and shot himself. This was not the first time Syria had chosen 'suicide' as a way to reshuffle power. But if it was an attempt to close the Hariri case by removing a fount of information as well as a possible suspect, it failed. On 14 October, Mohammed Nassif, a Syrian Mukhabarat chief, former confidant of Hafez al-Assad, and head of the pivotal Khayr Beyk Alawite clan, appeared in Washington, urgently seeking an audience with the Bush administration. The USA had been looking into its options in dealing with Syria – including alternatives to Bashar's rule.[41]

The Nassif mission looked like an attempt to strike a Libya-style deal with Washington, whereby Damascus would hand over plausible scapegoats for the Hariri murder, and end jihadi infiltration across its border into Iraq and other rogue activities. This still appeared to be the regime's tactics at the end of 2008, but three years earlier the time was not ripe. For a start, the deal struck by Libyan leader Muammar Gaddafi had been prepared by stages over not less than six years. Libya also had a lot of oil. As one Arab official remarked: 'you can repent, and get away with murder, provided you have oil. The Syrians don't really have that kind of oil.'[42]

The details of the Mehlis report, moreover, were more than sufficient for the Security Council to endorse a new resolution, 1636, requiring Syria to cooperate fully with an extended investigation into its role in Hariri's and other murders. The vote was unanimous and placed under Chapter VII of the UN Charter, allowing eventual use of force to bring the miscreant state into compliance. Had Hariri at the last got it right about Syria: that Bashar was walking down the same track as Saddam?

The difference between the Syria and Iraq cases is more important than the similarity. Although Washington had been looking at the option of a palace coup in Damascus – one possible explanation for the sudden demise of a man as powerful as Ghazi Kenaan – unlike with Iraq it was pursuing a multilateral course, carefully marshalling broad support behind its unlikely alliance with the French.

Arab public opinion, appalled by the carnage in Iraq and terrified US military action in Syria might widen the conflict and turn the Levant into a Balkans, was captivated as the Mehlis process ran its course. The Syria-in-Lebanon story was part Levantine conspiracy, part patriotic epic. Already it included Hariri's murder, a successful Lebanese uprising against the Syrian oppressor, the imprisonment in Beirut of four hitherto untouchable generals, the fall of Kenaan, and a Mehlis report that read like a thriller. Just as important, this US-backed UN legal offensive looked as though it was introducing, in a partial but exemplary way, the rule of law – which after the Iraq fiasco was so much more attractive in the region than any variety of shock and awe.

The USA crashed into Iraq, for its own motives (described in Chapter IV), careless and oblivious of the consequences. In dealing with the conjoined case of Syria and Lebanon, it was rummaging in a storehouse of the region's dreams and nightmares, a combination of the most advanced with the most backward, the most democratic with the most Balkanic. A great deal was riding on the outcome.

* * * * *

If any single event could be said subsequently to have changed the course of this history it was the summer war of 2006 between Israel and Hizbollah, set off by a 12 July cross-border raid by the Islamist guerrillas, who overran an Israeli army post and seized two hostages. But the 34-day bombardment of Lebanon that Israel launched in retaliation was about a great deal more than recovering two Israeli hostages.

At one level, the conflict could be read as the latest round in the struggle between Syria and Israel, who had occupied swathes of Lebanon for 29 and 22 years, respectively, and used it liberally as an arena for proxy war. That may help explain the outrageous threat by Lt Gen Dan Halutz, Israel's chief of staff, to 'turn back the clock in Lebanon by 20 years' – something his air strikes and artillery barrages, killing hundreds of civilians as well as carefully taking apart the civilian infrastructure put back after the 1975–90 civil war, were well on their way to achieving by the war's end. But, as we shall see, in terms of the Syria and Lebanon equation, this war threw into reverse the fragile process of political reconstruction launched by the Cedar Revolution – and helped chart a path for Syria to break out of its isolation.

Both sides in the conflict – Hizbollah with its reckless adventurism, Israel by unleashing disproportionate force to punish the population of Lebanon – seem to have been encouraged by the diplomatic vacuum that had opened in the Middle East. An under-examined reason for this was the debacle in Iraq, which, far from enabling the USA and its allies to pursue a radical new freedom agenda in the region, paralysed the Bush administration. One sign of this was that, whereas Washington was quick to claim credit for Lebanon's civic uprising as evidence of 'freedom on the march', by 2006 it had recoiled from tough action against Syria even though there was an international consensus to pursue the Assad regime for the assassinations of Hariri and a dozen other prominent opponents of Damascus. Syria was forced to withdraw from Lebanon, but Hizbollah, its ally, remained the single most powerful actor there.

Parallel to this, the USA lost its nerve about Arab democracy, as votes flowed to Hamas, Hizbollah and Iraq's Shia Islamists. Israel perceived this well, and noted the discomfiture of Washington's Sunni allies, Egypt, Saudi Arabia and Jordan, at Shia advances, as well as Iraq's descent into civil war between the Sunni and Shia: a propitious moment to try to persuade world opinion of the threat from Iran's growing power and that Tehran was behind every leaf that stirred in the region. In that sense, as I argued in Chapter I, Lebanon's summer war was a logical extension of the conflict in Iraq – or rather of the Anglo-American loss of nerve at the forces they had unleashed there.

Incontestably, Hizbollah provoked Israel by its cross-border raid. Sheikh Hassan Nasrallah, its leader and normally a politically astute operator, seriously misread sentiment internationally and within the region – as he would publicly acknowledge after the war. Neither side could easily claim the moral high ground, since Israel and Hizbollah had both used hostage-taking and assassination as instruments of policy and, all bluster aside, had established records of negotiating prisoner exchanges.

But Hizbollah was not just a militia. From its very inception after Israel's 1982 invasion, even while it established its bloody reputation with signature suicide bombings and the cult of martyrdom, by kidnapping westerners and hijackings, it was developing parastatal reach. Under Nasrallah it became not only a successful resistance movement but a national political and social force, with competent cadres providing good municipal government and exemplary constituency MPs, social welfare networks unparalleled by the state, including clinics and schools, even pioneering microfinance, *Qard al-Hasan* (the Good Loan), as early as 1984.[43]

Inspired by Iran and operating under licence from Syria, this latest edition of the states-within-a-state Lebanon habitually breeds nevertheless had a unique opportunity after Israel withdrew from the country under Hizbollah fire in 2000 and Syria pulled out its troops in 2005. Hizbollah could either take up fully its role as a national force – not just joining the government, but becoming a cornerstone of the solution to Lebanon's physical and political reconstruction – or it could become part of the problem by seeking vaingloriously to be the region's Islamist vanguard, in which case it would never lose the taint of a proxy army that was stoking conflict on behalf of Tehran and Damascus. It chose to try to do both.

In the summer war it appeared, at first, to get away with it because, not for the first time, Israel so violently overplayed its hand. Under a prime minister, Ehud Olmert, and a defence minister, Amir Peretz, who were not from the warrior class that has traditionally dominated Israel's governing elite, Israel seemed to be trying to re-establish its deterrence credibility, and allowing an army command – under an air force officer, Halutz – with its pride wounded by the cross-border raids to call the shots. Israel appeared to have forgotten that there was no Hizbollah until it invaded Lebanon in 1982, in an equally vain attempt to destroy the PLO that instead, after the siege of West Beirut had killed 12,000 people, destroyed its reputation. Or that its last, 17-day, assault on Lebanon in 1996 not only failed to crush Hizbollah, but saw the Shia Islamists emerge strengthened and Syria's role in Lebanon legitimized, with Israel's image further besmirched by the massacre of refugees in the UN base at Qana. Now public opinion was repelled by newscasts of Israeli forces pulverizing the homes and lives of ordinary Lebanese (as well as a new Qana massacre). While both sides targeted civilians, of the 159 deaths sustained by Israel, 39 were civilian and 120 were military. On the Lebanese side, Hizbollah eventually acknowledged 250 'martyrs', but the overwhelming majority of the around 1,200 dead were civilians.

While this went on, the Bush administration, with the lone support of its British acolyte, Tony Blair, provided further evidence of its diplomatic feck- lessness and faith in its (and Israel's) ability to bomb its way to a better future. In holding out against a ceasefire to give Israel time to crush Hizbollah and remove it from the regional equation, Washington and London used diplo- macy to try to achieve Israel's unrealizable war aims by other means. Condoleezza Rice, US secretary of state, blithely asserted that the world was witnessing 'the birth pangs of a new Middle East'.

This ill-judged metaphor – set against the background of the death-rattle of a recently resurgent Lebanon – caused widespread scandal among Arab leaders and public opinion alike, burying what was left of America's reputa- tion in the rubble of south Beirut and southern Lebanon. The assault on Lebanon had raised Hizbollah to the peak of its prestige, even among Sunni whose leaders regarded the Shia as idolaters and Hizbollah as Iranian stooges. This war, in which an Arab force was seen to match the might of Israel, aggrandized Hizbollah, while lethally wounding the pro-western and demo- cratically elected government of Fouad Siniora.

One legacy of the summer war was sectarian polarization: for the first time since the end of the civil war, the Lebanese threw off all restraint in overtly articulating their communalist prejudices. The political atmosphere visibly darkened. Another factor was the still pending Hariri case against Damascus and its alleged Lebanese collaborators. Hizbollah withdrew from the govern- ment after failing to secure veto rights on policy. This was widely seen as an attempt to block Lebanon's endorsement of the UN tribunal being set up to try the Hariri case. Even when, just over a year later, all sides reached agree- ment in principle on electing Michel Suleiman, the army chief of staff, to replace Lahoud as president, Hizbollah and its allies held out for a blocking minority on government decisions.

In that autumn after the war, however, the Shia Islamists mobilized their supporters and laid siege to Siniora's government and Lebanon's institutions, almost literally: setting up tent-cities in downtown Beirut to bring public life to a standstill. By the time of the crisis of May 2008, parliament had not met for 18 months and Lebanon had been without a president for six months. As the country polarized further, its political elite appeared to offer no project except suicide as a nation.

Intrigue and violence spread, highlighted by a three-month long assault by the army in the summer of 2007 on an Islamist militia at the Nahr al-Bared refugee camp near Tripoli in north Lebanon. This so-called Fatah al-Islam group was widely depicted as a jihadist movement linked to al-Qaeda, especially because most of its fighters were foreigners, not Palestinian refugees or Lebanese. But the group's background – like the al-Ahbash group implicated in the Hariri bombing – was as guns for hire with links to Syria's intelligence services. The assassination that December of Gen François al-Hajj, the army operations chief who led the Nahr al-Bared fight, was easily painted as straightforward revenge. But whoever placed the bomb that killed him, in Baabda, arguably the highest security zone in the country, was part of a powerful network. By the time of the May 2008 crisis, moreover, there were growing signs of Hizbollah's influence inside the Lebanese army.[44]

The dam finally broke after the Siniora government said it would close Hizbollah's secure telecommunications network and fired the Shia officer (a Hizbollah sympathizer) in charge of security at Beirut airport. Although the government had no visible means to enforce these measures, Hassan Nasrallah called them a declaration of war. His forces, allied with Amal and motley pro-Syrian groups, overran West Beirut during the morning of 9 May, closed down or torched Hariri-owned media outlets, and left the Sunni establishment and Siniora government reeling in a devastating show of unstoppable force. Army commanders, saying they would not risk splitting the military on confessional lines, stood aside.

There were several puzzling aspects to these disastrous developments. Why did Hizbollah launch such a sweeping response to measures everyone knew could not be implemented? The meticulous planning of its *coup de main* was not an improvised response to a provocation. Conversely, were the government measures, in view of their evident tokenism, an attempt to break the stalemate, smoke out Hizbollah and rob it of its dwindling cross-community mystique as a resistance movement once it turned its guns inwards? Complicating the picture further was the assassination in Damascus that February of Imad Mughniyeh. The bomb that killed this most secretive and deadly of Hizbollah's (and Iran's) operatives – who had been on the US most wanted list for 25 years

– was placed in an area of Damascus where security is normally airtight. Whoever did it – and most fingers pointed towards Israel – is widely assumed to have had top-level inside help. Be that as it may, Hizbollah (and Iran) lost faith in its Syrian ally and arms conduit, which in turn made their control over logistics and access to Beirut airport of paramount importance.

Nevertheless, the May events and, indeed, the whole trend of events since the confrontation with Syria began in 2004 highlighted two things. First, there seemed to be no limits to the depths into which Lebanon's politicians could dig the country many of them still treat as sectarian patrimony or the arena for proxy war. Their struggle for power had become fatally tied to the visceral contest between Sunni and Shia Muslims uncorked across the region by the US invasion of Iraq (Lebanon's Christians were on the sidelines of the May fighting).

But, second, US policy from the 2006 war had fatally undermined a democratically elected government that wanted to ally with the West, leaving them with the taint of collaborators with Israel and their country hopelessly polarized. The Bush administration, seeing everything through the prism of the 'war on terror' and the regional conflict it had done nothing to resolve, cut the ground out from underneath Lebanese and Arab reformers and democrats.

Other Arab governments in the region, friends and foes, took due note. They had already concluded that Bush and his allies were dangerous adventurers after the Iraq fiasco. Now they were reaffirmed in their view that the USA would always back Israel unconditionally, brushing aside the consequences for its allies, whether democrats or autocrats, and even at the risk of creating another failed state. We will look more closely at US policy towards Israel in the next chapter. Suffice to say that Lebanon faces a crisis that, while currently contained, has in no way been resolved.

On 21 May 2008, the Lebanese political class – locked in a hotel in Doha under Qatar's mediation – put a temporary end to the crisis. Michel Suleiman was duly elected president, the government's measures against Hizbollah were reversed, and the formula for the new government gave the opposition a blocking minority. Though irreversibly diminished in Lebanese eyes, Hizbollah remains the strongest force in the land. Its actions in May restarted a pattern of sectarian fighting and may well have invited the beginnings of a Sunni jihadi backlash. Come the next crisis, the army could well split, leading to rival governments – repeating the ultra-violent experience of the last two years of the civil war in 1988–90. The problem of who rules Lebanon has only been postponed.

For Syria, by contrast, things were looking up. The conclusion to the May crisis brought it back into Lebanon's political game, entrenching its allies.

France, now led by President Nicolas Sarkozy, invited Bashar al-Assad, persona non grata under President Chirac, to Paris for a regional summit – and to stay on for Bastille Day in July 2008. Paris (and, later, London and Berlin) praised Damascus for its help in resolving a May crisis that was in any case to Syria's advantage. Meanwhile, Assad had entered peace negotiations with Israel through Turkish mediation. While we do not know whether Syria was complicit in the Mughniyeh assassination, we do know the Assad clique's attraction to get-out-of-jail-free cards. At any rate, US pressure on Syria had visibly diminished. Whether the UN tribunal – due to convene in March 2009 – would be able to prosecute those elements of the Syrian regime its investigators appear to have identified as responsible for the Hariri assassination – and apply the rule of law – was now moot. The Assad regime had broken out of its isolation. The Syrian autocracy looked safe, while Lebanon's fragile democracy and its future as a nation were once more in peril.

VII

A Naked, Poor and Mangled Peace

While Israel was busy reducing Shia areas of Lebanon to rubble in the summer war of 2006, President George W. Bush, his secretary of state, Condoleezza Rice, and Tony Blair, the British prime minister, repeatedly justified their reluctance to demand an immediate ceasefire because conflict would inevitably recur unless diplomacy dealt with what they kept calling 'the roots of the problem'.

Yet examining those roots shows more than anything else that the USA and its allies have demonstrated a steadily diminishing ability to acknowledge the root causes of conflict in the Middle East, let alone the will to deal with them. The charge that Washington and its friends have applied 'double standards' in their lopsided dealings with the Israelis and the Arabs is an inadequate commonplace. Measured by the national interest – of the USA and its European allies, of Israel, of the Arabs in general and the Palestinians in particular – they have applied the *wrong* standards.

We have seen in the course of this book how damaging it has been to bank on despotism, to encourage an Arab Exception in a futile attempt to secure stability. Yet the single most important instance of these wrong standards is US collusion in Israel's elision of its legitimate demand that the Arabs recognize its 'right to exist' with Israel's right to remain in illegal occupation of all or part of the West Bank and Arab east Jerusalem. To repeat: Israel's right to exist is inalienable, but it has no right whatsoever to colonize occupied land. By mixing these things up so cynically it is compromising its right to exist.

The conflation is best captured in the demand that, first, the Palestine Liberation Organization, and now, Hamas, recognize an Israel that has never defined its borders – incrementally expanded since the creation of the state – and which continues to colonize Palestinian land.

This conflation of these two wholly distinct realities occasionally became explicit, as when Israel's then prime minister, Golda Meir, demanded impatiently of King Hussein of Jordan – at a secret meeting in a caravan on their common border in early 1974 – whether Jordan accepted Israel's 'right to be on the West Bank'. As Avi Shlaim has documented, Jordan held 58 clandestine meetings with Israel over the three decades between 1963 and 1994, 45 of which were attended by the king, the Arab leader who pursued with the greatest determination the strategic goal of an end to the conflict between Israel and the Arabs. Not once did Israel countenance the prospect of withdrawing fully from the West Bank and Arab east Jerusalem, which, since it captured them in the 1967 Six Day War, all Israeli governments without exception have continued to colonize with Jewish settlers.[1]

In reaching peace with Egypt in 1979, Israel was prepared (eventually) to return all of the Sinai peninsula captured in 1967. In its 1994 peace treaty with Jordan, it was ready to restore (with minor and mutual modifications) the East Bank land taken during the 1960s including that seized during the 1967 war, equivalent in size to the Gaza Strip. During the tantalizingly close but ultimately fruitless 1995–2000 negotiations with Syria – which has never recognized Israel – it was willing to give back the Golan Heights, seized in 1967 and defended bloodily against a nearly successful Syrian onslaught in the 1973 October, or Yom Kippur, war. Israel even relinquished its enclave in south Lebanon, amounting to 12 per cent of the Lebanese land mass, with no agreement or recognition of any kind, withdrawing in 2000 under heavy attrition from Hizbollah, its most militarily successful enemy.

At no point, however, has Israel been prepared to give up enough of the West Bank and east Jerusalem to seal an enduring peace with the Palestinians that would give them a viable state. While there were faults and fears on both sides during this seemingly eternal conflict, successive US governments, intervening for the most part as far from honest brokers between them, bear a heavy responsibility. It is important to remember that it was not always that way.

During the early years of the Israeli state, its leadership, dominated by David Ben Gurion, was as wary of US intentions as Washington then was of Israel's belligerence. Israel was closely aligned with the old colonial powers, France and Britain, and especially unnerved by American attempts to build alliances with the post-colonial Arab states, which not only had oil but were seen as potential bulwarks against the Soviet Union making inroads into the region. Israel's most reliable military supplier in the 1950s and early 1960s was France, no doubt partly for commercial reasons but mainly because of French antagonism towards Egypt's support for the FLN rebels in Algeria's war of independence – a modest role by Nasser the Israelis cannily exaggerated. It would be France, in 1957, which delivered the nuclear technology – a 24 megawatt reactor at Dimona – that eventually enabled Israel to make the strategic leap to atomic weapons, transforming the geopolitics of what was already becoming the most volatile region in the world.

An important facet of this volatility was Israel's unremitting aggression against its Arab neighbours, documented by a wave of revisionist Israeli scholars – the so-called New Historians – from the late 1980s. These examinations, exemplified by Avi Shlaim's later book *The Iron Wall*, showed how Israel, from Ben Gurion onwards, spurned any suggestion of an Arab olive branch as appeasement, preferring an aggressive policy of pre-arranged reprisals and provocations aimed at expanding the new state's borders, which its defence establishment, then as now, regarded as dangerously vulnerable if not indefensible.

Ben Gurion, backed by General Moshe Dayan, and usually using Arab infiltration as the pretext, attacked Jordan, Egypt and Syria across the 1948–9 armistice lines between 1953 and 1955. The officer who led the main operations, establishing early on his reputation for bloodthirstiness, was Ariel Sharon. While Israel was already under fire – not least from the USA – in the UN Security Council for trying to divert the waters of the Jordan river from inside the demilitarized zone separating it from Syria, Sharon, in an October 1953 commando raid on Qibya in Jordan, razed the village, dynamiting 45 houses over the heads of its inhabitants, killing 69 civilians including women and children.[2]

In Egypt, in the so-called Lavon Affair, an Israeli spy ring in July 1954 attempted to bomb Cairo cinemas, trying to spark a crisis that would torpedo a deal between Egypt and Britain for withdrawal of British troops from the Suez Canal. Nevertheless, Nasser and Moshe Sharett, Israel's dovish prime minister while Ben Gurion had temporarily stepped down, began exploring détente through emissaries and exchanges of letters. That too was dynamited upon Ben Gurion's return as defence minister, in a paratroop raid by Sharon into Gaza in February 1955 that destroyed the Egyptian army headquarters. In December that year, without provocation, the hyperactive Sharon led a devastating raid on Syrian positions on the north-eastern shore of Lake Tiberias in the Galilee.[3]

The Eisenhower administration, bilaterally and through the UN Security Council, vigorously condemned this aggression and, after the Tiberias attack, suspended negotiations with Israel on what would have been its first American arms package. While Israel was trying to break what it saw as the regional stalemate imposed by the inconclusive end to the 1948–9 fighting,

Israeli records excavated by the new historians and Arab documents captured during the 1967 war show that its Arab neighbours were, in the main, trying to quieten their common borders and prevent infiltration by Palestinian refugees.

The Palestinian 'question', in so far as it existed at that time, was generally treated as a refugee problem. While Washington opposed Israeli belligerence, it developed no real position on Palestinian political, much less national, rights. In response to the 1955 Gaza raid, however, Nasser began training and arming Palestinian refugees as *Fedayeen* irregulars to strike back at Israel. More ominously, he sought military support from the Soviet bloc, securing a significant arms delivery from Czechoslovakia. Israeli policy dragged the Cold War into the Middle East, charting a new and destructive course for the region. Israel's policy towards Nasser's Egypt overtly became regime change. The road to Suez had been opened.

The Suez war of 1956, a conspiracy between Israel, France and Britain to attack Egypt codified in the Protocol of Sèvres of October that year, revealed the reach of Ben Gurion's territorial plans. Like Ariel Sharon's invasion of Lebanon in 1982, or, indeed, the US invasion of Iraq in 2003, it was nothing less than an attempt to reorder the Middle East by force.

At the Sèvres meeting, on the outskirts of Paris between 22 and 24 October that year, Ben Gurion outlined his vision. The Hashemite kingdom of Jordan, seen by Israel as an unviable buffer, would be partitioned, with Iraq taking the East Bank and Israel taking the West Bank. Lebanon, too, under a plan Ben Gurion had developed with Dayan in 1955, would be partitioned: Israel would take the south up to the Litani river, and would help create a Maronite Christian and allied state beyond it. On the main front of the war meanwhile, with Anglo-French assistance, the Egyptian army would be destroyed, Nasser would be toppled, and Israel would take the Sinai peninsula and the Straits of Tiran.

There was, of course, as Ben Gurion himself admitted to the stunned, sinking colonialists with whom he had allied Israel, a 'fantastical' element to his plan. The Protocol of Sèvres itself set down the more limited objectives of dealing with Nasser. Nevertheless, Ben Gurion's vision of unbridled expansionism cannot be ignored – especially in the light of Israel's 1967 capture of the Sinai, Gaza, the West Bank and the Golan Heights, when Israel was widely seen throughout the world as the Jewish David versus the Arab Goliath. Israel's founding father foresaw a massive expansion: to the Suez Canal and the Red Sea, and to the Jordan and Litani rivers. In his victory speech after the 1956 capture of the Sinai and the Straits, he even spoke of 'the third kingdom of Israel'.[4]

President Eisenhower, as we know – and the Arabs remember – forced the British and French, and eventually the Israelis, to withdraw, at one point even threatening Israel with expulsion from the United Nations and, therefore, the loss of its hard-won legitimacy. There would in the future be plenty of work in the region for US diplomats, but not until the Cold War ended would any real direction emerge to test Israel's real intentions.

* * * * *

As the Cold War seized hold of international relations, and was replicated inside the Middle East – between the Arabs as well as between them and Israel – the Israelis could, from Presidents Kennedy and Johnson onwards, pretty much get their way in Washington and the councils of the West. Indeed, from Kennedy onwards, a trend whereby America's arming and strengthening of Israel made Israeli leaders steadily more intransigent and belligerent became clearly visible. Israel as David versus Goliath became transformed, in the words of Levi Eshkol, prime minister at the time of the 1967 war, as 'poor little Samson', insisting simultaneously on its unparalleled strength and unique vulnerability.[5]

It is not my purpose here to recount the well-documented story of the 1967 war. It was a fiasco for the Arabs. Following the pattern of provocation and skirmish established in the 1950s, featuring a new Israeli attempt to divert the waters of the Jordan river and Egypt's reckless closure of the Straits of Tiran, the Arabs, with Syria in the van, engaged in a criminally irresponsible game of overbidding, bombast and threats that, from the Arab League summit at Cairo in January 1964, pledged the liquidation of the state of Israel and set up a purportedly unified military command to carry it out. Israel, facing this threat to its existence, did not play games. It struck first with devastating effect, wiping out its adversaries' air forces. Without air cover the Arab armies collapsed, and Israeli forces, led by Moshe Dayan, seized as much land as they could.[6]

In the diplomacy that followed the war, UN Security Council resolution 242 called for 'the withdrawal of Israeli armed forces from territories occupied in the recent conflict'. The omission of the definite article – 'the' territories – was a triumph of British drafting obfuscation that left unclear the precise extent of any withdrawal. The Arabs may have interpreted it as Israel pulling back from all occupied land, but Israel set firmly about consolidating its hold on the new territory, particularly the West Bank and east Jerusalem – which it promptly annexed and expanded to include surrounding West Bank Arab villages.

The disaster of the Arab armies thrust the PLO and its *Fedayeen* guerrillas into the front line. It also put succeeding Arab leaders on their mettle. The October war of 1973 launched by Egypt, now under Anwar Sadat, and Syria, now led by Hafez al-Assad, was fought from the Arab side with conflicting aims. Syria's intent was to regain the Golan Heights and reverse the defeat of 1967; Sadat's goal was to advance far enough into the Sinai to recover his army's honour and establish a position of force sufficient to get Israel to negotiate. After leaving Syria militarily in the lurch in 1973, he eventually succeeded, through President Jimmy Carter's mediation, in negotiating the Camp David peace treaty with Israel, signed in 1979. That left the Palestinians politically in the lurch.

Menachem Begin, Israel's uncompromising Likud premier, was astute enough to realize that taking Egypt, the biggest Arab state with the biggest army, out of the game meant there would no longer be any combination of Arab armies that could convincingly threaten Israel by conventional means. He used Camp David not to go down broader avenues of peace, but to tighten Israel's grip on the West Bank and lash out at its neighbours. In the summer of 1981 the Israeli air force destroyed Iraq's Osirak nuclear reactor near Baghdad and the following summer Ariel Sharon launched a full-scale invasion of Lebanon. In the meantime, Begin made all of an expanded Jerusalem the capital of Israel.

Yet, as early as the 1973 October war, Henry Kissinger, President Richard Nixon's national security adviser and then his secretary of state – who saw the Middle East through the prism of the Cold War – had dismissed four different approaches from Yassir Arafat, all signalling the willingness of the Palestine Liberation Organization to recognize the existence of Israel and negotiate terms of peace with it. The PLO made an approach through Richard Helms, then US ambassador to Iran, in the summer of 1973; through King Hassan of Morocco, who offered to set up a meeting with Arafat, that August; through an intermediary in Beirut, four days into the war; and on 23 October, just as the war ended. Faced with such insistence, Kissinger finally sent Vernon Walters, deputy director of the CIA, to a meeting with an Arafat emissary in Rabat, with instructions to play a dead bat. As Kissinger saw it, the PLO was seen as 'refugees at the UN, as terrorists in the United States and western Europe, as an opportunity by the Soviets, and as a simultaneous inspiration and nuisance by the Arab world'. The arch-realist suspected Arafat of wanting to take over Jordan as a launch pad to regaining all of Palestine. He did acknowledge the danger that as time went on and the occupation continued, the PLO would become more established, undermining the proposition that a moderate course 'would return Palestinian lands to Arab control'. But he had bigger fish to fry. Walters, he reported with satisfaction, 'played for time, as was our plan'.[7]

Playing for time, in the event, amounted to 15 years and the onset of the intifada. The PLO, to be fair, was notoriously inclined to blow hot and cold; Arafat, in particular, embodied a kind of inarticulate ambiguity that was hard to pin down. Nonetheless, substantial subsequent PLO overtures got no further, even after Arafat, at Algiers in November 1988, won a historic majority in the Palestine National Congress (PNC) – a sort of Palestinian parliament-in-exile – recognizing the legitimacy of the Israeli state. That decision accepted all the main UN resolutions, including Security Council resolutions 242 of 22 November 1967 and 338 of 22 October 1973. These amounted to an internationally mandated package deal trading land captured by Israel in 1967 for peace: the seed of a two-states solution to the Israeli–Palestinian conflict. It took longer for Washington to arrive at that interpretation of resolutions 242 and 338.

While the administration of President Jimmy Carter (1977–81) flirted with the idea of some sort of Palestinian self-determination on the West Bank and Gaza, Ronald Reagan's administration (1981–9) believed the rights of the Palestinians amounted merely to some sort of autonomy under the supervision of Jordan, the former sovereign power in the West Bank and east Jerusalem – a role King Hussein declined, Arafat and the PLO could never contemplate, and Israel in any case summarily rejected.

The George H.W. Bush administration (1989–93), with James Baker as probably the most even-handed US secretary of state ever to deal with the Arab–Israeli conflict, in the wake of the 1991 Gulf War went importantly further, convening the October 1991 Madrid conference. Palestinians not overtly identified with the PLO were represented at Madrid in a joint delegation with Jordan, and the terms of reference of the conference were explicitly land-for-peace: based on Security Council resolutions 242 and 338. Yitzhak Shamir, the irredentist Israeli prime minister, dismissed the whole basis for the conference, maintaining that the conflict had nothing to do with land but Arab refusal to recognize Israel's legitimacy. Yet again, an Israeli leader conflated the Israeli state's right to exist with its right to remain in possession of the West Bank and Arab east Jerusalem.

Baker and Bush Sr held their ground and Yitzhak Rabin and the Labour party defeated Shamir at the polls in 1992. Not long after, secret and parallel negotiations opened between Israel and the PLO leading to the Oslo agreement, enshrined in the 1993 Declaration of Principles. This was based on mutual recognition and mapped out a gradual approach to Palestinian self-determination in unspecified amounts of the West Bank. The hitherto intractable issues – Israel's (and the future Palestinian entity's) final borders, the future of Jerusalem, the Jewish settlements on occupied land, and the fate of more than 5 million Palestinian refugees displaced by the creation of the state of Israel in 1948 and the 1967 war – were left to 'final status' talks to take place after interim Palestinian autonomy was established on incremental parts of the West Bank.

We will look later at the reasons behind the collapse of the 1993–5 Oslo accords, the abortive attempt to salvage an agreement from their wreckage at Camp David in 2000 under President Bill Clinton, and the Bush administration's de facto acquiescence in Israeli attempts to settle the issue by force by imposing terms on the Palestinians.

Suffice for now to underline that Oslo was nevertheless a watershed. Israel recognized the PLO. It also accepted the principle that the Palestinians had political and (still to be specified) national rights in former Mandate (British-administered) Palestine. The PLO, for its part, formally, with the backing of the PNC from the Algiers conference of 1988, and in treaty terms from Oslo in 1993, accepted a two-states solution, dividing what had been Mandate Palestine. Furthermore, the PLO accepted – to the horror of many hundreds of thousands of Palestinian refugees – that what was lost in 1948 was lost. It would have to build its state on what was left.

At the time of Britain's Balfour Declaration in 1917, promising the Jews a homeland in Palestine, the Jewish population numbered less than a tenth of the indigenous Arab population. After the defeat of the Arab Revolt against British rule and accelerating Jewish immigration in 1936–9, and Israel's triumph in the 1948 War of Independence (the *Naqba*, or catastrophe in Palestinian memory), defeating both Palestinian forces and the histrionic but half-hearted attempt by neighbouring Arab countries to crush the emerging state, Israel was left in possession of 78 per cent of Mandate Palestine. That compared to about 55 per cent of the Palestine territory it would have got in the 1947 UN partition plan the Arabs had summarily rejected. Under Oslo, the PLO accepted that Israel would keep all that land within its pre-1967 borders, but demanded the remaining 22 per cent captured in the Six Day War – the West Bank and Arab east Jerusalem in addition to the Gaza Strip – as the land for its independent state, to settle the conflict once and for all. Oslo brought Yassir Arafat and the PLO back to Palestine from Tunis, the last post of a wandering exile to which they had fallen back after their withdrawal from Beirut during the 1982 Israeli invasion. Oslo, in the eyes of the majority of, if not all, Palestinians, was to end the tragedy and injustice of 1948, to close the chapter on a historic defeat, to move on to a new era. It was supposed, in other words, to be a historic compromise. But it was not to be.

* * * * *

The political and diplomatic failure to seek a resolution to the battle between Arab and Jew over how (or whether) to share the cramped and combustible Holy Land is an astonishing abdication of western as well as Arab–Israeli responsibility, especially towards future generations who will have to deal with steadily more vicious attempts to settle it once and for all. This failure is all the more perplexing since there is no mystery as to what the outlines of such a settlement would have to be.

The solution lies in the parameters set by President Bill Clinton on 23 December 2000 and in the dozens of talks between Israeli and Palestinian negotiators, culminating at Taba, in Egypt, after the collapse of the Camp David summit that year; in the subsequent but informal Geneva Accord between former negotiators based on these; and in the adoption of their essentials by the Arab League at the Beirut summit in 2002. The Beirut peace initiative called for an end to the Arab–Israeli conflict, with full Arab recognition of – and relations with – Israel, in exchange for full Israeli withdrawal from all land occupied in the 1967 war. That, above all, means a Palestinian state on almost all of the occupied West Bank and Gaza, with Arab east Jerusalem as its capital, and what the Arab peace plan carefully calls 'a just solution' to the plight of the Palestinian refugees, which inevitably means compensation rather than right of return for the overwhelming majority of them.

We will look further at the all-important details of these outline solutions. But the political point is that, as a formula to end the conflict at the heart of the Middle East's chronic instability, it has never been tried. Oslo pointed hesitantly if hopefully in that direction, intending to light the way to a definitive solution. But the 1993–5 accords expired long before they were pronounced dead. They were killed principally by Israel's belief that it could continue to build Jewish settlements on Arab land without any reaction from the Palestinians.

The biggest expansion of these illegal settlements, it is important to understand, occurred during the heyday of the Oslo peace process. Under Labour governments in 1992–6, led by Yitzhak Rabin and Shimon Peres, the number of settlers in the West Bank grew by 50 per cent, four times the rate of population increase inside Israel proper. When Benjamin Netanyahu took office in 1996 with the overt intention of putting an end to Oslo, he quipped that he could hardly be expected to do less on the settlements than his Nobel Peace prize-winning predecessors.

At the heart of the settlement enterprise, Arab east Jerusalem has been encircled, mainly by four big clusters of settlements on expropriated Arab land: Giv'at Zeev north of the city, the giant Ma'ale Adumim to its east, and Efrat and Gush Etzion to the south and south-west. Every government since Oslo has been able to claim a rampart in the wall. The Right and the Left have used housing and zoning restrictions that inhibit any natural expansion of the Palestinian population – virtually banning all Arab building and regularly demolishing any that takes place – and discriminatory residence permits to filter out Palestinians and ensure a Jewish majority in the Arab east of the city – a milestone Jerusalem's then mayor Ehud Olmert reckoned was passed in 1996. As Ariel Sharon, Israel's now stricken leader, boasted at that time: 'In Jerusalem we built and created facts that can no longer be changed.'[8]

It is, of course, impossible to know whether things might have gone differently had Yitzhak Rabin not been assassinated in November 1995 by a Jewish religious zealot. We saw in Chapter II how Arafat had wilfully and autocratically allowed himself to be blindsided and outmatched during the Oslo II talks by Israeli negotiators, whose main tactic was to prise the PLO leader away from more knowledgeable aides who attended to detail. Yet, three days before Rabin was killed, Yossi Beilin, the most dovish of Israel's negotiators, and Mahmoud Abbas (Abu Mazen, who would later succeed Arafat) reached a draft agreement on 'final status' issues that amounted to a big step forward for the Palestinians. Israel would keep 6 per cent of the West Bank, mostly the area around Jerusalem that contained the bulk of the settlers. But even so, Israel would retain sovereignty over all of Jerusalem, giving a special status to the Haram as-Sharif – the Muslim holy places. This draft agreement is said only to have offered the Palestinians a capital outside the municipal boundaries of the city set by Israel.[9]

However great an advance this was on anything previously contemplated by Israel, it was still a deal that was unlikely to fly with Arafat or sit well with Palestinian or Arab public opinion. But, in any case, the Beilin–Abu Mazen ideas, pursued secretly in Stockholm unknown to either Rabin or Peres, were certainly not those of the soldier–premier. In an interview with the author not long before his death, Rabin made his most forthright statement on how he saw the final shape of the peace with the PLO. In his slow, nicotine-tuned growl, he said the Israeli right had wilfully misunderstood or misrepresented his position: 'I by no means have the intention of returning to the pre-1967 lines.' He spelt out that Israel would keep 'a united Jerusalem ... and beyond what is now united Jerusalem, under Israeli sovereignty'. Furthermore, he said, Israel would insist on 'defensible boundaries' and thus keep the Jordan valley and 'land annexed to it' as its main shield against attack from the east. The Palestinians would get 'a less than independent state'.

Arafat, Rabin said, could take it or leave it. 'When could Arafat dream that a government of Israel would give him control of Gaza and Jericho, and the six major towns and cities of the West Bank – and as a stage towards a permanent solution?', he asked gruffly: 'Without the policy of the present Israeli government he could have stayed in Tunis for the next 20 years without getting anything, and have so-called ambassadors all over the world, but no leg anywhere in what used to be Palestine under the British mandate. He could pretend, but would have nothing.'[10]

But the whole question of final status became academic, and the status of the interim Oslo accords became moot, as soon as Netanyahu defeated Peres, Rabin's successor, at elections in May 1996, after a series of devastating Hamas and Islamic Jihad suicide bombings early that year turned the tide of Israeli public opinion. Another factor that may have swayed the Israeli mood was the damaging (if unsubstantiated) charge by Netanyahu that Peres planned to divide Jerusalem.

More generally, Oslo could not withstand the political and security upheavals on both sides of the Israeli–Palestinian divide. One of the intrinsic problems of Oslo was that its gradualist timetable failed to build confidence because there was no agreement – within or between each side – on the final destination. Anything seen as a 'concession' along this meandering path enraged maximalists, in plentiful supply on both sides, and the very length of the journey allowed extremists to exercise a veto.

When Netanyahu came to power in 1996, Oslo was already well behind schedule. Five months into his government, 49 of the agreements reached were between six months and three years overdue, by Palestinian count, but the Rabin and Peres governments were partly to blame for this. More than 4,000 Palestinian prisoners should have been released under Oslo I, for example, and a Palestinian 'safe passage' established linking Gaza to the West Bank. Yet, while Palestinians wondered whether Oslo was a confidence trick, a mechanism for them to collaborate in their own subjugation, Netanyahu rejected its very principles.

Beyond Israel's religious claim to the Israel of the Bible, *Eretz Israel*, Netanyahu believed Israeli security required a buffer of occupied land – including most of the West Bank – to insulate it from its Arab neighbours. The whole Arab–Israeli equation was, for him, a zero sum game. He told his supporters he would go no further down the road charted by Rabin and Peres, arguing that his predecessors had raised Palestinian and Arab expectations, which he would now bring back to earth. Faced with determined Israeli leadership, he averred, they would moderate their demands.

Egged on by neo-conservatives in Washington (as we saw in Chapter IV), and well before 9/11, Netanyahu was trying to position Israel alongside the West in a conflict with the Arabs and Muslim world that would allow Israel to retain a wall of occupied Arab land as its shield. Israel was not going 'to shrink itself to indefensible boundaries', he said, echoing Rabin. Conceptually, however, he went far beyond Rabin. Land for peace would be replaced by peace for peace; the new currency of negotiation would be security; that is, Israel's security. Although he never formulated an offer, his ministers suggested the Palestinians would get no more than half the West Bank, or 8 to 10 per cent of historic Palestine, hemmed into cantons by Israeli troops. Historic compromises were out. 'I will not make compromises with Israeli security', he said: 'The Palestinians will have to compromise.' His solution was that Israel 'retains part of the defensive wall' in the West Bank it acquired by conquest. 'The Palestinians should have those areas where they live and run their own lives' – a sort of supra-municipal government, but no state, which he regarded as part of a dangerous 'proliferation of the idea of unbridled self-determination'. The Palestinians could not expect a nation.[11]

Things did not go quite as smoothly as Netanyahu anticipated. Outbreaks of fighting in the West Bank, punctuated by Hamas suicide bombings, dented his image as Mr Security. The Clinton administration found itself dragged in regularly as firefighters. Netanyahu did make two agreements: a partial withdrawal from Hebron, a West Bank tinderbox where 34 settler families lived in a militarized cocoon surrounded by 130,000 Palestinians; and the October 1998 Wye Plantation deal, whereby he agreed to withdraw troops from a further 13 per cent of the West Bank. He never fulfilled this. His preferred technique was to keep on either reopening or postponing existing agreements – pending Palestinian ability to provide Israel with a level of security Israeli troops had never been able to deliver – and, when pushed, roll them forward into final status negotiations he had no intention of beginning.

The other villain of Oslo, of course, was Yassir Arafat. Oslo to Arafat was about political survival: to avoid being marginalized by the internal leadership of the intifada by regaining a foothold inside Palestine. So anxious was the PLO leader to assume the trappings of statehood, and so incompetent at statecraft, that he ended up being swindled and swindling his people. Arafat never understood, nor attempted to understand, the Israeli psyche. His primary activity upon returning to Palestine was to suppress internal challenge to his supremacy. Just like his Arab peers, he devoted his political energy to ensuring no new leaders emerged. As we saw in Chapter II, his autocracy hamstrung his ability to negotiate, much less build a state. His main ideas to bolster his position were to rely on the Americans to deliver on his demands of Israel, while simultaneously allowing the 'armed struggle' option to stay dangerously in play. While so fearful of a rupture in the Palestinian consensus, he often followed his people rather than led them. His authoritarian instincts, clandestine conditioning, cronyism and patronage, and his basic inarticulacy, could never permit him to mobilize them: behind the existential demands of the Palestinian nation or the determined and methodical process of nation-building in which his Israeli adversaries had so purposefully succeeded.

As I have already argued, the assembled ranks of Arab autocrats, though prodigal in outpourings of ritual solidarity on the Palestinians' behalf, attended primarily to their own regime maintenance needs by giving voice to the outrage of their subject citizens. Whether formally at peace with Israel like Egypt and Jordan, or not, like Saudi Arabia and Syria, Arab leaders had become adept at navigating the rapids of 'no war, no peace'. Stalemate helped justify the emergency powers through which they exercised their despotism and monopolized their country's resources.

The USA, meanwhile, the only power with the influence to end this stalemate, regressively declined to do so. That was not new either. As former secretary of state James Baker lamented in 1996, warning presciently that expanding settlements would kill any hope of peace: 'We have gone from calling the settlements illegal in the Carter administration, to calling them an obstacle to peace in the Reagan and [George H.W.] Bush administrations, and now [under Clinton] we are saying they are complicated and troubling.' But however many times the USA vetoes criticism of Israel's colonization policies in the Security Council, and however inventively it moves the semantic goalposts on its ally's behalf, this has not and will not disguise the hard fact: Israel could have land or peace. It would eventually have to choose.[12]

* * * * *

Events and – above all – the way they were managed have conspired to postpone that choice. Indeed, Israel's policy of expansion has contrived to foreclose on the outcome, to pre-empt ever having to negotiate over final borders and Jerusalem and instead present the Palestinians and the world with a fait accompli. At Camp David, in the summer of 2000, there was a serious attempt to negotiate a solution. It misfired disastrously, and would prove ruinous to already crumbling Israeli–Palestinian relations, as well as the PLO's newly minted relationship with Washington.

Published accounts of Camp David by participants from all sides, including Robert Malley, Clinton's adviser on Arab–Israeli relations, Shlomo

Ben-Ami, Israel's foreign minister, and Akram Haniyeh, from the Palestinian delegation, while differing in emphasis and, of course, agenda, taken together paint a nuanced picture of a 'Tragedy of Errors', as the Malley account was titled.[13]

To begin with, the Israelis and Palestinians had wholly different preoccupations. Israeli prime minister Ehud Barak was mindful of the fragility of his governing coalition, and aware of how far out in front of public opinion Rabin had reached – and the price he had paid. Temperamentally, moreover, this cold and clinical new soldier–premier wanted everything settled at once. With so many unfulfilled agreements on land restitution, Arafat suspected he was being led into a trap, being corralled into a process of continual renegotiation aimed at prising away from the Palestinians big slices of the residual 22 per cent of historic Palestine they had settled for in the PLO's historic compromise.

Camp David, which appeared to promise so much, and in which Bill Clinton invested the last months of his presidency, turned into a diplomatic fiasco. As Malley and Agha summarized it: 'the path of negotiations imagined by the Americans – get a position that was close to Israel's genuine bottom line; present it to the Palestinians; get a counterproposal from them; bring it back to the Israelis – took more than one wrong turn. It started without a real bottom line, continued without a counterproposal, and ended without a deal.' It was indeed a tragedy of errors, a poignant prelude to the real tragedies to come.

The outbreak of the second intifada at the end of September 2000 followed quickly after the collapse of Camp David that July. But it is hard to make a convincing case (as many Israelis maintain) that it was pre-planned by the Palestinians, or (as many Palestinians insist) that it was deliberately provoked by Israel. Among the Palestinians, frustration at the failure of Oslo to end the occupation had been building to a pitch of despair no leader – and certainly not Arafat – could presume to control. That was not least because of popular bitterness directed against the PLO and Fatah, the national liberation movement that had flown the flag of Palestinian statehood for nearly four decades, but many of whose leaders had become bywords for corruption, incompetence and brutal disregard for human and democratic rights, as they scrabbled for spoils amid the despair of their people. On the Israeli side, there was a growing sentiment that returning West Bank towns to the PLO had not brought them security and stability; that Oslo could not protect them from suicide attacks on their shopping malls and restaurants, buses and markets. They were already receptive to the mendacious message manufactured by Ehud Barak: that Arafat had spurned Israel's hand of peace at Camp David.

When Ariel Sharon took his famous walk through the Haram as-Sharif on 28 September 2000, chaperoned past the al-Aqsa mosque towards Temple Mount by hundreds of Israeli riot police, this was unquestionably a deliberate provocation. Yet it cannot properly be said to have caused the intifada, any more than a hit-and-run traffic accident in Jabaliya refugee camp in 1987 can be said to have caused the first intifada. All the ingredients for an explosion had long been present. Sharon's role was to throw a lighted match onto a powder trail already well laid by the failure of Oslo. The second uprising of the Palestinians since the 1967 occupation was essentially the Oslo war.

Nothing better encapsulates this than the career of Marwan Barghouti, the young Fatah activist who came to personify the al-Aqsa intifada. Barghouti was the outstanding leader among the new generation of grass roots activists that emerged in the occupied territories and the refugee camps before and during the first intifada, when the historic leadership of the PLO and Fatah was in exile in Beirut and then Tunis. The Islamist tendency typified by Hamas was an important part of this phenomenon, especially in Gaza, but it was the new, home-grown Young Guard of Fatah that predominated in the West Bank. Born near Ramallah, Barghouti entered the fray as a teenager, rising to the leadership of the first intifada, interspersed with long spells in Israeli jails where he not only continued his education, but learned perfect Hebrew and came to admire many facets of the Israelis, particularly their determined and democratic approach to nation-building. He returned from exile in Jordan in 1994 strongly committed to Oslo as the means to end the occupation and create an independent Palestine with democratic institutions, on the West Bank and Gaza, with east Jerusalem as its capital.

A charismatic, compact fireball of a man with a reputation for personal honesty and forthright opinions, his emphasis on reform, on institution building, and on strengthening civil society, all brought him into collision with Arafat and his Tunis coterie, who tried repeatedly but unsuccessfully to side-line him. Barghouti's emphasis on democratic legitimacy as the foundation of the future nation was a threat to their hegemony. 'In the past', he said (with heavy emphasis on the future), 'Fatah earned its right to lead the Palestinian national movement by virtue of the armed struggle of its fighters and the blood of its martyrs. Now we have a Palestinian National Authority on Palestinian soil we must earn our legitimacy from the democratic choice of its people.'

Barghouti, now serving a life sentence after being convicted by Israel of ter-rorist offences, was arguably also the most conspicuous Palestinian bridge builder, cultivating a network of relations with Israeli politicians across the political spectrum, not just with the peace camp. But as the occupation expanded, he began to speak out ever more stridently, against the colonization of Arab land and against the feckless and corrupt Palestinian leadership that was passively watching it happen. In sharp contrast to Arafat's disdain for detail, he pointed out that Israel had built almost as many housing units in the West Bank settlements in 1993–2000 – under the umbrella of Oslo – as it had in the first 26 years of the occupation. We recognize Israel, he said, the problem is that it does not recognize us.

Eventually, as Palestinian anger started to boil over, he would famously say that 'we tried seven years of intifada without negotiations, then seven years of negotiations without intifada: perhaps it is time to try both simultaneously'. Fifteen months into that intifada, he set out his position in an Op-Ed in the *Washington Post*. It is worth quoting at some length, since it not just his manifesto but a summary of the present state of the conflict and how to resolve it:

> 'The only way for Israelis to have security is, quite simply, to end the [then] 35-year-old Israeli occupation of Palestinian territory. Israelis must abandon the myth that it is possible to have peace and occupation at the same time, that peaceful coexistence is possible between slave and master. The lack of Israeli security is born of the lack of Palestinian freedom. Israel will have security only after the end of occupation, not before.
>
> Once Israel and the rest of the world understand this fundamental truth, the way forward becomes clear: End the occupation, allow the Palestinians to live in freedom and let the independent and equal neighbours of Israel and Palestine negotiate a peaceful future with close economic and cultural ties.
>
> Let us not forget, we Palestinians have recognized Israel on 78 percent of historic Palestine. It is Israel that refuses to acknowledge Palestine's right to exist on the remaining 22 percent of land occupied in 1967. And yet it is the Palestinians who are accused of not compromising and of missing opportunities. Frankly, we are tired of always taking the blame for Israeli intransigence when all we are seeking is the implementation of international law.[14]

With the collapse of Camp David, the outbreak of the intifada, the implosion of the Barak government, and the looming end of the Clinton administration, the fevered negotiations that went on through the second half of 2000 and into January 2001, leading to the Clinton parameters and the Taba talks, cannot really be described as a 'missed opportunity' – unless anyone imagines that Ariel Sharon, who by then was obviously the premier-in-waiting, would give these plans a moment's consideration.

But as I have already argued, the parameters and Taba are the only realistic framework within which the Israeli–Palestinian conflict can peacefully be resolved. Clinton's plan, drawn up on 23 December 2000, required both sides to give ground – although, needless to say, there are still discrepant interpretations of who would give exactly how much.

A sovereign Palestinian state would be built on between 94 and 97 per cent of the West Bank, with the Palestinians getting a land-swap from Israel in exchange for the areas it annexed (mostly north, south and east of Jerusalem and in the Ariel salient to Jerusalem's north-west), equivalent to between 1 and 3 per cent of the West Bank. Israel would abandon its strategically obsolete obsession with keeping the Jordan valley as its eastern border, which would instead be patrolled by a multinational force. Palestine would get all of Gaza, with Israeli land alongside it to let its teeming population spread out, plus a sovereign safe passage linking the strip to the West Bank.

The Clinton parameters proposed the division of Jerusalem to create two capital cities, one Israeli and one Palestinian: Yerushalayim and al-Quds. The Jewish areas of the city would be Israeli and the Arab areas would be Palestinian. Regarding the holy sites, the Palestinians would have sovereignty over the Haram as-Sharif, while Israel would have sovereignty over the Western Wall of the ancient Jewish Temple. All this was a bold move. But it did not resolve whether the areas of Arab east Jerusalem colonized by Israel to create a Jewish majority were to be evacuated and returned to the Palestinians or to remain under Israeli rule, thereby legitimizing a land-grab. The same question applied to the settlements ringing east Jerusalem. Would they all be annexed by Israel? Would the future al-Quds, in consequence, be cut off, by hitherto illegal settlements, from Ramallah to its north and Bethlehem to its south?

All that would – if and when the occasion arises – have still to be worked through. But Jerusalem is and will remain at the heart of the conflict. It is much, much more than a Berlin, a Belfast or a Beirut, or any other city that has been riven by history, by ideology or by theology. This thrice holy city, sacred to Jews, Christians and Muslims, all of whose traditions are in the grain of its stone, is built on a combustible myth.

For the Jews, the history that matters is embedded in the Old Testament. According to the second Book of Samuel, King David made this 'fortress of Zion' his capital around 1000 BC. Psalm 137 emblazons its importance: 'If I forget thee, Oh Jerusalem, let my right hand lose its cunning.' In Jewish tradition, the First Temple, of Solomon, was destroyed by the Babylonians in 586 BC. The Second Temple, later associated with Herod the Great, was destroyed by the Romans in 70 CE after the Jewish Revolt, leaving only the

Western Wall, on the western flank of Temple Mount, which miraculously survived the razing of Jewish Jerusalem by the Emperor Hadrian in 135 CE after another rebellion against Rome. Always the object of profound religious emotion for Jews, the Western Wall, after the 1967 capture of east Jerusalem, was transformed into a centre of national consciousness, indeed of Israeli identity, even though many of the pioneers of Zionism disdained Jerusalem as redolent of a Judaism that had failed its people. But the reunification in 1967 of a resurgent Israel with this relic of a once glorious Jewish past changed all that, even for secular Zionists.[15]

Christians of all denominations have their churches in the holy city, and share the majestic Holy Sepulchre, where, in 327 of the Christian era, what they believe was the tomb of Jesus Christ was discovered. Jerusalem's association with Christ's passion and crucifixion was, of course, already long established. But this new resurrection, from underneath a temple the Romans had erected to Aphrodite, came to symbolize the triumph of Christianity over paganism and, as Karen Armstrong has written, with the conversion of the eastern Roman or Byzantine empire to the Christian faith, its victory over Judaism, giving the Christians a powerful and aggressive new identity. Christians were responsible for one of the bloodiest chapters in Jerusalem's blood-soaked history, slaughtering as many as 70,000 Muslims and Jews when they captured the holy city in 1099 during the First Crusade.

When Saladin recaptured Jerusalem from the marauding Crusaders in 1187, he reminded the departing Richard the Lionheart that it was from the Temple Mount (the Haram as-Sharif), the third holiest place in Islam, that the Prophet Mohammed, in Muslim belief, ascended to heaven in his 'night journey'. The Dome of the Rock, completed in 691 on the site from which the Prophet (in 620 or 621) was held to have journeyed to Allah and the prophets on his steed Buraq, is if not the earliest surviving mosque certainly the oldest great monument of Islamic architecture, stirring the emotional and spiritual attachment to Jerusalem of more than 1 billion Muslims. Jerusalem, indeed, preceded Mecca as the *Qibla*, the direction towards which Muslims turned in prayer. As Saladin wrote to Richard: 'Jerusalem is our heritage as much as it is yours. It was from Jerusalem that our Prophet ascended to heaven, and it is in Jerusalem that the angels assemble.'[16]

These three, deeply emotive and profoundly embedded religious traditions – the sacredness to each of the three monotheistic faiths of the Israelite Holy of Holies, the site of Christ's crucifixion and resurrection, and the Dome of the Rock – have collided across the millennia. I point to them not to place any one set of beliefs and claims above the others, but to underline that they are not to be trifled with.

In particular, the unreflecting obeisance paid by the overwhelming majority of US politicians to Israel's oft-stated goal of an eternally united and indivisible Jerusalem is breathtakingly irresponsible. To begin with, near unanimity in American discourse on this issue is not shared inside Israel, where dividing Jerusalem in the context of an eventual peace settlement remains a legitimate subject of lively debate. Second, foreclosing on this option would, without a shadow of a doubt, put beyond reach any end to the Israeli–Palestinian and, indeed, wider Israeli–Arab conflict. But third, it would turn a conflict that can still, at this late stage, be settled in terms of a division of land into a rocket-fuelled clash of politico-religious identity – a twenty-first century war of religion.

The late Faisal Husseini, the paramount Palestinian leader in Jerusalem, warned before his death of the consequences if Israel and its American allies put the rival traditions of the holiness of the holy city into political play. Husseini, descended from Hajj-Amin al-Husseini who, before the PLO existed, led the Palestinians as Grand Mufti of Jerusalem, and the son of Abd al-Qadir al-Husseini, commander of Palestinian forces in the 1948 war, made a despairing plea, as Israeli bulldozers cleared more ground for the Jewish colonization of Arab east Jerusalem in 1996. 'Please, don't open the religious issue', he said. Nobody can afford to 'give new legitimacy and motivation' to Islamist or any other extremists in Palestine and the Middle East. The paradox for Palestinians was quite simple. Without Jerusalem and its combustible layers of religion and myth, the Palestinians arguably would command little more international attention than other peoples without a state in the region, such as the Kurds. But Palestinian nationalists could not use Jerusalem as a weapon. 'The PLO holds the most important card in the Arab world because Palestine has Jerusalem in it', he said: 'But the PLO is secular and we cannot use this [religious card]. But if that card drops from its hands, the only ones who can pick it up are the Islamist organizations. Please do not let it drop from our hands.'[17]

The other Arab–Israeli minefield which can still be traversed with a pragmatic compass concerns the fate of the roughly 5 million Palestinian refugees – still used by rejectionists on both sides as the reason why no reconciliation of this tragic history will ever be possible.

The Palestinian refugees, driven out by the 1948 and 1967 wars, and the PLO, insist on their right of return. That they were actively driven out under an Israeli policy of 'transfer', as well as forced to flee the fighting, has now been established beyond doubt: by the Israeli new historians mentioned earlier, by the Palestinian historian Nur Masalha, and, not least, by the accounts of such as Yitzhak Rabin, a commander in 1948, whose account of the expulsion of the Palestinians of Ramla and Lydda on the orders of David Ben Gurion was censored from the first edition of his memoirs in 1979 (though leaked to the *New York Times*) and only restored in a posthumous 1996 edition. With the departure of around 750,000 Palestinians in 1948, moreover, Israel physically obliterated more than 400 of their towns and villages.[18]

The 1967 war added another 250,000 refugees from the West Bank. By now, the total of Palestinian refugees and their descendants totals 4.5 million, according to the register of the United Nations Relief and Works Agency (UNRWA) responsible for their welfare. These refugees of war – the Shattat, or diaspora – are to be distinguished from earlier waves of emigration, beginning under Ottoman rule in the nineteenth century. Israel opposes the return for any part of the Palestinian diaspora, arguing that this would irreversibly change the demographic balance of the Jewish state, which would then cease to be Jewish. This is a real concern that has to be addressed. So it would be as well to begin with its reality.

First, the UNRWA numbers, though juridically correct, are not, in reality, accurate. In Lebanon, for example, it had 374,000 refugees on its books in 2002, spread out in 12 camps. Fearful of its delicate confessional balance, Lebanon denies Palestinians not only citizenship, but the right to own property or work in 71 specified professions, a policy it claims is to safeguard the refugees' eventual right of return. In consequence, many Palestinians able to leave, using UNRWA-acquired educations as their passport, have left. The actual number remaining in Lebanon in 2002, UN officials privately confirmed, was 192,000. This is doubly important because Israeli officials often point to the Lebanon Palestinians, who are mostly from the Galilee, as among those most likely to swarm back into northern Israel if they agreed to the right of return.[19]

Second, apart from the real numbers involved, how many among them, 60 years on, would actually exercise their right to return? Khalil Shikaki, a reputable Palestinian pollster, in 2003 asked refugees in Jordan and Lebanon if, given the choice, they would return to Israel, or accept compensation. In Jordan, which hosts the biggest concentration of about 2.8 million refugees who, unlike in Lebanon, enjoy Jordanian citizenship, only 5 per cent opted for return; in Lebanon, predictably given the hospitality of the host country, it was 23 per cent.[20]

These two factors, taken together, give some idea of the real dimensions of the right of return problem. Furthermore, just as UNRWA's register for Lebanon is numerically overstated, its overall tally is almost certainly a good deal higher than the actual number of refugees in the Arab states neighbouring Israel. The reason for the discrepancy is that the UN agency has the mandatory obligation to safeguard the legal rights of all the refugees, wherever they are, against eventual compensation they may receive under a settlement of the conflict. Which brings us onto the third element in the reality of the problem: compensation.

The Clinton parameters, according to Shlomo Ben-Ami, give the refugees the right of return to 'historical Palestine', but 'no explicit right of return to the state of Israel', which could limit the numbers it admitted. The rest of the refugees would be covered by a multi-billion dollar compensation and reset-tlement programme. The Arab League peace offer agreed at Beirut in 2002, as we have seen, proposes 'a just solution' to the right of return that quite obvi-ously foresees compensation for the majority of refugees.[21]

Israeli officials complain the Clinton parameters and Beirut plan are too nebulous, offering no guarantees on the right of return. That is, at best, disin-genuous. Israel is in control of its frontiers, its internal as well as its external borders; it has had little problem, for instance, in excluding Arab citizens of Jerusalem, in open defiance of international law. Most of all, however, Israeli officials know full well they negotiated just such a deal in 2000, with Syria, under US mediation. That package fell apart because, although Israel was pre-pared to return the Golan Heights, it refused to allow Syria back onto the last metres of land down to the water's edge of Lake Tiberias or the Sea of Galilee. But there was agreement in principle, Israeli and American officials say privately, on an overall, internationally funded package, then worth up to $17 billion, covering items including early warning stations on the Golan, but mostly to compensate the registered 450,000 Palestinian refugees in Syria.

The right of return conundrum, in other words, is pragmatically soluble. Israel knows this because it has already been down that path – and the path is still open. It will stay open, for a time, so long as it is clearly understood that no Palestinian leader – and certainly not President Mahmoud Abbas, who has lost Gaza to Hamas, has nothing concrete to show for his peace-making efforts, and is in danger of being branded the Palestinian Petain – can possi-bly yield on the rights of the refugees, as opposed to negotiating how those rights are honoured.

The cost of an overall compensation package has been variously estimated at between $50 billion and $80 billion; benchmarked against the Syrian pack-age, it is more likely to exceed $100 billion, likely to be financed by the USA, the European Union and the Gulf states. Expensive? That rather depends on the alternatives. Apart from the question of justice, of righting a wrong which is not just historical but actual, the idea that Israelis can enjoy security inside a ring of dozens of refugee camps – not just in neighbouring states, but inside the West Bank, Gaza and east Jerusalem – is delusional. Already the phenomenon of al-Qaeda style jihadism has begun to surface in the camps –

in Gaza, in Nahr al-Bared in Lebanon (see Chapter VI) and in Jordan – not least because the refugees' own institutions are collapsing in the implosion of the PLO, which led and policed the camps.

It is not in the interests of Israel, of a future Palestinian state, of the Arab states, or indeed of anyone with the remotest interest in the stability of the Middle East – which is to say pretty much the world – to let this continue. If these desperate huddles of misery are allowed to fester further, cut off from any hope of a decent future, they will become the new universities of jihad. No Israeli wall will be proof against that.

* * * * *

Ariel Sharon's wall, the 'security barrier' to separate the Palestinians from Israel, is alleged by its apologists to be no more than a legitimate response to Palestinian suicide bombers. It is more realistic to say that Sharon, upon taking power in February 2001, knew how to take full advantage of the collapse of Camp David, the international backlash against all forms of terrorism after 9/11, and the politically suicidal tactics of the Palestinian militias in targeting Israeli civilians.

Those who argue that Israel's robust response under Sharon was no more than a justifiable response to the irresponsibility of the Palestinian leadership and the second intifada need to explain why the land he identified for Israeli annexation – everything except the roughly 46 per cent of the West Bank enclosed in disconnected cantons inside the so-called security barrier – was identical in its essentials to the map first drawn up by Sharon in 1982 (see Chapter II). Or, indeed, why possession of all or part of the West Bank and east Jerusalem has, as we have seen, been a constant in Israeli policy since the creation of the Jewish state.

The unrestrained violence of Sharon's reconquest of the West Bank in 2002, and its destruction of Palestine's incipient institutions, was more than just new evidence of the Israeli leader's well-established brutality. Everything about it sent a message: from the trashing of the databases of the Palestinian education ministry, to the siege of Arafat's compound in Ramallah, confining the PLO leader to four rooms in a ruin, over which flew the Star of David, in an operation wittily dubbed 'Matter of Time'. As Israel pounded heavily populated Palestinian areas with heavy weapons, General Moshe Ya'alon, the army chief of staff leading the assault in 2002, summed up the strategy: 'The Palestinians must be made to understand in the deepest recesses of their consciousness that they are a defeated people.' There was to be no let-up. Israel was interested only in their capitulation. In the three years from June 2001, all the Palestinian groups called, and largely observed, four ceasefires, ignored by Israel. In the total 28 weeks of these truces, three, relatively insignificant, Palestinian attacks took place. Israel, during the same period, killed around 350 Palestinians, and assassinated 21 of their leaders in 'targeted killings', including Sheikh Ahmed Yassin, Hamas' spiritual leader, and Abdel Aziz al-Rantisi, its political leader in Gaza.[22]

Sharon had tactical reasons, too, for unleashing this violence. He had hatched his long-term plan. In early 2004, he let it dribble out that he intended to withdraw from Gaza. 'I am working on the assumption that in the future there will be no Jews in Gaza', he said. Sharon's erstwhile friends among the settlers called it death by 'friendly fire'. The hostility of the Gaza settlers, along with the calculated circumscription of the West Bank, prompted Israeli commentators to wonder whether Sharon had abandoned the goal of Greater Israel, the Biblical dream of *Eretz Israel*. It was he, after all, who evacuated the Sinai settlements in 1982, they suddenly remembered. Had the old warrior turned into a statesman? It also served Sharon's purposes when the irredentist Likud split over the Gaza withdrawal in 2005, and he went on to set up the Kadima (Forward) party, which won the largest number of Knesset seats in the 2006 elections. For the first time in his life, Sharon emerged, as if by magic, as an ostensible moderate, in the politically geometric if not ideological centre, with Benjamin Netanyahu left to play the unreconstructed extremist on his right flank at the head of a rump Likud. The assault on the Palestinians, moreover, demonstrated to Israelis that he was not pulling out under fire, drawing a contrast with Ehud Barak's withdrawal from Lebanon in 2000 under Hizbollah's guns, widely seen by Israelis as having encouraged the PLO and Hamas to launch the second intifada.

Sharon had always been unsentimentally practical. In Gaza as with Sinai, moreover, Israel made no real historical, ideological or religious claim on the land, as it did with the West Bank. The Gaza settlements were not just morally indefensible – 7,576 colonists lived in garrisoned enclaves among 1.5 million Palestinians, but used 40 per cent of a land scarcely bigger than Martha's Vineyard or the Isle of Wight – but physically undefendable. The so-called 'ideological' colonies in and around the Jordan Valley were costly and difficult to protect. As for the hundred or so settler 'outposts' – little more than caravans on West Bank hilltops Sharon himself had encouraged the colonists to take – they were never intended as more than pawns to be given away once the chess game began. Policing all of the West Bank, moreover, required more than 500 checkpoints in an area not much bigger than Delaware in the USA or Lincolnshire in the UK. The essence of the Sharon strategy was to grab as much as he could of the geography with as little as possible of the (Palestinian) demography. Politically, being denounced as a traitor by the settlers – not a popular constituency with many Israelis – did him no harm, while appearing to give up so much would make it so much easier to take elsewhere – in the West Bank. Sharon was pursuing a calculated annexation plan, without reference to Oslo or the Palestinians. The Gaza withdrawal was explicitly meant to reinforce Israel's strategic control of the West Bank. As General Ya'ir Naveh, who headed the Israeli occupation in the West Bank, put it: 'In Gaza we are leaving and closing the gates behind us. We have no intention of leaving Judea and Samaria [the West Bank]. We will remain here in one way or another for tens and thousands of years.'[23]

The Bush administration, sincerely or cynically, fell for it. Even while the Israeli assault on the occupied territories continued, President Bush called Sharon a 'man of peace'. More American praise gushed forth after the Israeli prime minister signed up to the internationally mandated 'road map' – another doomed series of incremental and interim steps on the Oslo model. A seminal moment in America's unconditional support for Israel, as mentioned in Chapter I, occurred on 14 April 2004, when, at a meeting in Washington with Sharon, Bush endorsed an Israeli letter that in effect took the right of return of Palestinian refugees off the negotiating table and assigned to Israel the big blocs of West Bank settlements. Tony Blair, while protesting full support for a two-states solution, for all practical purposes endorsed this blatantly one-sided and illegal new policy that, if it stands, would make that solution impossible. This second Balfour Declaration within weeks drew heavy fire from 52 British and 50 American former ambassadors, in an undiplomatic démarche that extended well beyond the usual Arabist suspects; the principal signatories to the public letters were committed Atlanticists dismayed at Anglo-American policies in the Middle East they rightly saw as doomed to failure. When Washington gave something between an amber and green light to Sharon's launch of a new round of settlement expansion that August, it became clear that the Israeli tail was wagging the American dog. US refusal to object to, let alone rein in, inflammatory Israeli behaviour in violation of international law and the Fourth Geneva Convention, while its forces meanwhile pulverized Fallujah and Najaf in the war of choice in Iraq, cut the ground from under moderate and democratic opinion in the Arab world, making the belief that the West was in a war against Muslims no longer extremist but mainstream.

If there was any doubt that the Sharon strategy was intended to settle the conflict by force and Palestinian capitulation, it was dispelled that October, when Dov Weisglass, the prime minister's closest aide, spilled the beans to

Ha'aretz. It was Weisglass who drafted and negotiated with Washington the Sharon letter endorsed by Bush (and Blair).

Disengagement from Gaza, Weisglass explained, was a gambit to freeze the Middle East peace process indefinitely, hang on to nearly all the Israeli settlements in the West Bank, deny the Palestinians a state, and set aside for ever the future of the refugees, the status of Jerusalem and where Israel's final borders would be drawn. The Gaza plan, he said, 'supplies the formaldehyde that is necessary so there will not be a political process with the Palestinians'.

'When you freeze the process, you prevent the establishment of a Palestinian state', reiterated Weisglass, in case his interviewer had not grasped the point: 'Effectively, this whole package called a Palestinian state, with all it entails, has been removed indefinitely from our agenda.' All this, he crowed, had won the blessing of the USA, even as it formally still purported to be pursuing a negotiated solution to the problem at the heart of the Middle East conflict through the 'road map'.

What Weisglass had outlined with such triumphalist candour had been his boss's plan for at least two and a half decades. The only new feature was that the USA had signed off on it. It left the Palestinians, and their hapless president, Mahmoud Abbas, unable to demonstrate the ability to reverse the occupation by the peaceful means of negotiation – the dilemma they, Israel and the USA still confront and will not be able to ignore. It was, furthermore, just more confirmation that the different parts of the Israeli political spectrum continue to believe that managing this conflict is about negotiations between themselves, whereas, as Yitzhak Rabin pointed out, peace is something you have to make with your enemies.

VIII

Pax Arabica: the Middle East and the West

In 2008, the last year of the irresponsible Bush administration that presumed to make its own history in a twenty-first century caricature of nineteenth-century manifest destiny, the world's sole superpower painted a sorry picture in the broader Middle East. Bogged down in two wars, in Iraq and Afghanistan, US diplomacy in the region was conspicuous by its absence. Its moral authority was rock bottom, its democratic message in tatters.

On his last, farewell, visit to the insulated Green Zone of Baghdad that December, George W. Bush inadvertently offered up an indelible image for his presidency and its principal, if far from only, debacle. At a press conference alongside Nouri al-Maliki, Iraq's prime minister, Bush was forced to duck a volley of shoes from an enraged Iraqi journalist, who called him a 'dog'. The president professed to be perplexed: what possible beef could any Iraqi have with him? This was an epic insult aimed at a serial bungler but, like the shoes, it went straight over his head.

Bush's successor, Barack Obama, by contrast awoke real hope across the region. 'We've got a unique opportunity to reboot America's image around the world and also in the Muslim world in particular', he told the *Chicago Tribune* in an interview published on 10 December 2008. But it was hard to overstate the magnitude of his task.

The year 2008 saw a number of partial deals and tentative diplomatic openings. But, in terms of such engagement as there was, the USA was not in or near the driving seat. In May 2008, as we saw in Chapter VI, it was the small, gas-rich emirate of Qatar that patched together a deal between Lebanon's feuding factions to end the Lebanese crisis and, at least, postpone the threat of a relapse into sectarian war. It was Turkey, almost simultaneously, that emerged as the mediation channel in the re-establishment of peace feelers between Israel and Syria. It was the Saudis who established tentative contact between the beleaguered and western-allied government of Hamid Karzai in Kabul and the most tractable elements of the Afghan Taliban. Egyptians and Germans tried to broker deals with Hamas and Hizbollah, while the diplomatic effort to engage Iran continued to be led by the three big states of the European Union or EU3 – Britain, France and Germany – fronted by Javier Solana, the EU foreign policy chief.

The obvious riposte to this is: of course. The Bush administration had set its face against dealing with Iran and Syria, much less Hamas and Hizbollah, which it tended, in any case, to see as one largely undifferentiated phalanx under the command of Tehran. But that was always more an attitude, and a petulant one at that, than a policy. Its framing moment was May 2003, contemporary with George W. Bush's 'Mission Accomplished' photo opportunity aboard a US aircraft carrier.

That moment ostensibly marked a USA at the height of its hyperpower. Baghdad had fallen, Saddam Hussein's Iraq was no more. Bush in that month disdainfully rejected an offer from Iran, passed on through Switzerland, of a 'grand bargain' to sort out all the differences between the Islamic republic and the American republic, including Tehran's nuclear ambitions and meddling in Arab countries on the one hand, and its quest for security guarantees and regional recognition from the USA on the other. Iran, the administration presumably reasoned, was suing for peace because it was weak and awed by the might American forces had just demonstrated in Iraq. Tehran surely feared that it, as a charter member of Bush's 'axis of evil', might be next. Yet, as we have already seen, this administration had immeasurably enhanced the reach and influence of the Islamic Republic throughout the region, not least by bringing its Shia allies to power in Iraq and overturning a near millennium-old balance of power, strengthening revolutionary Iran at the expense of the Sunni status quo. Iran had cooperated with the USA, mostly at arms reach, in both the war and post-war in Afghanistan. It has also offered cooperation, as well as competition for influence, in Iraq where, as I argued in Chapter IV, the US position would have become wholly untenable had Iran really got up to everything Washington has claimed. After Iraq and its Shia apotheosis, moreover, the settlement of the most significant conflicts in the Middle East – Iraq, Palestine and Lebanon – required Iran to support, or at least not obstruct, their resolution.

But the barely contained armistice with Iran, and the flurry of regional side-deals I have mentioned above, amounted to little more than band aids. It can, of course, be argued that local forces taking local ownership of local conflicts is a positive development. Yet, the greater work of reaching a resolution of the Palestinian question and an end to the Arab–Israeli conflict, of dousing the flames of Sunni–Shia sectarianism ignited by Iraq, and of establishing a regional security architecture that binds in Iran and gives it a stake in the stability of the Middle East, awaits US rediscovery of the force and uses of vigorous diplomacy and engagement. The USA *is* the indispensable (if not the only) power in the region, which is waiting for America to come to its senses – and which knows, to retrieve the late Yitzhak Rabin's remarks once more, that peace is something you have to make with your enemies.

As I have already remarked, the vigour and pluralism of the debate inside Israel about its future and its security stands in accusatory contrast to the totemic and cowering uniformity of mainstream US political debate. Israeli leaders desperately trying to scrape a majority in the Knesset can enjoy the rare balm of wrap-around unanimity on their visits to the US Congress. It is not just that the USA is not offering its Israeli ally the candid views of a loyal friend. The idea that the current status quo in the Middle East can be maintained is delusional – and dangerous to Israel's long-term security. The current state of violent stalemate is not only devastatingly destructive but, just as important, not on long-term offer. Israel, moreover, would be short-sighted to rely on the fawning support of American politicians. The USA's need to look to its own national interest, and to claw back its credibility with more than 50 Arab and Islamic countries and the world's 1.2 billion Muslims, will at some point cause it to review the behaviour of its closest Middle East ally and, in particular, to question how the Israeli tail manages to keep wagging the American dog.

M.J. Rosenberg, writing in his weekly column for the Washington-based *Israel Policy Forum*, which he directs, sums up the default position of most US politicians with caustic accuracy:

> Think about it. There is no political downside to simply going with the crowd on the Middle East. A politician knows that all they have to do is say that they are for Israel, and against the Palestinians, and they will be deemed a 'staunch supporter' of Israel and the campaign money will flow their way.
>
> In short, supporting the status quo is the path of least resistance. It is the default position for every politician, easy and risk-free. But it is also the one that only adds to Israel's security problems—and America's declining strategic position in the Middle East.
>
> Unfortunately, many in the pro-Israel community seem not to understand this. They believe that the status quo—and specifically the last eight years—have been good for Israel when, in fact, they have been disastrous.[1]

It is not that other leaders were doing much better. In July 2008, Nicolas Sarkozy, president of France, presided over the re-presentation in polite geopolitical society of Bashar al-Assad, as we saw in Chapter VI. Persona non Grata in Paris since a UN investigation in October 2005 implicated members of Syria and Lebanon's security services in the murder of Rafiq Hariri and a campaign of assassinations against Syria's opponents in Lebanon, Assad was given a front-row seat at Bastille Day celebrations. Mahmoud Abbas, the beleaguered Palestinian president who has risked his life and reputation to negotiate an end to the Israeli occupation to no avail, was confined to a back-row seat alongside the delegate from Somalia, another failed state. As a message, what could be clearer?

By November, David Miliband, the British foreign secretary, had journeyed to Damascus to announce that Syria was a potential force for stability in the region. The glee with which Damascus exploited these vain attempts to peel Syria off from its alliance with Iran was almost palpable. This tactic was an evasion. It avoided the need for a real strategy to deal with the real problem: Iran.

There is, in any case, a distinction to be made between shallow realism, rubbing along with a sort of Hobbesian realpolitik, and strategic clarity. That distinction is not made either in rewarding and therefore encouraging Israel's policy of illegally colonizing Arab land, or in turning a blind eye to Syria's attempts to intimidate and vassalize its Lebanese neighbours. Nor, as we have seen in numerous examples throughout this book, is it a clear or compelling strategy to promote democracy as a political panacea, and then recoil from its consequences when Islamists win or do well – in Iraq, Palestine, Lebanon, and even Egypt.

A distinct but equally supine western example of double standards was offered by the government of Tony Blair in the al-Yamamah affair. In December 2006, Britain's Serious Fraud Office (SFO), under direct pressure from the government, abandoned a two-year-long investigation into whether BAE Systems, the defence company, paid kickbacks to unspecified members of the Saudi royal family on a £43 billion arms deal, known as al-Yamamah. The government's argument was that to continue the investigation would seriously damage UK–Saudi relations and, by extension, Britain's national security. Lord Goldsmith, the then attorney general, made the specious assertion in parliament that the SFO 'had to balance the need to maintain the rule of law with the wider public interest'. Saudi officials had indeed threatened that the investigation would jeopardize a new arms deal worth perhaps another £40 billion. Just as they had done two decades earlier to clinch the terms of the original al-Yamamah contract, the Saudis ostentatiously held meetings in France to discuss alternative suppliers. A British cave-in duly followed.

This not only trampled on Britain's policy that governments cannot interfere with the rule of law, it amounted to issuing a general invitation to blackmail. Britain's sermons on transparency and good governance, as well as its adherence to international anti-bribery conventions, would rightly be blown away in gales of derision. It is, moreover, questionable whether pouring arms into Saudi Arabia advances western strategic aims, or really contributes to the kingdom's defence. As we saw in Chapter V, Saudi military spending, at about three times the average for a developing country, is partly a mechanism for distributing wealth and power within the top ranks of the House of Saud – and a bloated absolute monarchy squandering fabulous public wealth is not exactly a recipe for stability.

A coruscating judgement by the High Court (later overturned by the Law Lords, the UK's most senior judges) ruled the decision to drop the investigation unlawful. It found that Prince Bandar, former Saudi ambassador to the USA and son of Crown Prince Sultan, the defence minister, had directly intervened with the British prime minister's office, which 'failed to recognise that the threat uttered was not simply directed at this country's commercial, diplomatic and security interests; it was aimed at its legal system'; and the Blair government made no attempt to persuade the Saudis that 'their threat was futile', since the courts would uphold the rule of law.

But the domestic backwash is only part of the story. The message sent to the Middle East by this behaviour was devastating. King Abdullah himself, according to an eminent former US official involved in tracking international corruption, said he was dismayed at the British decision to drop the inquiry. He saw it as undermining his gradual attempts to introduce reform, including limits to the ruling family's share in Saudi wealth. That is not the least damaging aspect of this shameful episode.

The West as a whole presents a sorry spectacle to the Middle East. Admired as it is for its technical and cultural achievements, and even, against all odds, for aspects of its political culture, its embrace is seen as increasingly threatening, not to say downright poisonous. How could it be otherwise, when we not only collude with tyrants, connive in land-grabs, turn a blind eye to murder, and facilitate corruption, all in the name of security and stability? Any healthy and even notionally practicable policy for dealing with the Arab world and the broader Middle East not only needs to review its strategic aims, and the means to achieve them. It needs the West, beginning but not ending with the USA, to recover its standing: its honour and integrity, its clarity and its credibility. As I have argued throughout this book, it is the Arabs who need to do most – by far the most – to make their countries successful societies. But, we must be clear: they have the right to expect from us that we do not support almost every countervailing trend preventing them from doing so.

*   *   *   *   *

In the course of a conversation with a senior US policy strategist on the Middle East, in the spring of 2006, I was startled when he admonished me to stop paying attention to what American leaders said: 'look at what we do, not what we say', he said. The peoples of the Middle East have long since learned that lesson. Arab nationalists, liberals, and Islamic revivalists alike, have been made painfully aware through experience of the discrepancies between American rhetoric and practice. In the aftermath of the First World War, in particular, they greeted with enthusiasm the advent of a new, anti-colonial superpower to balance Europe's colonizing powers. Their expectations were not met, but their hopes persisted, flickering episodically into life when, for example, as we saw in the previous chapter, Eisenhower used American power before and during the 1956 Suez crisis to confound Israel's expansionist plans and spoil the last hurrah of Anglo-French colonialism in the Middle East. Yet, had they known America better, the Arabs would surely have detected a persistent strain of tension between a libertarian and anti-colonial attachment to the ideas of self-determination and freedom, and the needs of an emerging and expansionary power to establish spheres of influence, throw itself into balance of power politics and, on occasion, trample on the rights of others. They might also have detected strains in American thinking that would make it difficult for the country's leaders and people to see the Middle East in all its clarity – and which were there from the beginning.

America, a republic founded on an idea, Thomas Jefferson's empire of liberty, has always believed unshakeably in its righteousness and its goodness. It has also believed, despite periodic setbacks, in its military ability to spread this. Its role in bringing two world wars to an end provided a firm buttress for this conviction but, as Joan Hoff, in her recent study of US foreign policy from Woodrow Wilson to George W. Bush, puts it, there has always been an 'exceptionalist belief in the country's "rightness" and military capability'.[2]

Part of that vocational conviction is captured incandescently in the famous line from 1630 of John Winthrop, the Puritan leader of the early Pilgrims: 'for we must consider that we shall be as a City on a Hill, the Eyes of all people are upon us'. This luminous statement was often quoted by Kennedy and Reagan, and permeates the rhetoric of succeeding leaders. Thus, Madeleine Albright, Clinton's secretary of state, would, for example, assert that: 'The United States is good. We try to do our best everywhere.'[3] George W. Bush, in his 2003 State of the Union speech, on the eve of invading Iraq, told Americans: 'as our nation moves troops and builds alliances to make our world safer, we must also remember our calling as a blessed country is to make the world better'.

Let us hear once again what President Obama told the ecstatic crowd at his victory rally in Chicago in November 2008: 'To those who would tear the world down – we will defeat you. To those who seek peace and security – we support you. And to all those who have wondered if America's beacon still burns as bright – tonight we proved once more that the true strength of our nation comes not from the might of our arms or the scale of our wealth, but from the enduring power of our ideals: democracy, liberty, opportunity and unyielding hope.'

When the Monroe doctrine was formulated in 1823, it was, at one level, based on the principle of self-determination throughout the Americas, in opposition to the predatory designs of the European colonial powers. But it also asserted the right of the USA to act against those powers, which turned into a general warrant for hemispheric intervention, of which the USA took full advantage. For this was the era of Manifest Destiny. Coterminous with America's expansion from the Atlantic to the Pacific, the USA would take nearly half of what was then Mexico in the 1846–8 war against Santa Ana, conquer the Philippines and Cuba in the 1898 wars against Spain, in addition to more or less licensing assorted filibuster adventures in Central America, and launching 20 US military actions in the Caribbean Basin between 1898 and 1920. It is not too hard to see how this experience – the story of a nation of settlers – would later feed into an instinctive sympathy for Israel's regional position and its desire to improve it, and a lack of empathy for Arab revolutionary nationalism and self-determination, once America graduated from hemispheric to world power.

As far back as Winthrop, the Puritan tradition believed that the Israelites had 'special commission' from God, as revealed in the Bible, to drive out the inhabitants of their land. In the American context, by the mid-nineteenth century, Francis Parkman, one of the republic's first great historians, would argue that America's native Indians were 'destined to melt and vanish before the advancing waves of Anglo-American power, which now rolled westward'. One is tempted to think that many Americans, hearing the Zionists voice their ambition to recreate *Eretz Israel*, the Biblical Land of Israel, from the river (Jordan) to the (Mediterranean) sea, heard not only the echoes of the Bible but the first and last chorus of the hymn America the Beautiful: 'America! America! God shed his grace on thee, And crown thy good with brotherhood from sea to shining sea.'

The idea of the USA as the redeemer nation chosen by God and providence is a common thread through American history, shared by almost all its leaders. Woodrow Wilson, for example, believed that through establishing the League of Nations after the First World War, America was leading in the 'redemption of the world'. Within this shared conviction, however, one strand of more apocalyptic thinking has gathered particular strength in recent decades – a fundamentalist, Protestant evangelism that looks to the 'end of days' and the return of Christ to defeat Satan, which would be triggered by the return of the Jews to all of Biblical Israel. This religious Right, powerful not only in the Republican party but gathering strength, for example, in Britain's Conservative party, offers unconditional support to Israel and any policy – such as the invasion of Iraq – that appears to benefit Israel and advance its own millenarian aims. These so-called Christian Zionists have no interest in actual Jews, except as ciphers in fulfilling a Biblical grand design from which Jews will be excluded. The power of this lobby is not the least of the constraints under which American policy operates.

For their part, the Arabs heard from America its ringing cries of freedom, a freedom it had seized for itself from the British Empire. The Arabs, one must never forget, had set enormous store on the 14 Points on self-determination and freedom issued by Woodrow Wilson as the First World War drew to a close, bringing the curtain down on the Ottoman empire. In 1919, General James Harbord, after visiting the Middle East on behalf of Wilson, reported to the president that 'without visiting the Near East, it is not possible for an American to realize even faintly the respect, faith and affection with which our country is regarded throughout that region'. This, he said, was because of 'the world-wide reputation which we enjoy for fair dealing'.[4]

But the USA failed to deliver on the exaggerated promise of self-determination in the region. The findings of the 1918 King–Crane commission, including that the Palestinian Arabs overwhelmingly opposed the establishment of a Jewish state in Palestine, were not published until 1922, by when the Arabs had been delivered into a sort of Anglo-French condominium in the region and the Balfour Declaration had been approved by both houses of the US Congress.

American consciousness of the Middle East, as Douglas Little has shown, developed over subsequent decades under the influence of *National Geographic* magazine and its stereotypical view of alien Arab exoticism and Israeli pioneer pluck. Hollywood epics from *The Thief of Baghdad* to *Aladdin*, openly propagandist best-sellers such as the 1958 novel *Exodus* by Leon Uris (also a four-hour biopic of Israel starring Paul Newman) and its racist follow-up, *The Haj*, or the venomous vignettes of the Arabs to be found in books from Mark Twain's *Innocents Abroad* to James Michener's *The Source*, reinforced these stereotypes.[5]

There is little new in this. Aeschylus (whose *Persians* of 472 BCE is the earliest surviving play) and the classical Greek tragedians won many pan-Hellenic Oscars by manufacturing an image of a cruel, effeminate and decadent despotism of the East, building up Greek identity and cultural superiority. The great tragedians were the first and most accomplished demonizers of 'the other'.[6]

As a tactic, this recurs throughout history. In Chapter III, I remarked on how Europeans had forged their identity in opposition to Islam. As David Levering Lewis has shown, this could involve almost literal forgery or, at least, literary fabrication. The mediaeval *Chanson de Roland* turns the debacle that befell Charlemagne at Roncesvalles (Roncevaux) in 778 into a civilizational foundation myth. Charlemagne was, in fact, retreating from an unsuccessful foray over the Pyrenees into Muslim Iberia. His rearguard, including the heroic Breton Roland, was destroyed by Basques, angry that the Christian paladin of the Franks had sacked their (Christian) city of Pamplona. Almost three centuries on, and in the run-up to Pope Urban II's declaration of the First Crusade in 1095, this humiliation at the hands of the Basques was transmuted into a nation-moulding clash between Franks and Saracens, between Christians and Muslims, an epic of Greater Frankland as well as a constitutive myth of Christendom.[7]

But American popular consciousness of Arabs and Muslims, ground up with episodes in the expansion of the USA through the Mexican and Indian wars, percolated up to the very top of government where it eventually seeped into the Cold War fixation about communism penetrating the Middle East. President Johnson, it was said, saw Nasser as a cross between Ho Chi Minh, the Vietnamese revolutionary leader, and Geronimo, the Apache warrior. His Texan aide, John Roche, once told the president: 'I confess that I look at the Israelis as Texans and Nasser as Santa Ana.'[8]

As William Fulbright, long-time chairman of the Senate foreign relations committee, would point out in his 1966 book *The Arrogance of Power*, America, despite its own revolutionary history, was not capable of empathizing with Third World upheaval and the appeal of revolutionary nationalism. A Nasser was utterly alien. All this coincided, moreover, with a tendency to confuse power with virtue, 'and a great nation is particularly susceptible to the idea that its power is a sign of God's favour, conferring upon it a special responsibility for other nations – to make them richer and happier and wiser, to remake them, that is, in its own shining image'.

This aspect of American conviction, seen most vividly in the invasion of Iraq, is a bit like a syllogism: We Americans are good and freedom-loving; our intentions in the Middle East are selfless and honourable; mostly everything we do there is therefore good. But that is not how US behaviour is seen inside the region, and not only by the Arabs. The uplifting vision of the Liberty Bell pealing throughout the lands of the Middle East, summoning Abu Jeffersons to the cause of liberty, is at odds with America's record of mistrust of democracy there. America's history in the Middle East is, indeed, about the difference between what it says and what it does.

* * * * *

One of the hostages to that history is Iran, which, as I have argued, after the invasion of Iraq upturned the Sunni order and immeasurably enhanced Iranian influence through Shia empowerment, must now be taken into account in any attempt to resolve the principal conflicts of the Middle East. Iran is a critical player in the region; so, to an important if lesser extent, are other big, non-Arab countries such as Turkey and Pakistan. In this section I wish to look at their roles in the Middle Eastern drama, and at the pattern of US relations with them.

Whether Iran would be part of the solution or part of the problem depended on whether the USA and Iran could overcome their visceral historical animosities and resolve their differences. The far from impossible alternative – whereby either the USA launched a strike against Iranian nuclear facilities, or, more likely, Israel did, drawing the Americans in – risked setting fire to a Middle East already in turmoil and unleashing Iranian retaliation within and beyond the region.

The Bush administration, after contemptuously rejecting the Iranian reformist president Mohammad Khatami's offer of a 'grand bargain' in May 2003, has, as we saw in Chapter IV, had tentative bilateral contacts with Iran over Iraq. In the summer of 2006, it offered to join the EU3 in direct talks with Iran, but set the killer precondition that Tehran first suspend all uranium enrichment activities. There, for the moment, the matter lies. Yet there was nothing substantive, in any event, to suggest that Iran and the USA were ready to talk, let alone negotiate on what divided them. There was simply too much bad blood on both sides.

The USA has never forgotten how its forces were driven out of Beirut by pro-Iranian truck bombers during the Lebanese civil war, and never forgiven the Tehran embassy siege after the 1979 revolution and the botched attempt to rescue its hostages. Nor has it forgotten the Americans held hostage in Beirut in the 1980s and the Iran–Contra fiasco where it was suckered into arms-length arms deals with Tehran to try to release them. It has, moreover, never accepted the survival of Hizbollah.

Iran, for its part, neither forgives nor forgets the 1953 Anglo-American coup against the elected, nationalist Mossadegh government and the restoration of the Shah (nor that it was H. Norman Schwarzkopf, father of the US commander in the 1991 Gulf War, who equipped the Shah's autocracy with its police force). Whatever they think of it now, probably a majority of Iranians felt the 1979 revolution was carried out not only against the Pahlavi dynasty but its American sponsors. No less can Iranians forget how the USA and the West condoned Iraq's 1980 invasion of Iran, and then armed Saddam Hussein as he rained rockets on its cities and chemical shells on its troops. All that was long before Bush made the mullahs eligible for regime change in his 2002 'Axis of Evil' speech.

These are livid scars on the psyches of both these proud nations, a legacy that is very much alive in the mutual mistrust of their rulers. Despite its proud Persian history and defiant Shia Muslim tradition, Iran has been invaded by Greeks and Romans, Arabs and Mongols, Seljuk and Ottoman Turks. As it struggled towards modernity early in the last century, it was the plaything of Russian and British imperial interests. To a greater or lesser extent it was able to soak up these invasions. The US intrusion, however, proved harder to cope with, especially as the imposed western modernity of the Shah's 'White Revolution' opened up fractures and provoked dislocation across Iranian society.

For the Americans, the legacy of Beirut is particularly hard to overcome. The Shia forces in Lebanon sponsored by Iran – which would later coalesce into Hizbollah – inflicted arguably the worst humiliation suffered by US forces since Vietnam. The American embassy in West Beirut was destroyed by bombers in April 1983 and its annexe in Christian east Beirut was blown up a year later, rubbing salt into the wound of the 52 Americans held hostage for 444 days at the embassy in Tehran. Worse still was the truck bombing that killed 241 US marines (and 58 French paratroopers) near Beirut airport in October 1983, triggering the withdrawal of American forces four months afterwards. Twenty years later, Richard Armitage, deputy secretary of state in the first Bush administration, would describe Hizbollah as 'the A Team' of international terror – more lethal than al-Qaeda – and owing a 'blood debt' to Americans the USA intended to collect.[9]

But Iran's scars from serial invasion and foreign meddling in its politics are vivid too. All Iranians, including the many who despise the ruling mullahs, have hardwired into them how Britain and Russia invaded their country during the Second World War to seize the trans-Iranian railroad, forcing Reza Shah Pahlavi to abdicate in 1941 in favour of his son, Mohammad Reza Pahlavi. The 1953 Anglo-American plot to topple Mohammad Mossadegh for presuming to nationalize the oil industry is so totemic that the theocrats who now rule in Tehran easily use its echoes to present western opposition to Iran's nuclear ambitions as a new attempt to deprive the country of resources and technology, rather than to stop Iran becoming nuclear-armed. Iran, moreover, is the one country in recent times that has actually experienced the terror of being attacked by weapons of mass destruction – Iraqi chemical weapons that ultimately can be sourced to western suppliers – a fact that makes the West's arguments about Iran's nuclear plans additionally suspect in Iranian eyes.

None of this makes for a promising backdrop for even tentative talks let alone hopes of détente. Yet there have been tantalizing opportunities. When Mohammad Khatami, a former culture minister forced out of office for 'permissiveness' in 1992, was elected in a reformist landslide in May 1997, he asserted the dormant republican ideas of the Islamic republic and appeared to offer not only the prospect of marrying Islam with democracy, but an opening to reconciliation with the USA and the West.

The theocrats, who had consolidated their power, their puritan hegemony and their dense network of material interests in the shadow of the 1980–8 war to repel Iraq's western-backed invasion, were left reeling by this determined electoral uprising in favour of reform, which gave Khatami 70 per cent of the vote on a nearly 90 per cent turnout. More than 20 million votes, predominantly from the under-25s, who make up two thirds of Iran's population, and from Iranian women, could not be denied. One year on, popular support for the then 55-year-old cleric bordered on adulation. In May 1998, on the first anniversary of his victory, I watched tens of thousands throng into Tehran university to celebrate. Only after a 15-minute ovation could Khatami speak, and promise them he would not be deflected from creating a freer society with a government accountable to the people, under the rule of law. 'If religion comes into conflict with freedom', he said, 'then it will be religion that suffers'. He called for 'a politics free from coercion, based on human rights, popular sovereignty, the rule of law and tolerance, with respect for thought per se, respect and reverence for freedom [as a value in] itself'. These beguiling calls changed the political debate in Iran, but provoked fear among the vested interests and competing power centres of the clerical regime.

Conventional analysis of this power structure portrayed an opaque and impregnable Islamist fortress immune to change. All real power, in this view, flowed from Ayatollah Ali Khamenei, successor as Supreme Leader to the late

Imam, Ayatollah Ruhollah Khomeini, inspirer of the revolution that replaced the Shah's autocracy with theocracy. Khamenei controlled the army, the Revolutionary Guards, the intelligence services, the judiciary and foreign policy. Moreover, parastatal fiefs such as the *Bonyads* (ostensibly charitable foundations built from the assets of the Shah and leading monarchists), which along with the state controlled about 80 per cent of the economy, producing some 5,000 goods and services but no new investment or jobs, were accountable only to him. The private sector was dominated by the Bazaar, a conservative trading community biased against entrepreneurship and happy to exploit the loopholes in a rigged economy, which was held to be in his pocket. The Leader further controlled both the conventional and traditional mass media: broadcasting and the mosque.

Nevertheless, at that time, the forces of Islamist reaction that the mercurial and messianic Mahmoud Ahmadinejad would come to personify after his presidential victory in 2005 could manage only a ragged response, amounting more to random provocation than a cohesive strategy to roll back the Khatami project. And this project, although it did not question the legitimacy of the Islamic republic, was a democratic project. As a Khatami aide put it at the time, 'one of [the president's] main objectives is to get a political structure that allows the winner of an election to take power'.[10] Khatami, not just an admirer of de Tocqueville but a translator of Machiavelli, moved quickly to replace all provincial governors (who control elections), sacked some 200 political appointees in the civil service and, most telling of all, got rid of the commander of the Revolutionary Guards.

All this was being watched closely across the region. Sheikh Hassan Nasrallah, the Hizbollah chief, was one of those to applaud. Khatami, he told the author, 'is presenting a model and an example. There are lots of models, some of them dangerous like the Taliban phenomenon, which, with Made in USA collusion, wants to show Islam as ignorance, savagery, the degradation of women and the regression into factional warfare. In Iran, what is now being prescribed is an enlightened and tolerant Islam that is genuine and authentic and based on the origins of Islam. This model is going to have a gradual and positive impact on the Arab world, both at government and popular level.'[11]

This was, in other words, a potentially pivotal moment in the life not only of Iran but of the Middle East. In contrast to, say, a Mikhail Gorbachev, admired more abroad than at home, Khatami had vast reserves of domestic popular support but needed to acquire real international standing. He put out his initial feeler to the USA in an interview with CNN in January 1998, calling for 'a dialogue of civilizations' with 'the great American people' to break down 'the wall of mistrust'. With liberty and the rule of law at the centre of his programme, he harked back to America's own revolutionary and dissident religious traditions.

It looked for a while as though President Bill Clinton would go for it, and seek a rapprochement with Iran analogous to Richard Nixon's breakthrough with China 25 years earlier. When Clinton called for 'genuine reconciliation' on the occasion of that year's Iran versus USA football match in the World Cup, the parallels with the 'ping-pong diplomacy' that preceded détente with Beijing were unmistakeable. But the moment passed, briefly resurrected, as we have seen, by a now immeasurably weakened Khatami in May 2003. The silky and smiling Iranian president was rebuffed on both occasions. But it was the earlier approach in 1998, when Iran's theocrats had been stripped of their legitimacy and were unsure of the loyalty of their enforcers, when Khatami had the chance to take power as well as office, that was the best opportunity. By 2003, the reformists had been sabotaged by the politically isolated but institutionally powerful clerics and powerbrokers grouped around Khamenei, and the Iranian political elite was debating whether, in the light of the invasion of Iraq, it should power ahead with its nuclear programme.

Khatami, to be sure, contributed to his own downfall. He chose not to confront head on a power structure in which the Khomeinist concept of 'the rule of the jurisprudent' vests supreme power in unelected clerics who can overrule popularly elected politicians. He opted instead to try to persuade Khamenei that his survival and that of the Islamic republic depended on reform. But his cautious reformism underestimated how determined the regime was to protect its power and privileges. Preferring to fuel public debate with ideas rather than lead, Khatami failed to protect his closest associates from impeachment, ducked confrontation with the Majlis (parliament) on constitutional reform, nailed his colours to the fence during the July 1999 student uprising, and put too much faith in shaky alliances with Akbar Hashemi Rafsanjani, his ambitious predecessor and the arch-fixer at the heart of Iranian realpolitik.

It is impossible to know – but a legitimate question – whether a more determined American and European effort to engage with Iran, and to emphasize and welcome its democratic evolution, would have strengthened Khatami's hand, and his backbone. What is certainly true, however, was that Khatami had overwhelming popular support among Iranians, who are, at the same time, probably the most instinctively pro-American of the Middle Eastern peoples. That was the size of the opportunity that was spurned – a genuinely democratic opportunity that the West largely ignored. Instead, Ahmadinejad and the opponents of reform were able to show that Khatami had led the country up a blind alley into the Axis of Evil.

In 2003, the rebuff was not just because the Bush administration's hawks, led by vice president Dick Cheney and defence secretary Donald Rumsfeld, were so pumped up by ostensible victory in Iraq. After all, at this seeming peak of its power, Washington had still managed to hold its nose and sit down at the same table as the North Korean Stalinists, already well on their way to nuclear arms capability. Iran's road map – which offered to address US concerns on nuclear weapons and terrorism, sort out their differences on Iraq, and cooperate in pursuit of a two-states solution in Israel–Palestine – was even greater in scope than the disarmament agreement that had just seen Libya and the promiscuous terror-sponsor Muammar Gaddafi graduate from the ranks of rogue states. There is simply something more visceral about Iran.

The Bush administration, as we saw in Chapter IV, soon began to discern the hand of Tehran behind every leaf that rustled in Iraq and the region. It showed signs of using the Mujahedin e-Khalq, an Iraq-based and cult-like paramilitary group on the US terrorist list since 1997, as a pawn against Tehran, amid reports that US special forces were stirring up Iran's Arab, Azeri, Kurdish and Baluch minorities against its Persian, Shia, majority. Nothing Iran might offer, it seemed, would be sufficient so long as it remained an Islamic republic while, as I have already remarked, the US posture looked more like an attitude than an executable policy.

Iran's attitudes are confusing, too, mixing victimhood with the innate sense of cultural superiority of an ancient civilization, vulnerability with a sense of entitlement as a regional power. The Islamic republic is paranoid but breast-beatingly arrogant and belligerent at the same time – though it is the latter of these characteristics that is most visible in the outpourings of President Ahmadinejad, especially his now well-rehearsed provocation calling for the elimination of Israel. Yet Iran's confidence is not baseless.

After Afghanistan and Iraq, Iran is almost encircled by US forces. Yet, as we have seen, it is the clearest beneficiary of the Iraq invasion, and American forces are bogged down in both theatres. In Tehran's eyes, America blinked first by authorizing its then ambassador in Baghdad, Zalmay Khalilzad, to open talks with Iran on Iraqi security. If attacked, moreover, Iran has the ability to retaliate through proxies in Iraq, Afghanistan, Lebanon, Syria and Palestine, as well as to destabilize the Gulf. It has other reasons to feel confident, at least for now.

Oil revenues were high and demand for its oil riches had never been higher. The worldwide downturn triggered by financial crisis and recession in the rich countries cut the oil price to around one third of its peak by the end of 2008. But while this was bad news for Ahmadinejad – who liberally looted oil revenue to fund populist schemes that struggled to keep pace with the inflation they unleashed – the medium-term outlook for oil prices was radically different. The chronic structural deficit in investment in oil exploration and output across major oil producers points to sharp price rises once economic recovery starts.

With Ahmadinejad's election, moreover, the theocrats are political masters in their own house – even amidst growing public resentment at the government's economic incompetence. The sanctions that first the USA and then the international community have placed on Iran are smarter than the devastating embargo on Iraq – targeting banks (and therefore trade and investment), strategic industries and prominent Iranian cadres. Even so, the diplomatic siege has tended to unite the nation, making the right to technology and deterrence a totem like the nationalization of the oil industry more than half a century ago.

Iran's security concerns are now so mixed up with its sense of entitlement that any bargain with the USA and the West would have to give it status as well as security. Washington may have moved, but so far it seems to have steeled itself only to try to deal diplomatically with a problem, not to consecrate a regional power, much less set it up as a rival hegemon to Israel. That is the nub of the diplomatic and strategic problem.

* * * * *

Before moving on to consider the policies that might have a chance of successfully addressing this and the other strategic problems that we have looked at in the course of this dismal record of failure in the Middle East, I would like to touch on two countries whose affairs have an impact on the region: one a broadly hopeful example, Turkey; the other, much less so, Pakistan. The US invasion of Iraq not only excited widespread Muslim and Arab animosity. It empowered Iran with significantly enlarged influence. It alienated Turks to the point that Turkey is at risk of sliding out of the western orbit. And the whole thrust of US policy since 9/11 is in danger of turning Pakistan into a failed state.

Pakistan, as I argued in Chapter IV, presented the most real example of the potentially deadly combination of dangers the Bush administration and Blair government affected to see in Iraq, namely the possible intersection of nuclear weapons with the rising influence of jihadism. As a strategically positioned country, at the intersection of the Middle East, Central Asia and South Asia, as a nation declared by the Bush administration to be a 'major non-NATO ally', it is also a federation being pulled apart by a complex mix of ethnic, tribal and Islamist insurgency, exacerbated by the thinly disguised military dictatorship the USA supported in Pakistan from October 1999 to August 2008.

When General Pervez Musharraf took power in a bloodless military coup in October 1999, many Pakistanis dared to hope for an end to decades of misrule, by civilians as well as generals, which had bankrupted the country and buckled its institutions. Pakistan's allies and adversaries, meanwhile, while tut-tutting on cue about the vulgar anachronism of a military coup, were privately relieved that a newly nuclear-armed state, which had just fought a small war in the Himalayas with arch-rival India, was firmly in the grip of an officer with an ostensibly modernist outlook: a whisky liberal in an Islamic republic, an admirer of Mustafa Kemal Ataturk, father of secularist Turkey, as much as of Mohammed Ali Jinnah, the revered founder of Pakistan. How naïve that view would later come to seem.

True, those who hoped or believed in Musharraf seemed vindicated when he threw his weight behind the USA after the al-Qaeda attacks of 9/11 – even though, given the fierce pressure from Washington, he did not have much choice. As the manager of an initially civilian team, moreover, the general secured some positive change, such as fiscal reform and privatization for a rickety economy, and in the social arena by enhancing the rights of women. But this was nothing like enough, and only by the time of the political and constitutional crisis that broke out in 2007 was its price becoming clear.

The general had the chance to re-lay the foundations of stability and democratic rule. He constantly told visitors to his Army House residence in Rawalpindi that he would restore democracy as soon as he had put in place the accountability essential for it to work – accountability so foreign to the neo-feudal elites who had lorded it over Pakistani politics. Whereas previous military rulers had superimposed martial law on civilian rule, leaving its weak structures intact, he aimed to change them. 'What we're involved in is not minor adjustments, what we're doing is the political restructuring of the entire democratic system', he protested. Surrounded by gilded ceremonial swords and exquisite Moghul miniatures, the general said: 'I could have imposed martial law, but if you put a military superstructure on top of civilian structures when you leave [power] you leave the civilian structure as it was. I did not want to do that. Better to let the civil system improve, reform and perform.'[12]

He did indeed change the structure of power, but in a way that sought to institutionalize and prolong his supremacy, which he appeared to regard as consubstantial with the national interest. Musharraf's larger purpose was shown to be to cling to power, civil and military. In this he had full backing from the USA, which, disdainful of democracy, had come to equate Pakistan with the general.

Like many of his Arab peers, Musharraf was a master tactician. He managed to convince Washington that only he could deliver up the al-Qaeda cadres Pakistani security episodically killed or captured; that only he, survivor of three near-miss attempts on his life, could prevent the country falling to the jihadis; and, therefore, that it was he who must stay at the head of the army, Pakistan's last working institution, to banish the spectre of mullahs with nukes. The USA has pumped roughly $12 billion in aid into Pakistan in the years since 9/11, along with new F-16 fighter jets. According to Husain Haqqani, Pakistani ambassador to the USA, American aid to Pakistan over the past half century has totalled $24 billion at today's prices, $21 billion of which has gone to the military, while there were long periods, mostly coinciding with civilian rule, when aid stopped flowing.[13]

Washington, moreover, tacitly endorsed for as long as possible General Musharraf's double-hatted but unconstitutional role as president and army chief of staff. While it was 9/11 that wrenched Musharraf into overt alliance with the USA, it was also 9/11 that gave the Bush administration the insight that despotism breeds extremism. It made no attempt to reconcile this in the case of Pakistan. The 'exceptionalism' the USA and the West applies to the Arab world extends to the broader Middle East.

Inside the army and the intelligence services, Musharraf bought off some generals with sinecures, but secured the support of others by letting them abet jihad – in Afghanistan through aiding the resurgent Taliban, including against NATO troops, and in Kashmir, the divided, mainly Muslim territory at the heart of Pakistan's warring with India. Irrespective of their religious or ideological make-up, some Pakistani officers, especially in ISI military intelligence, have long believed in the need for 'strategic depth' in Afghanistan as part of the primordial contest with India, as well as denying the Indians a foothold there. In the Kashmiri conflict, licensing a few thousand jihadis to hold down up to half a million troops in the Valley of Kashmir long seemed an ingeniously successful use of asymmetric warfare by the weaker party in the broader sub-continental contest. Yet these tactics, it should now be clear even to the sorcerer's apprentices who practised them, have willy-nilly given the jihadis a run of territory from Kashmir to the Hindu Kush.

The USA, fixated on its strongman's ability to deliver in the 'war on terror', failed to grasp the extent to which Musharraf was beholden to the ISI and the security apparatus to keep him in power, not to mention alive.

General Musharraf's approach to domestic politics proved equally disastrous. His methodical marginalization of the mainstream parties – the Pakistan People's Party (PPP) of the late Benazir Bhutto and the Pakistan Muslim League faction led by Nawaz Sharif (PML-N) – forced him into an alliance with the religious right. Before the rigged 2002 elections, in which they won 11 per cent of the popular vote, Islamist parties in Pakistan had never made it into double figures. Afterwards, they started to swagger across the national stage, Talibanizing the country. Musharraf, the whisky liberal, led Pakistan back 30 years, to the time of the coup by another American protégé, General Mohammed Zia ul-Haq, that first set the country on an Islamist course under military tutelage. As so often the case throughout the broader Middle East, his success in damming up Pakistan's political mainstream gave violent force to the Islamist tributaries.

In 2007, Bush sent Dick Cheney to Islamabad as evidence mounted that al-Qaeda had rebuilt its command and training structures in Pakistan's tribal areas along the Afghan frontier, with whose leaders Musharraf had concluded a truce. It was, as not only Musharraf loyalists pointed out, sickeningly rich that Cheney, the vice-president who after 9/11 had pushed so hard to go after Saddam Hussein rather than finish off Osama bin Laden, should be lecturing anyone about the international jihadism he and his superficially muscular policies had done so much to proliferate. It was also a pity Washington had no grasp of, and nothing to say about, the way the camouflaged military rule it supported in Pakistan was visibly piling up the country's problems, as well as giving a fillip to the jihadis. It is also fair to say that Pakistan, more perhaps than any other country, was still struggling with the 'blowback' from the anti-Soviet jihad the USA sponsored in Afghanistan in the 1980s, which has so coloured the politics of the region. But Musharraf, a man who started by admiring Ataturk but ended up looking like just another Mubarak, made all this worse.

By the time of the 2007–8 political and constitutional crisis, it was scarcely an exaggeration to say that Pakistan was flirting with failure as a state. Its federation was fraying at the edges. The tribal areas, notwithstanding periodic truces, were in revolt. In the North-West Frontier province, where Musharraf had given a big leg-up to the Islamists, Pashtun nationalism was fusing with Islamism; an indigenous Pakistani Taliban emerged in alliance with their Pashtun allies in Afghanistan. The crushing of opposition in resource-rich but dirt-poor Baluchistan, in order to favour pro-Taliban allies, had rekindled a nationalist insurgency. Reliance on gangster–politicians in Sindh as a counterweight against the PPP was helping revive ethnosectarian conflict.

Yet Musharraf eventually blundered too far. When democracy pulls together all the tiny slivers of power held by its citizens it can be a humbling force. After the general sacked the chief justice, Iftikhar Mohammed Chaudhry, in February 2007, the hitherto supine judiciary reacted to the affront and became the catalyst for a much wider backlash against dictatorship from Pakistani civil society, re-energizing the mainstream parties, parliament and the press. Benazir Bhutto and Nawaz Sharif had each had two goes at governing before the 1999 coup and had proved venal and incompetent, temporizing with the army and the jihadis. Yet Pakistan needed their supporters to build a democratic bloc against extremism, and to reinvigorate Pakistan's institutions and restore the credibility of its rulers so that nation-building could begin anew.

The USA, over-invested in its Pakistani generalissimo whom it had come to regard as indispensable in the campaign against al-Qaeda, panicked. Washington tried to match-make an alliance between Musharraf and Benazir Bhutto, a stitch-up that would for all practical purposes bypass Pakistani voters and civil society. US officials pointed in mitigation to the vigour with which Musharraf had cleared jihadis out of the Red Mosque in Islamabad in July 2007. Yet, had he acted in January, when the jihadis started their open challenge to the state, moving in from the frontiers to the capital to occupy the mosque, there might have been fewer dead in the bloody clash and fewer reprisal bombings. But in the face of the jihadi onslaught, Musharraf got away with postponing elections and having himself anointed to a second term as president by his placemen in a rump parliament, in the expectation that Benazir, amnestied out of a self-imposed exile fleeing corruption charges, would soon furnish a fig-leaf of legitimacy. As the jihadi terrorism Musharraf's US-backed policies did so much to stimulate spread, highlighted by an attack on Bhutto's homecoming motorcade that massacred 136 people, the general imposed emergency rule that November – arresting lawyers, human rights activists and politicians, and shutting down critical press outlets. In other words, the regime turned its guns on civil society, the real indispensable ally in the struggle against jihadism.

The successful assassination of Benazir Bhutto on 27 December 2007 left Washington adrift. She had presented to the world an example of courage and a plausible face of modernity: a young, glamorous woman in a male-dominated society, educated at Oxford and Harvard, fluent in the idiom of western capitals, and politically attuned to what they wanted to hear. Under her ruthless command, the PPP was more of a feudal hierarchy than a political party.

The PPP came first in the subsequent elections, in which Musharraf's political vehicle was all but destroyed. Asif Ali Zardari, Benazir's widower, known as 'Mr 10 per cent' after allegations of corruption when he was a former minister in her governments, became its de facto leader. After a brief and rocky coalition with Nawaz Sharif – with Musharraf still in the presidency – Zardari replaced the general after the army forced him to step down in August 2008. The Bush administration became increasingly unhappy at the new government's attempts to reach an understanding with the panoply of insurgents it faced, and growing evidence of ISI involvement with Taliban, al-Qaeda and Kashmiri jihadi elements on both sides of the Pakistani border with Afghanistan. In the summer of 2008 the CIA accused the ISI of complicity in the 7 July bombing of the Indian embassy in Kabul. Menacingly, jihadis from across the wider region were flocking into Pakistan and towards its lawless borders, providing the sort of magnet Iraq had been for itinerant holy warriors until the Sunni tribes turned against al-Qaeda. But Washington seemed to be most unhappy at the end of the apparent neatness of clear-cut rule by an army strongman.

The conclusion the incoming US administration should draw is that Musharraf and the military destabilized immeasurably further – we will eventually see by how far – a country already badly weakened by decades of misrule. Rule by a generalissimo may look neater, but Musharraf, by clinging on to power, by allowing the military to parasitically monopolize the scarce resources of the state, and by licensing the ISI to abet jihadism in Afghanistan and Kashmir, assisted in the Talibanization of Pakistan. The Pakistani military, by simultaneously if sporadically attacking the jihadis, turned the state into a target and – as the November 2008 attacks on Mumbai showed – encouraged the jihadis to widen their sights and attempt to blow up any hope of détente between Pakistan and India that would resolve or reduce the conflict on which the radical Islamists thrive. This was a textbook replica of the errors of judgement the USA has made across the Middle East, with very high stakes. It was a prime exhibit of the flimsiness of US commitment to the difficult work of democracy.

*　*　*　*　*

In Turkey, the stakes are different, but also very high. It is hard to think of a more overarching geopolitical imperative at the beginning of the twenty-first century than to demonstrate that Islam and democracy can be bound successfully together. Turkey may be on its way to proving that, in an experiment that is resonating far beyond its borders. It is the Turks, of course, who are responsible for making a success of this great challenge. But their partners in Europe and NATO must rise to it too.

At the centre of this experiment is the ruling Justice and Development Party (AKP) and its charismatic leader, Recep Tayyip Erdogan, Turkey's prime minister. His has not been an easy passage. His turbulent career in Turkey's Islamist politics is at odds with his look – tall, self-assured, tailored and groomed – that makes him seem more like a Mediterranean football manager than a mullah on the make. Erdogan, improbably, has come to embody Muslim Turkey's attempt to win (eventual) promotion into the hitherto Christian league of the European Union, a promotion a big and diverse fan club of Turks were initially rooting hard for.

At the head of a 15-month old AKP, Erdogan came to power in a landslide in November 2002, with Turkey still mired in its worst financial crisis since the Second World War, the imminent war in Iraq looming on its southern front, a fierce test of wills with the EU over Ankara's European ambitions in prospect, and every possibility of a clash with Turkey's generals and secular establishment, suspicious of the AKP's neo-Islamist colours and its leader's past.

A popular mayor of Istanbul in the 1990s, Erdogan was jailed in 1999 on a spurious charge of 'religious incitement', after reciting a nearly century-old poem by a nationalist writer – reputedly a favourite of Turkey's founding father, arch-secularizer Kemal Ataturk – that described the city's majestic minarets as 'our bayonets'. The incident came after a coalition led by the Islamist Welfare party, with which Erdogan was at the time affiliated, was forced out of office after 11 months by Turkey's powerful military, without a murmur of dissent from its NATO allies. That conviction meant Erdogan could not stand in the 2002 election, but the size of the AKP landslide, the depth of Turkey's crisis, and the fact that – this time – Ankara's EU and NATO allies treated Erdogan as the leader of a democratic government, forced the establishment eventually, and ungraciously, to give way.

Erdogan's success in consolidating a solid economic recovery, delivering political reform and stability, and foreign policy success greatly strengthened his position. In particular, in the interests of getting closer to the EU, he engineered a reversal of three decades of policy towards Cyprus – the Mediterranean island partitioned between Greek and Turkish Cypriots – and acceptance of a UN unification plan that, in the event, the Greek Cypriots rejected in a referendum. In December 2004, that helped win Turkey a date to start EU accession talks in October 2005, after more than four decades in Europe's ante-room – a genuine moment of history for Europe and Turkey. The AKP survived a big early hiccup when, on the eve of the Iraq war, the parliament it dominated voted against allowing the USA to use Turkish soil to open a northern front in its invasion of Iraq. Washington's reaction (as we saw in Chapter IV) was to lean on the generals to lean on the politicians, and it withdrew an offer of a $24 billion aid package to help dig Turkey out of its financial crisis. Even that redounded in the new government's favour. As an EU official put it, the vote was 'saying that the US cannot assume it can pick up the telephone, talk to the military, haggle over the financial prize and sign the cheque. Things have changed and that is Erdogan's challenge.'

By 2007, however, as EU negotiations stalled and Turkish reform ran out of steam, it became clear the clash with Turkey's overmighty generals had only been postponed. The crisis erupted in April after the army issued an elliptical ultimatum – on its website – against the presidential candidacy of Abdullah Gul, Erdogan's urbane foreign minister, saying in effect that Turkey's secular heritage could not be entrusted to a man who had entered politics as an Islamist and whose wife (like the prime minister's) wears the Muslim head-scarf. As this constitutional crisis raged and the urban secular middle classes held vast demonstrations in defence of a lifestyle they felt was under threat, Erdogan called early elections. The AKP was returned with a hugely increased share of the vote: 47 per cent on an 84 per cent turnout, up from its 34 per cent tally in 2002. Turks stood four-square with democracy as the generals tripped over their clumsy digital démarche. It looked like a moment in the country's history akin to Spain's experience after Franco, when Spaniards elected the Socialists in a 1982 landslide after a failed army coup in 1981.

Before the AKP emerged in late 2001, the army had ousted four govern-ments – and closed four Islamist parties – in four decades. This resounding vote showed Turkey had changed and that it had done so, to the horror of its cosmopolitan and secular elites, under a neo-Islamist banner. Precisely how that happened is important, and not just to Turkey.

Three reasons for the AKP's success appear to stand out. First, it helps to be competent and to have a national project. When Erdogan's party first won office in 2002, the nationalist right was a howling irrelevance, the left a museum-piece, and the liberal and social democratic centre had fragmented into shrinking personality cults for giant egos, cut off from the conservative heartland of Anatolia and, indeed, the lives of ordinary Turks they had done so little to improve. The AKP, by contrast, was a considered and democratic project. Recycled from the wreckage of two banned Islamist parties, liberally seasoned with mainstream conservatives and Turkey's new business class, Mr Erdogan and his friends did their homework while they were putting the party together. They interviewed 41,000 people across the country, learning that ties to Europe and an economy in its worst recession since 1945 overwhelmingly dominated Turkish concerns; headline issues such as headscarves came a distant ninth.

The AKP has since provided good governance, with high economic growth and stability, rocketing inward investment, 2.5 million new jobs and near doubled per capita income, while raising spending on education and infra-structure. It has also, as part of Turkey's attempt to meet the criteria, presided over a constitutional revolution: abolishing the death penalty and criminaliz-ing torture, introducing democratic freedoms of expression and association, and minority rights for the Kurds, with whom Ankara had been locked in a 20-year insurgency. Above all, these reforms subordinated the army to civilian authority, without which Turkish EU membership would be a non-starter. This was possible as long as the army saw in the EU project the fulfilment of the European vocation Ataturk foresaw for Turkey, and the AKP saw in the democratic club rules of Europe a shield against the generals. EU accession provided not just a mighty engine of reform, but the glue of political cohesion.

A second reason for the AKP's success is its astute reading of the social transformation of the country. The party is now the chosen path to modernity of the socially conservative, religiously observant but at the same time dynamic and entrepreneurial middle classes of central Anatolia, who now demand their rightful share in power, hitherto monopolized by a self-perpetuating secular elite. The AKP's appeal, in other words, is aspirational, about giving people the chance to build fulfilling lives; but reassuring, by holding fast to the moorings of family, religion and the villages from which many Turks are just a generation away. In Islamist terms, this is a traditionalist world-view that looks forward, rather than a radical outlook that harks backwards in a violent lament for past glory. It is, above all, democratic.

The AKP's symbol is a light-bulb with seven beams to signify the seven regions of Turkey. It is a modern and traditional symbol, emblematic of an enlightenment after darkness – a recurring theme in orthodox Muslim as well as Islamist literature, which speaks of a *Jahiliyya*, or dark age of ignorance, preceding the revelation of the Quran. 'This is something the people of Anatolia can understand', says Erdogan. He bridles at being described as an Islamist. 'We do not accept being characterized as an Islamist party', he says. 'That carries with it too many misperceptions and anti-democratic associations. If you call yourself an Islamist, it suggests you are trying to impose some sort of Jacobin and intolerant uniformity. We, furthermore, believe religion is a personal issue.' He added: 'just as no race is better than any other, so no one religion is superior to any other'.[14]

Many Turkish secularists know full well this is not, as some of them claim, theocracy by stealth. Certainly, like its secularist predecessors, the AKP has proved adept at packing the civil service and public offices with its followers. This is about spoils not *shari'a*, an attitude, unfortunately common to all Turkish parties: 'we won, it's our turn'. But there is an unmistakeable whiff of class animus in the resistance of the urban elites to the shift in the balance of power to Turks from the provinces and the countryside – captured in sneers about 'black Turks' who only talk about family and football. There are, too, fears about the survival of the secular lifestyle, stoked by, for example, local mayors who ban alcohol consumption. These are genuine fears and they have to be addressed. But they do not add up to theocracy by the back door. The outlook of some secularists is ossified. Too many of them have a lazy sense of entitlement to power and influence; unable to win elections any more, they resort to inciting the army and the courts. Others are shrine-keepers to Mustafa Kemal Ataturk who, like many who built republican Turkey from the remains of the Ottoman Empire, was a refugee, regrouping behind what became an essentially defensive political (and military) culture.

The AKP's third ace – and Turkey's – has been Europe. EU membership, though negotiations are now in the doldrums, is still a popular and unifying idea in Turkey. Just about. As mentioned earlier, the Kemalists and the neo-Islamists cohered behind the European project and the reforms needed to make it possible. That was until reluctant EU partners such as France, Germany and Austria started raising the bar for Turkish entry. But despite the maladroitness of its politicians, and the thinly disguised racism of some of them, Europe's soft power is still seductive enough to arrange a marriage between Islam and democracy, bound by EU vows. Put another way, the modern interaction between Europe and Turkey is creating the Muslim world's first, as it were, Christian Democrats. Like Christian Democrats in government across Europe (and parts of Latin America), these Muslim Democrats differ from the mainstream centre-right – over moral issues or social justice, for example – but they should be easy to recognize. When I first put it to Erdogan, in October 2002, that this was the essence of his project, a fully democratic republic with a Muslim identity, led by Muslim Democrats, he said: 'we have a conservative outlook and many similarities [with the Christian Democrats] including our similar attitudes to family issues and to traditional values and ethics'. Unable to resist a sideswipe, however – undoubtedly aimed at German Christian Democrat leaders then thundering about Turkey not being a European country – he added: 'I dislike their xenophobia – we are more universal.'[15]

But some of the hiccups and upsets in the EU negotiations are the result of unresolved internal tensions. The failure to amend adequately or – better still – repeal Article 301 of the penal code, making it a crime to insult Turkishness, used by the xenophobe nationalist lobby to hound writers and journalists, is one example. Another is its failure to confront the dying Ottoman Turkey's role in the mass murders of the Armenians from 1915 onwards, to establish once and for all whether this was a centrally directed, attempted genocide. Turkey will never enter the EU until it settles this account with history. The continual skirmishing between the secular establishment and the new AKP political elite will also have to be resolved. The judiciary pulled back from banning the AKP – and Erdogan and Gul and 70 of the party leaders – in the summer of 2008, imposing a fine instead after the public prosecutor accused the government of trying to institute *Shari'a* law in Turkey. That concluded a battle, however, resulting in a draw, rather than resolved the war.

The prize of success, for Turkey, the West and the surrounding region, remains huge: the creation of the Muslim world's first Christian Democrats, a so much better bet than the autocrats of the Middle East who, even when ostensibly enlightened like the Shah of Iran and his White Revolution, create social dislocation and breed extremism. There is something, too, in Erdogan's claim to be more 'universal' than the Christian Democrats. Encouraged by the AKP government, Turkey's religious establishment was in 2008 close to completing a modern reinterpretation of Islam. Theologians at Ankara University, backed by the *Diyanet*, the state authority for religious affairs, were re-examining the *Hadith*, the sayings and deeds attributed to the Prophet Mohammed. These were not codified until two centuries after the Prophet's death in 632. While the Quran is held by Muslims to be the revealed word of God to the Prophet, the orally transmitted *Hadith* are the origin of the majority of *Shari'a* law. Modern scholars believe that embedded in many *Hadith* are cultural traditions and mechanisms of social control – especially of women – alien to the original message of Islam. The 'Ankara school' aims to use contextual techniques to strip away the accretions and apocrypha, to arrive at a truly modernized Islam.

Turkey, obviously, cannot do this alone. Wahhabi fundamentalists in Saudi Arabia and Muslim conservatives in Egypt will, furthermore, paint post-Ottoman (and post-Caliphate) Turkey as warped by secularism and confined to the periphery of Islam. But Islam too is undergoing a form of globalization. And Turkey's success in coming up with modern and identifiably Muslim politics might just give its religious modernism an edge. Because the whole point about Turkey and the AKP is not to sell it as a model but to make it a success – because success does sell.

That is why the AKP's electoral victory against the generals in 2007 and score-draw against the attempted coup by the judiciary in 2008 are such milestones. Europe should respond energetically to this, and stop behaving as though the Turks were still menacing the gates of Vienna.

The assertion, especially in France, that Turkey shares none of Europe's heritage is not only politically obtuse but ahistorical: unless there was no Byzantium, no eastern Roman empire, no classics of Greek science and philosophy (as well as Arab mathematics and medicine) that, transmitted through the world of Islam, dragged Europe out of the Dark Ages. This is a country embedded in the history of Europe and Christendom as well as Islam, a precious commodity it would be criminal to squander.

* * * * *

The USA and the West have squandered opportunities, in these three different experiences and in the Arab world whose dilemmas they help illuminate. The Turkish experience, in particular, dramatizes the imperative need to weld Islam and democracy successfully together.

It is not the job of the West to 'redeem' the Arab and Muslim worlds, much less at the point of a tank barrel. Our job is to keep faith with our values and beliefs and to put in place a policy framework with an unerring bias towards freedom. It is their job to make of that what they will, without being hobbled by what hitherto has been our almost uniform preference for dealing with tyrants and strongmen.

As I hope I have made clear, this is not a short cut to stability. There are big risks, the process will be messy and marked by upheaval for what may be uncomfortably prolonged periods. But those risks, we must be clear, have to be balanced against the already manifested risk of the wholesale alienation of the Arabs and Muslims, of nearly one fifth of humanity, which sees in the policies of the USA and its allies a war against Islam intended to hold them back and deny them their freedom. That is the reality and it is pointless to start from any other place. We have to find a way of navigating through these risks if the Arabs are ever to be able to feel they are reclaiming their destiny.

As I argued in Chapter I, of course the Arab countries need better economic management and more transparent governance. Of course they desperately need modern infrastructure. Of course they need more investment in job-creating activities. And of course they need an overhaul of education and training to emphasize critical, independent thinking and problem-solving skills. But as I said in Chapter II, the idea that getting the economics right will cause everything else to fall into place is crudely determinist, when not downright evasive.

Western policy should not be about regime change or, for that matter, about supporting this individual leader or that particular movement or party. Such intrusion is resented and counterproductive; we cannot overtly take sides when we are perceived as so toxic. As I remarked in the Preface, we need to develop institutional links with these countries. Our ideas and values, moreover, are still attractive, though repudiated by many because we act as though they do not apply to them.

In the full knowledge that more open political systems across the broader Middle East will, at least in the short term, open the way to Islamicized politics and Islamist parties, western policy needs nevertheless to demonstrate its faith in democracy and its underpinnings. It needs to demonstrate by its actions its commitment to the rule of law. It needs to channel its resources in ways that promote and extend education and the empowerment of women, rather than the power of military and security elites. In a path-breaking UNDP report on Arab human development in 2002, its predominantly Arab authors cite failures in these areas as the main factors behind underdevelopment of the Arab world. Will our pursuit of these aims not, too, be regarded as intrusion? Not if the USA and its allies recover legitimacy and respect through the other policies they must pursue in the region: above all in Israel–Palestine, in Iraq, in Iran – and in the increasingly damaging war in Afghanistan.

The US-led NATO mission in Afghanistan is not winning against the Taliban. This graveyard of empires is once again in danger of failing as a state and being overrun by insurgents, this time sustained by almost limitless funds from opium production. The counter-insurgency effort is looking bad, and not just because insufficient troops have never managed to force more than tactical retreat on the Taliban and its jihadi allies, which in 2007–8 began spreading the war into Pakistan, and even beyond, to India. The US and NATO's reliance on air power was killing too many civilians; even if they hit the right targets, such wars are won through the patient accumulation of popular support, not by stacking up corpses. The West needs a re-focused strategy, built around security and jobs, and a democratic alliance between Kabul and the new, democratically elected Pakistani government, to win that support. Together they needed to break the cycle of lawlessness and corruption rotting any advance in nation-building.

It may be the shocking case that the might of the West is unable to beat the Taliban militarily. But it should be able to hold and expand secure territory while it helps create a state: building up local administrative and security capacity and spreading the rule of law. For that to put down roots and have the attractive capacity to outflank the Taliban needed accelerated development: not just schools and clinics but power and irrigation; roads and markets for farmers to sell legitimate produce, made increasingly more valuable relative to poppy production by the commodities boom. Any chance of success needs the creation of jobs, not just through infrastructure spending, but through, for instance, developing the country's mineral resources. It may not sound as exciting as the Global War on Terror, but secure lives and livelihoods are the only way forward.

In Chapter VII, I argued that the outline of a solution to the conflict between Israel and the Palestinians has long been clear. It simply has not been tried and, because of Israel's expansion in the West Bank, the opportunity to do so is receding. The tentative revival of talks at Annapolis in 2007 between

Mahmoud Abbas, the fatally weakened Palestinian president, and an Israeli government crippled by the fraud allegations against its now defenestrated prime minister Ehud Olmert, failed to produce advances on any issue of substance; all that advanced was Israeli colonization and Arab alienation and anger.

Partly that was because of Israeli, US and western attempts to isolate Hamas, the victor in the 2006 Palestinian elections, unless it accepted three preconditions: to recognize Israel, forswear violence, and accept the validity of all previous agreements between Israel and the PLO and Palestinian Authority. Undoubtedly Hamas, as a terrorist organization as well as a political and social movement, presents a real problem. But boycotting Hamas while promoting the democratic process through which it emerged triumphant has been self-defeating. It failed to exploit the Islamists' desire for legitimacy and recognition. It exposed the West, rightly, to the charge of hypocrisy. It was the political equivalent of holding one's nose. The three tests did nothing to dispel that impression.

First, there is no legal or moral reason why Hamas – or anyone else – should recognize a state that refuses to define its boundaries, which are being expanded daily on Palestinian land. What Hamas must eventually recognize is an Israel, and its right to exist in peace, behind the borders that will be defined at the *conclusion* of negotiations to end the conflict, and, indeed, the organization has agreed in principle to abide by the results of a referendum on such an outcome. If a Palestinian state were to be established on virtually all the land Israel captured in the 1967 war, there is little doubt it would command the support of a big majority of Palestinians. Hamas would have to accept that or go out of business.

Second, Hamas can rightly point out that the right to resist foreign occupation is enshrined in the UN charter. Fine. But it is also a cornerstone of international law that combatants should not target civilians – and Hamas has an atrocious record of targeting Israeli civilians. That is what it must undertake to stop if it wants any sort of seat at the table. Politically, Hamas and all Palestinian rejectionists should also reflect on where violence has taken their people: into the prison of Gaza and the Bantustans of the West Bank. It is true that it did take violent resistance to upgrade the Palestinians from refugees to political actors; we may regret that but it is a fact. But it no longer holds true, despite the frustration and anger at the failure of Oslo that devolved into the second intifada. That uprising has failed. Militant Palestinians have allowed themselves to be seduced by the example of Hizbollah, which evicted Israel from Lebanon. But Israelis had no emotional, religious or ideological claim on Lebanon, and Hizbollah, for the most part, fought their soldiers, not their civilians. The only way forward for the Palestinians is not force – at which Israel will always better them – but the moral force of their argument and their undeniable rights. Civic resistance and diplomatic war are the arms that might deliver these rights.

Third, the recognition of past agreements is useful, but moot. As part of the 2007 Mecca agreement on a (short-lived) national unity government with Fatah, Hamas did in fact recognize all the 1993–8 Oslo agreements and endorse the 2002 Arab League peace offer spurned by Israel. But Israeli governments have trampled over so many of their Oslo undertakings that it is hard to know any longer what they mean. Much more useful would be to retrieve the essence of past agreements and incorporate them into a new framework of negotiation that targets the final destination of a definitive agreement. That, as I have argued, can only be an independent Palestinian state on nearly all the West Bank and Gaza, with east Jerusalem as its capital. No more road maps, no more confidence building, and no more interim agreements: there is only one deal to be done and the chance of doing it is fast ebbing away.

That must be the goal of a US and western policy that throws its weight unequivocally behind bringing it about. That will not happen if the West continues to treat Israel and the Palestinians as equal parties, and allows Israel what in effect is a veto on any viable path to Palestinian emancipation. Israel has to be told that it can no longer hold hostage what has long since ceased to be a regional conflict at the expense of international stability, not to mention its own security. Yes, that will mean the USA and its allies using all the leverage at their disposal, their largely unused arsenal of diplomatic and commercial power, their economic and military aid, to nudge Israel towards compromise. It is often said that would be counterproductive. That hypothesis has not often been tested and, on the rare occasions it has been, has had interesting outcomes. We do not have to go back all the way to Eisenhower and Suez.

In 1982, after then secretary of state Alexander Haig gave at least an amber light to Israel's invasion of Lebanon, President Ronald Reagan made it eventually stop the siege and aerial bombardment of West Beirut. In 1991, after the first war against Iraq and in the lead-up to the Madrid conference, the first Bush administration withheld billions of dollars worth of housing loan guarantees aimed at helping the assimilation of Jews from the former Soviet Union into Israel, unless the government of Yitzhak Shamir stopped expanding settlement activity. There was a fierce political storm, in the USA and Israel. The loan guarantees were eventually restored. But we should not forget that Shamir was voted out of office by Israelis in favour of Yitzhak Rabin, the patron of Oslo. Israeli voters were not prepared to risk jeopardizing their all-important alliance with the USA.

The behaviour of some of the pro-Israel maximalists purportedly defending that alliance inside the USA has also been suggestive. In the spring of 2006, there was an extraordinary backlash against a critical study of the way the Israel lobby shapes US foreign policy in Washington by two prominent American academics, Stephen Walt, from Harvard's John F. Kennedy School of Government, and John Mearsheimer, from the University of Chicago. Only a UK publication, the *London Review of Books*, was prepared to carry their argument – later turned into a book – that extraordinarily effective lobbying had created a consensus that American and Israeli interests are inseparable and identical.

The most strident cheerleaders of the pro-Israel lobby liberally used moral blackmail – working on the fear that any criticism of Israeli policy and US support for it amounted to anti-semitism – to shut down the debate, target other dissenters on American university campuses, and carry out character assassination campaigns against figures such as Robert Malley, a former adviser to Bill Clinton on the region (see Chapter VII). At one level, this was a self-inflicted wound no society built on freedom should be anything but ashamed of. Honest and informed debate is not only the foundation of freedom and progress, but the precondition of sound policy; important sections of the US establishment, in no way representative of mainstream American Jewish opinion or the vigorous debate inside Israel, attempted to force dissent offshore or reduce it to the status of *samizdat*. But this extraordinary deployment of heavy artillery looked to me, at least, like a sign of fear – fear of being unable to continue dictating the terms of democratic debate.

As I have already argued, Israelis tend often to be more pragmatic than Americans and Europeans, subsumed as they are in their hypocrisy and guilt, and keep open a far broader debate about realistic policy options. They would, wouldn't they? It is, after all, their future at stake, not ours.

Israeli officials have discreetly facilitated, for example, the diplomacy that Marwan Barghouti has carried out from his jail cell, which has helped negotiate two ceasefires: the 2007 Mecca agreement mentioned above, and the Prisoners' Document of that year which amounts in effect to a united front in favour of a two-states solution based on the 1967 borders – with all the emotional weight that prisoners hold in Palestinian society. Barghouti, as we saw in the last chapter, has a complex and difficult history for the Israelis. He may not be the Nelson Mandela his admirers claim, but Israeli officials know that it is with leaders like him – capable of delivering not just the rank-and-file of Fatah but Islamist factions like Hamas too – that they will have to deal if they ever want to resolve this conflict. Western policy can only operate on the basis that they do, indeed, want to end it once and for all. It is still the case that a majority of Israelis and Palestinians look to the USA – and to a lesser but not negligible extent its European allies – to lead them out of the morass.

Iraq does not have an obvious blueprint to resolve its catastrophic state of prostration. Despite the undeniable success of the 'surge' in reducing apocalyptic levels of violence, that is all, as we saw in Chapter IV, fragile and reversible. The political reconciliation the surge was meant to create the space to accomplish has not taken place. New fronts, such as between Arabs and Kurds in dispute over the future of Kirkuk and its oil-rich surroundings, or between the American-backed Sunni militias of the Sons of Iraq and the Shia-dominated Baghdad government that by the autumn of 2008 was provocatively reining them in, could erupt at any moment. The assertiveness of the government of Nouri al-Maliki in 2008 looked less like new-found confidence, more a politically expedient response to the demands of the Sadrists, of Ayatollah Sistani, and of Iran. The relative pacification of Baghdad, moreover, was overstated. France won the Battle of Algiers in 1954–62, but it lost Algeria. Apart from lacking a new Sunni–Shia entente, moreover, Iraq was missing almost its entire middle and professional classes, dispersed among the 5 million scattered abroad and across the country by war, insurgency and ethnosectarian cleansing. It was being policed, essentially, by rebadged militia. It was still hard to see how this broken country could put itself back together again.

At worst, Iraq could become a shell state divided into mini-emirates, like post-Soviet Afghanistan, prey to warlords and militias, and the seedbed of rival Taliban: on the Sunni side, a lethal hybrid of Islamism and irreducible nationalism that has not faded with the partial retreat of al-Qaeda's allies; on the Shia side, a fusion of Shia puritanism with tribal tradition. That would create two spectres that could haunt the Islamic world and its relations with the West for generations. Alternatively, one side – the majority Shia – could resolve their leadership struggle and impose their writ on the country. Or – the least bad outcome – Iraq could emerge exhausted into a loose confederation, with a weak central government with agreed tasks such as the allocation of oil revenue.

By the end of 2008, Baghdad and Washington had managed to agree a new Status of Forces Agreement to regulate a continuing US military presence and – just as important – point the way to a structured and orderly withdrawal. US troops were to withdraw from all urban areas by the end of June 2009, and from Iraq as a whole by no later than the end of 2011 – and at *any time* before that if demanded by either side. Under Article 27, moreover, the USA was not allowed to use Iraq as a launch pad for attacks on other countries.

An orderly withdrawal required the USA to stay long enough to avert a new bloodbath, but leave soon enough to make Iraq's high wire faction leaders – their safety net removed – reach some sort of modus vivendi.

That outcome would be eased by some sort of rapprochement between Shia Iran and Sunni Saudi Arabia (which is possible), and if Washington buried the past and sought a diplomatic grand bargain with Tehran (which might, conceivably, be made possible under President Obama). The starting point would be to recognize that solving not just Iraq, but many of the conflicts of the Middle East, now requires Iranian cooperation.

I would note here, in passing, one interesting straw in the wind at the time of the Iraqi Status of Forces Agreement. While I have argued that it will be almost impossible to establish stability in Iraq without Iran, recent, prima facie evidence of this was by no means unhopeful. The Iraqi cabinet that rejected the SOFA in October 2008, unanimously, agreed to essentially the same document in November. There was, of course, still significant opposition, especially among the followers of Moqtada al-Sadr. But it would appear that Abdel-Aziz al-Hakim, leader of the Islamic Supreme Council of Iraq, Iran's closest and most powerful Iraqi ally, telephoned his instructions to change the vote on the SOFA from Tehran. What had really changed between those two Iraqi votes, of course, was the Americans' vote for Barack Obama.

A grand bargain between the USA and its allies and Iran is essential to the future stability of the Middle East. The threat of the current regime in Tehran's nuclear ambitions has to be woven into that. As I detailed above, the USA has missed one opportunity and spurned another to close any such deal, the outlines of which are clear: security and status for an Iran that ceases to be a threat to its neighbours (including a nuclear threat) and has a stake in their stability and common prosperity. Analogous to the Bush administration's mishandling of North Korea, which now has a nuclear bomb, Iran is now close to theoretical nuclear weapons capability. There is still a chance to stop it at that theoretical level, and deflect Iran towards détente and shared stability. We can achieve that. There may, indeed, be a brief window before the 2009 presidential elections in Iran – an opportunity maybe even to influence their outcome, especially if Mohammad Khatami bows to the clamour of the reformists and runs against Ahmadinejad. Before then, however, the USA will have to use its power to prevent Israel from unilaterally attacking Iran – an adventure that would undoubtedly end by sucking in America and its allies. Equally, a serious policy would cease chasing the chimera of trying to hive off Syria from its tactical alliance with Iran. Yes, there might be some short-term benefits from this – at the price of rehabilitating a narrowly based despotism that tramples on the rights of its people, remains lethally entrenched in Lebanon, and has no coherent view of Syria's national interest. The western (at this stage primarily European) embrace of Syria is a betrayal of the human and democratic rights of Syrians and Lebanese. But it is also a way of evading the main policy task: getting a workable arrangement with Iran.

I have insisted throughout this book, above all, on the need for the West to uphold its values and demonstrate its belief in democracy in all its dealings with the broader Middle East, to secure the inestimable prize of the eminently achievable marriage between Islam and the freedom that an overwhelming majority of Muslims yearn for – but are frequently denied because of our malign intrusion in the affairs of their countries.

It may seem, to some readers, paradoxical therefore that I also insist on constructive and conditional engagement with political Islam. I have outlined the terms of engagement with Islamists: including the suggestive if inconclusive terms worked out within the region through Jordan's National Charter of 1989 (Chapter II), the Iraqi constitution (Chapter IV) or the terms of debate of the Khatami administration in Iran mentioned above. I do not propose that we offer privileged engagement to Islamists – in a way that deprives their fellow citizens of alternatives and drives them into their arms, and fosters the kind of identity politics so expertly promoted by western policy to date – merely that we recognize that they are there, they are a big and growing part of the political equation, and that we now have to work to ensure they are part of the political solution. In a place like Saudi Arabia, as I said in Chapter V, they may even be the main part of the solution. If we ignore this it is because we are ignorant.

And, just as we have betrayed Arab and Muslim liberals, we will end up losing Islamist reformers, and open the gates to the jihadi element that, as I have argued, still has every chance of entering the mainstream so long as western policy continues on its destructive path.

Until now, we have deployed a lethal mix of implacable but misaimed military might and politically ingenuous sleepwalking that has overturned the balance of power in the region, and at the same time shown its mistrust of the weapons of democracy to transform it. There is no reason for anyone to take our values seriously unless we do. Everyone knows that Arab tyrants use Palestine demagogically as a shield and an alibi. But what, exactly, are we doing? We support tyrants and decline to resolve the Palestinian question on the basis of justice and law, to destroy that shield and remove the alibi in a transformative way. The policy of the Bush administration, in particular, has essentially been to tell anyone it dislikes in the region: 'You surrender, then we'll talk'. But what we have, in fact, done is disarmed ourselves and armed our enemies.

One of the greatest mistakes we have made, through our deceitful collusion in tyranny and dispossession, and the self-regarding exculpation and evasions of the 'they hate us for our freedoms' industry, is to have forced an entire civilization into the politics of a wounded identity.

Identity, admittedly, is an aspiration common to us all. But why then have we not insisted on those aspects of western identity that are common to us all, which are universal but not uniform, and which number foremost among them freedom, and the countless ways in which it was achieved, through periods of darkness and tyranny that eclipse anything that has befallen the modern Arab and Islamic worlds? Can it be that we so mistrust our own values and the institutions and collective methods that embody them that we so fatally condescend to others?

Amin Maalouf, the historical novelist, an Arab Christian from Lebanon who writes in French, wrote an important essay at the end of the 1990s – after the intercommunal bloodletting in Lebanon and the Balkans, and the Rwandan genocide – arguing that people tend to see themselves in terms of whichever of their multiple allegiances is most under stress or attack: language, nation, colour, class, religion. Religion, no less than the others, could not be used by those struggling with the memory of past sufferings or faded glory to carry out 'collective crimes of passion, regrettable but comprehensible'. There was no excuse, he argued. Religions shape the people who adhere to them, but those peoples also shape their religion. The relationship is dialectical. The 'Christian' West won through to modernity in the teeth of clerical reaction. 'Christianity today is what European societies have made of it', Maalouf says in a marvellous phrase, 'through countless little touches of the chisel'.[16]

Islam, as I argued earlier in this book, was for centuries a triumphant civilization, sure of itself and therefore open and tolerant. When it ceased to be dynamic and innovative it started to slide towards the politics of wounded identity. But, as I have also insisted, in the collision with a confident and expansionist Europe, above all from the late eighteenth century, it was not the spontaneous choice of the Arabs and Muslims to retreat into Islam. It was only when balance of power politics and subsequent western support for tyranny in the interests of stability and cheap oil thwarted nationalist (and sometimes liberal) attempts at modernization that Islamic revivalism acquired legs, and devolved into Islamism. That has become an identity and a political currency and we, no less than the Arabs and Muslims, have to deal with it. From the West's point of view, our point of entry can only be the stress on shared values: all the great religions have values in common, the problem is to translate them into policy.

The policy changes we need to make include pursuing relentlessly a just solution to Israel–Palestine, the embrace of Iran in a workable bargain that helps free Iranians from the faux-nationalist blackmail of the mullahs, and above all the decision to cease supporting despots and start supporting education, modernization, institution-building and everything in the region that opens a path towards democracy. To use Maalouf's metaphor, we need to put down the hammer and start patiently to chisel.

* * * * *

There are choices to be made. The realpolitik school of policy makers will point out cogently the reasons for their choices.

Israel is a democracy and a strategic ally. It is, above all, a sanctuary for the Jews after the horror we visited upon them in the last century. We have to stand by it and them – and by their choices, whether or not we entirely agree with them or think these choices contribute to strengthening Israel's security. Furthermore, the reality of American (and German) politics is that we cannot change this: there is no alternative.

Egypt's despotic regime guarantees us, at a relatively modest price, transit through the Suez Canal, a vital lifeline for our trade flows as well as our ability to deploy our forces quickly. It holds the ring in the most populous Arab country, even though this will not always look decorous, much less Jeffersonian. Furthermore, look at the alternative: another blur of men in turbans.

Saudi Arabia holds one quarter of the world's proven oil reserves, and is key to the control of the Gulf, which, as a whole, contains about two thirds of the world's oil reserves. Coddling the House of Saud and colluding in its corruption, ignoring its mediaeval absolutism, and even turning a blind eye to the export of its religious extremism (and extremists), is a small price to pay for this great prize. Furthermore, look at the alternative: Osama and his friends.

Fine. But choices have consequences, especially if the choosers overestimate their assets and flatter their bottom line – leaving out the already huge and growing liability of those who feel robbed of their heritage and their freedom.

If these are the choices, then do not howl in incredulous outrage when forces incubated by them – however alien and evil – fly airliners into your buildings, bomb your resorts and hotels, your train systems and your embassies, your churches and your synagogues. Above all, do not when this happens keep insisting that 'they hate us for our freedoms' or that 'the world has changed'. It has not, precisely because you have chosen not to change it.

Do not complain that most of your foreign aid budget, your overstretched military capacity and your diplomatic ingenuity and dwindling political capital is tied up in serial firefighting in a region that, somehow and inexplicably, 'doesn't get it'. They get it all right. They get your choice to continue unconditionally supporting Israel's creeping colonization of Arab land, which forecloses on any viable Palestinian state and rings Israel with a seething diaspora of dispossessed Palestinians, and they have every reason to understand your default position of propping up every dictatorship in the region; they bear the scars on their backs. So no more hand wringing, please, about chronic instability, insurrection and terrorism, backwardness and stagnation. You have connived in the 'Arab exception' for short-term advantage. No Arab, not even the dwindling band of friends whom you have betrayed, who regard you as the custodian of a universal heritage of freedom, will ever see this as other than an assault on Islam as well as freedom – their freedom.

Above all, do not complain when wars of choice (Iraq, 2003 and counting; Lebanon, 2006; Iran?) result in the humbling of your military might. Even the most crackpot strategists should know you cannot take even the best football team in the world to play a basketball game. If you disdain knowledge of your enemy, if you wilfully misidentify the nature of your strategic threats, if you think conventional warfare can defeat irregular warriors, if you think air power can defeat your enemies on the ground rather than multiply them, you are going to get thrashed, however spectacular the damage you can do (which will in any case rebound against you). You will get nowhere, moreover, so long as you continue to make simple category errors: the Global War on Terror (GWOT) comes to mind. The Romans did not do particularly well against the Parthians (who ruled most of Mesopotamia and Persia) for about a century and a half after the legions of the triumvir Marcus Licinius Crassus were destroyed near the Euphrates in 53 BCE (driving a final nail into the coffin of the Roman Republic). But no historian records that they thereafter declared a Global War on the Parthian Shot (GWOPS).

I have made clear throughout this book that it is, in the first place, for the Arabs (and Iranians, Turks, Pakistanis and so on) to start making their own choices. But no one can pretend these will not be influenced by our choices. That is a monstrous evasion far exceeding the reach of the meaning of hypocrisy. I do not claim our choices are easy (nor are theirs); much less that there are any quick fixes, or assured outcomes. Quite the contrary. I have insisted that whatever happens, whatever we do or do not do, the road ahead is treacherous. Of course it is.

This is, after all, our last chance. If it is to become a lost chance, that is our choice too.

Notes

Chapter I: The Arab Political Jungle

1   Interview with US official, Washington, 11 September 2005
2   See 'CIA holds terror suspects in secret prisons', by Dana Priest, *Washington Post*, 2 November 2005
3   I quote from a comment Cordesman posted on *The Washington Note*, 18 March 2006

Chapter II: The Despot in his Labyrinth

1   See 'The Chameleon King', by Roger Matthews and David Gardner, *Financial Times*, 8 February 1999. I personally witnessed some of the jostle of the impending succession at a royal banquet presided over by Crown Prince Hassan in the Diwan, 30 August 1998
2   *Lion of Jordan: The Life of King Hussein in War and Peace*, by Avi Shlaim (Allen Lane, 2007), p. 98
3   *The Modern History of Jordan*, by Kamal Salibi (I.B.Tauris, 1993), pp. 197–9
4   *The Jordanian National Charter* (*al-Mithaq al-Watani al-Urduni*), December 1990. See 'Can Islamists be Democrats? The Case of Jordan', by Glenn E. Robinson, *The Middle East Journal*, Volume 51, Number 3, summer 1997. In private conversation on 14 October 1995, King Hussein told me he had intended to appoint an Islamist prime minister. Marwan Qassim, then head of the royal court and also present, implied that this would have been 'a bad idea' and that His Majesty did not really mean it. Hussein returned to the theme in a formal interview with me two days later, on 16 October 1995, making large claims. 'One of the greatest

weaknesses of the Arab world is the absence of pluralism, democracy and human rights', he argued. Jordan's restoration of democracy since 1989, he said, was 'an example that works'. He said he had the legitimacy to see it through: 'We are Hashemites, after all'. He again said the time would come ('the time will be ripe') when an Islamist would be Jordan's prime minister, 'and they and the people will see what government is about and who can do it'. The time would never be ripe. See 'Court of the chameleon', by David Gardner and Julian Ozanne, *Financial Times*, 17 October 1995

5   Fouad Ajami's *The Arab Predicament* (Cambridge University Press, 1981), which retrieves the most important post-1967 Arab writing on the debacle, notably Sadek al-Azm's *Self-criticism after the Defeat,* and his *The Dream Palace of the Arabs* (Pantheon, 1998), remain good guides to this 'moment' – irrespective of Ajami's subsequent enthusiasm for invading Iraq

6   This figure is based on interviews with two Egyptian ministers in March and April 1996; a senior Egyptian interior ministry officer, April 1996; an interview with Mustafa Mashhour, Supreme Spiritual Guide of the Muslim Brotherhood (Cairo, 7 April 1996); conversations with Egyptian NGOs; and my own research. Mashhour expressed every confidence the Brotherhood's patient strategy for a creeping theocracy would triumph: 'They have the police and the army, and on the surface they look like the winners. But we have been able to change society. In time, we'll be the winners'

7   Bahraini minister, March 1996. See 'Democracy out of reach', by David Gardner, *Financial Times*, 12 April 1996

8   Interview with Mahmoud Zahhar, Hamas leader, Gaza, 3 February 1995; see *Hamas: Unwritten Chapters*, by Azzam Tamimi (Hurst, 2007); and *Inside Hamas*, by Zaki Chehab (I.B.Tauris, 2007)

9   French and Syrian sources told me of the (Syrian branch of the) Brotherhood's influence, including on a brother of Osama bin Laden who used family company trucks to help the assailants enter the mosque. It was, of course, plans of the layout of the holy compound furnished by bin Laden Construction that eventually enabled French and Saudi forces to flush out the Mahdists and end the siege. See 'A Modern Assassin; Osama bin Laden', by David Gardner, *Financial Times*, 22 August 1998

10   Steve Coll's *Ghost Wars* (Penguin Press, 2004) is a monumental reconstruction of this episode

11   I am quoting a knowledgeable and, to my mind, enlightened US official who has headed three embassies in the region

12   There are exceptions. I attended in Cairo in 1998 a reception for Daniel
      Kurtzer, the Jewish US ambassador, organized by Osama al-Baz,
      Mubarak's chief foreign policy strategist, intended to put an end to a
      public murmur channelled by the media asking why Israel now had 'two
      ambassadors' in Cairo

13   It is hard to settle on any perfect illustration of this: the competition is
      fierce. But, for sheer surrealism, the Arab League summit in Beirut in the
      spring of 2002 takes some beating. On the one hand, the summit
      endorsed King Abdullah of Saudi Arabia's comprehensive peace offer to
      Israel; but not before officials acting for Lebanese president Emile
      Lahoud physically cut the loudspeaker system cables the moment PLO
      leader Yassir Arafat started to speak

14   Direct quote from leading regime reformist in April 1998. I asked him
      whether he still felt the same way four years later, and the answer was yes.
      I am bound to report, nonetheless, that he has re-entered the Egyptian
      government to have one last try

15   Declaration of interest: my wife, Samia Nakhoul, was the author of the
      Reuters Imbaba reports. Her informant confirmed to me the details of
      how they were insinuated into Mubarak's hands. For the Imbaba siege,
      I am indebted to an Egyptian officer who led the assault – and who was
      badly wounded on the second day

16   Ganzouri interview with author. See *Financial Times Survey of Egypt*,
      20 May 1996

17   Boutros Ghali interview with author, Cairo, 13 April 1997

18   Mubarak interview with author, Cairo, 7 May 1995

19   Edward Said interview with author, London, 18 June 1997. See 'A
      generation never taught to serve aces', by David Gardner, *Financial
      Times*, 9 August 1997

Chapter III: The Janus of Islamic Revivalism

1   I first heard this formulation – 'return to ourselves' – from Mahmoud
      Zahhar, the Hamas leader, in Gaza on 3 February 1995. He put jasmine
      on my hands in his cramped office in the Islamic university, as he marked
      anatomy exams and explained to me the logic of suicide bombings

2   See 'An eye for an eye for', by David Gardner, *FT Weekend*, 13–14
      October 2001, my initial analysis of the politics of bin Laden in the
      aftermath of 9/11. Osama bin Laden's and Ayman al-Zawahiri's corpus of
      pronouncements can be found in a rising pile of al-Jazeera transcripts

and on jihadi websites; in US government compilations (http://www.fas. org/irp/world/para/ubl-fbis.pdf). Among the most instructive pre-9/11 interviews were those by John Miller (*Esquire*, February 1999); Robert Fisk (*The Independent*, 6 December 1993; 10 July 1996; 22 March 1997); Scott MacLeod (*Time*, 6 May 1996); 'Abd al-Bari Atwan (*Al-Quds al-Arabi*, 23 August 1998)

3   See Steve Coll's *Ghost Wars* (Penguin Press, 2004), pp. 162–4 and 379–81

4   The Zawahiri text, 'Knights under the Prophet's Banner', was published in excerpts in the London pan-Arab daily *As Sharq al-Awsat* in December 2001, FBIS translation: http://fas.org/irp/world/para/aymanh_bk.html. See also Steve Coll's *Ghost Wars* (idem), especially pp. 382–3; Gilles Kepel, *The War for Muslim Minds* (Belknap Press, 2004), especially Chapter 3; and 'The Man behind bin Laden', by Lawrence Wright, *The New Yorker*, 16 September 2002. See also Lawrence Wright's *The Looming Tower* (Knopf, 2006)

5   See, for example, *The Muslim Jesus*, by Tarif Khalidi (Harvard University Press, 2001), which came out fortuitously on the eve of 9/11

6   See *Mohammed: a biography of the Prophet* (Harper, 1993), and *A History of God* (William Heinemann/Vintage, 1993), both by Karen Armstrong. I use the term Manichean here in its Oxford English Dictionary definition, not its historical religious sense

7   See, for example, the brilliant *God's Crucible: Islam and the making of Europe, 570–1215*, by David Levering Lewis (W.W. Norton, 2008)

8   I have taken this typically perfect phrase from the French–Lebanese writer Amin Maalouf's extraordinary essay *On Identity* (Harvill, 2000)

9   I have benefited enormously in my understanding of this from: *Arabic Thought in the Liberal Age, 1798–1939*, by the late Albert Hourani (Cambridge University Press, 1983 – although first published by the OUP in 1962); Rashid Khalidi's recent *Resurrecting Empire* (I.B.Tauris, 2004); and the Maalouf essay mentioned above

10   Hourani (ibid) pp. 114–20

11   Ibid pp. 122–4

12   *Faith and Power: the Politics of Islam*, by Edward Mortimer (Faber & Faber, 1982), pp. 237–50; on Abduh, see Hourani (ibid), pp. 139–44

13   Hourani (ibid), p. 228

14   Hourani (ibid), p. 235

15   Hourani (ibid): on Abduh, p. 149; on Rida, pp. 230–1; Mortimer, *Faith and Power* (ibid), pp. 245–6. See Chapter V on Wahhabism

16   Mortimer (ibid), pp. 250–1, describes Hassan al-Banna, founder of the Muslim Brotherhood, as 'fully in sympathy with the ideas of Afghani and

Abduh, as conveyed by Rida and al-Manar'. That 'as conveyed by' is an important modifier

17 *The Anatomy of Fascism*, by Robert O. Paxton (Allen Lane, 2004), p. 155

18 'General casts war in religious terms', by Richard T. Cooper, *Los Angeles Times*, 16 October 2003; 'The Religious Warrior of Abu Ghraib', by Sidney Blumenthal, *The Guardian*, 20 May 2004

19 See, for example, *Pew Global Attitudes Project: 17 nations survey*, 14 July 2005; See also: 'The politics of the wounded identity', by David Gardner, *Financial Times*, 29 July 2005

20 Lest I be suspected of hindsight, let me state – before the next chapter, devoted to Iraq – this was the conclusion of a column I wrote before the invasion ('War in Iraq will only hinder the war on terror', *Financial Times*, 27 January 2003). I always argued that an assault on Iraq would proliferate a new blend of Arab nationalist and Islamist extremism

Chapter IV: The Time of the Shia

1 *My Year in Iraq*, by L. Paul Bremer III, and Malcolm McConnell (Simon & Schuster, 2006). This is an epic of solipsism. See my review 'Diplomatic Baggage', by David Gardner, *FT Magazine*, 4–5 February 2006, pp. 28–9

2 GAO-07–711 of 31 July 2007

3 GAO-07–639T and GAO-07–444 of 22 March 2007

4 'Iraq: the Politics of the Local', by Charles Tripp (*Le Monde Diplomatique*, January 2008; published on *Open Democracy*, 25 January 2008)

5 'A Ministry of Fiefdoms', by Ned Parker, *Los Angeles Times*, 30 July 2007

6 On Wahhabi bridgehead in Mosul, see 'Iraqi Christians fear post-Saddam Islamists', by Samia Nakhoul, *Reuters*, 17 March 2003

7 See 'GIs forge Sunni tie in bid to squeeze militants', by Michael R. Gordon, *New York Times*, 6 July 2007; 'Iraq: the Politics of the Local', Charles Tripp (*Le Monde Diplomatique*)

8 See 'Iran helped end Iraq fighting', *Reuters*, Tehran, 4 April 2008, quoting Mohsen Hakim, SCIRI chief's son

9 US (and British) support for Israel's Lebanon war in the summer of 2006 gave added impetus to the fury of the Shia, who suspected Washington had changed sides

10 'Whatever Happened to Iraq?', *American Journalism Review*, June/July 2008

11 GAO-08–837 of 23 June 2008

12   Netanyahu interview with author, 11 February 1998, Jerusalem

13   'Talking to Iran', by Elaine Sciolino, *New York Times*, 21 December 1997

14   Derived from author's interviews with senior Egyptian security officials (Cairo, April 1997) and leading member of Iran's Expediency Council (Tehran, May 1998)

15   *Republic of Fear*, by Kanan Makiya, 1989

16   Mubarak interview with author, Cairo, 15 February 1998

17   Mubarak (ibid). After two wars, sanctions and stifled rebellion, no successor was likely to be an improvement, in Mubarak's view. 'What makes anybody think such a person will not be even more dangerous and vengeful?', he asked

18   See 'Shots in the Dark', by David Gardner, *Financial Times*, 18 December 1998

19   Defense Planning Guidance of 18 February 1992, reported in *New York Times* of 7 March 1992; see als: *Daydream Believer*, by Fred Kaplan (Wiley, 2008), pp. 124–5

20   'A Clean Break: A New Strategy for Securing the Realm', *Institute for Advanced Strategic and Political Studies*, July 1996

21   Fred Kaplan, *Daydream Believer* (Wiley, 2008), p. 126

22   'War in Iraq will only hinder the war on terror', by David Gardner, *Financial Times*, 27 January 2003

23   See also 'Iraq: The War of the Imagination', by Mark Danner, *New York Review of Books*, 21 December 2006

24   See Woodward, *State of Denial*, and Danner (idem); also *Rise of the Vulcans*, by James Mann (Viking, 2004), pp. 362–3

25   Wolfowitz would later say: 'The truth is that for reasons that have a lot to do with the US government bureaucracy, we settled on the one issue that everyone could agree on which was weapons of mass destruction as the core reason.' *Vanity Fair* & Pentagon transcript of Wolfowitz interview, May 2003

26   'Putting the meaning of the words back together again', by David Gardner, *Financial Times*, 7 February 2004

27   *Financial Times*, 1 June 2001

28   Kaplan, *Daydream Believer* (Wiley, 2008), pp. 53–76

29   *Out of the Ashes: the resurrection of Saddam Hussein*, by Andrew Cockburn and Patrick Cockburn (Harper Collins, 1999), pp. 13–30

30   The quotations from Iraqi Shia clerics here and in the rest of the chapter are from interviews conducted by the author in Najaf, Kerbala and Baghdad, in June and July of 2003

31   Fadlallah interview with author, 27 June 2003, Beirut

32 *Muqtada al-Sadr and the Fall of Iraq*, by Patrick Cockburn (Faber & Faber, 2008), pp. 149–58

33 *The Shi'ite Movement in Iraq*, by Faleh A. Jabar (Saqi, 2003)

34 *Al-Ahram*, 29 August 2003

35 'Iraq: the Politics of the Local', by Charles Tripp (*Le Monde Diplomatique*, January 2008; published on *Open Democracy*, 25 January 2008)

36 Cockburn, *Muqtada al-Sadr and the Fall of Iraq* (Faber & Faber, 2008), pp. 107–14

37 'Shi'ite Politics in Iraq: the role of the Supreme Council', from the International Crisis Group, *ICG Middle East Report* 70: 15 November 2007

38 On Hizbollah losses in siege of Najaf, Hizbollah official, Beirut, October 2004

Chapter V: Arabia Infelix

1 I happened to be on a reporting trip to Saudi Arabia in May–June 2004 when the Khobar siege took place. See 'Chaos Theory', by David Gardner, *FT Magazine*, 31 July 2004, pp. 16–21

2 Muqrin's call was on the *al-Sawt* jihadi website in May 2004

3 Senior Saudi official, Riyadh, 3 June 2004

4 Mohsen al-Awajy, interview with author, Riyadh, 1 June 2004

5 See *The House of Saud*, by David Holden and Richard Johns (Sidgwick & Jackson, 1981); *A History of Saudi Arabia*, by Madawi al-Rasheed (Cambridge University Press, 2002), which observes that 'without Wahhabism, it is highly unlikely that Dir'iyyah [the first al-Saud capital] and its leadership would have assumed much political significance' (p. 18); *The Saudi Enigma*, by Pascal Menoret (Zed Books, 2005); and 'The 'Imama versus the 'Iqal: Hadari–Bedouin conflict and the formation of the Saudi state', by Abdulaziz H. al-Fahad (*European University Institute working papers*, RSC 2002/11)

6 Al-Rasheed (ibid), pp. 191–200. Ibn Saud, nevertheless, initially had to recognize some diversity: the Hijaz constitution of 1926 was based on Shura

7 The Shia had their revenge, assassinating the Saudi leader Abdul Aziz in the mosque of their capital Dir'iyyah in 1803. Perhaps they are enjoying a second revenge through Shia majority rule in Iraq, derived from the tribes the Wahhabis drove out of Arabia into Mesopotamia

8   In fact, the Roosevelt/Ibn Saud bargain almost predates their famous
    encounter. The USA made non-belligerent Saudi Arabia eligible for US
    aid under the wartime Land Lease Act in 1943. See *American
    Orientalism*, by Douglas Little (I.B.Tauris, 2002), p. 49

9   See 'Lingerie stores urged to employ female staff', *Gulf News*,
    27 December 2005

10 Interview with author, Riyadh, 30 May 2004

11 Al-Rasheed, *A History of Saudi Arabia* (Cambridge University Press,
    2002), pp. 1993–2000; on textbooks own research

12 See Chapter III

13 Interview with senior Saudi diplomat, London, May 2004

14 Private conversation with author, Oxford, September 2003

15 Interview with author, Riyadh, March 1995

16 Interview with author, Riyadh, 2 June 2004

17 Senior Saudi official, Riyadh, 3 June 2004

18 I happened to be nearby when the November 1995 bombing took place
    and, in the nearly two hours that elapsed before Saudi police secured the
    scene of the attack, formed a clear impression from residents and work-
    ers in the National Guard centre that it was the work of Arab Afghans.
    Saying this in print, while the authorities and local diplomats busily
    blamed Iraq and/or Iran, caused me visa problems with Saudi Arabia for
    nearly a decade. See 'An uncharacteristic lapse in control-obsessed
    Riyadh', by David Gardner, *Financial Times*, 14 November 1995

19 Jamal Khashoggi, interview with author, London, May 2004

20 Mohsen al-Awajy, interview with author, Riyadh, 1 June 2004

21 *A history of Saudi Arabia*, Madawi al-Rasheed, pp. 106–34; Steffen
    Hertog, 'Shaping the Saudi State', *International Journal of Middle East
    Studies* 39, 2007

22 Interview with author, Riyadh, 31 May 2004

23 See, for example, 'The Shi'ite Question in Saudi Arabia', by the
    International Crisis Group (*Middle East Report*, Number 45, 19 September
    2005)

24 See Hertog, *Shaping the Saudi State*; and *America's Kingdom*, by Robert
    Vitalis (Stanford University Press, 2006)

25 See 'Between Islamists and Liberals: Saudi Arabia's new Islamo-liberal
    reformists', by Stephane Lacroix (*Middle East Journal*, Volume 58,
    Number 3, summer 2004)

26 Abdulaziz al-Qassim interview with author, Riyadh, 2 June 2004

Chapter VI: Getting Away with Murder?

1 *The St George Hotel Bar: International Intrigue in Old Beirut*, by Said K. Aburish (Bloomsbury, 1989)

2 Figures from *Lebanon Shot Twice*, by Zaven Kouyoumdjian (Chamas, Beirut, 2003)

3 Walid Jumblatt, interview with author, Mukhtara, 29 October 2004

4 *A House of Many Mansions*, by Kamal Salibi (I.B.Tauris, 1988)

5 241 US marines and 58 French paratroopers were killed in the bombings; see Chapter VIII passages on Iran. For background to the war, see *Pity the Nation*, by Robert Fisk (Simon & Schuster, 1990); and *The Tragedy of Lebanon*, by Jonathan Randal (Hogarth Press, 1990; first published in the USA by Viking, 1983, as *Going all the way: Christian warlords, Israeli Adventurers and the War in Lebanon*)

6 Syria's priorities became plain within hours of Israel's withdrawal from South Lebanon in 2000, when Farouk Shara'a, then Syrian foreign minister, pronounced the pull-out incomplete because Israel still held Sheba'a farms, which few Lebanese not resident there had heard of and the United Nations assigned to Syria

7 Samir Franjieh interview with author, Beirut, 26 October 2004

8 Fouad Siniora, then finance minister of Lebanon, interview with author, Beirut, 27 October 2004

9 Rafiq Hariri, interview with author, London, 6 July 1999

10 Rafiq Hariri, interview with author, Qoreitem, Beirut, 29 October 2004

11 Michel Mouawad, interview with author, Beirut, 30 October 2004

12 Samir Franjieh, interview with author, Beirut, 8 September 1998

13 Nasser Saidi, interview with author, Beirut, 28 October 2004

14 On port 'tax': interviews with Lebanese businessmen, bankers and officials over several years

15 Patriarch Sfeir interview with author, Dimane, 10 September 1997

16 Rafiq Hariri interview with author, Fakha, 6 September 1998

17 Rafiq Hariri and Samir Franjieh interviews with author, Beirut, 11 September 1997

18 Rafiq Hariri interview with author, 6 September 1998, Fakhra

19 Another visitor of Hafez al-Assad's recounts a conversation in 1999, in which the Syrian president struggled to remember the name of Ronald Reagan

20 Rafiq Hariri, interview with author, London, 6 July 1999

21   Interviews with two senior US state department officials, Washington, 6 October 2005

22   Ibid

23   Ibid

24   Interview with senior Lebanese politician, Beirut, October 2004

25   Ibid

26   Interview with Walid Jumblatt, Mukhtara, 29 October 2004

27   Ibid

28   Interview with Nayla Mouawad, Beirut, 30 October 2004

29   Interview with Rafiq Hariri, Qoreitem, Beirut, 29 October 2004

30   Interview with senior state department official, Washington, 6 October 2005

31   Interview with Rafiq Hariri, Qoreitem, Beirut, 29 October 2004

32   According to French foreign ministry officials. These letters, admittedly, included one lobbying for a $700 million gas contract that instead went to a little known consortium with ties to the Assad family circle. 'This is the inebriation of corruption', said one person familiar with the details

33   This is my interpretation based on conversations with Rafiq Hariri; an interlocutor with Damascus on his behalf; officials in Beirut and Washington in 2004 and 2005; and the confidential version of the 'Report of the United Nations International Independent Investigation Commission established pursuant to Security Council resolution 1595 (2005)', by Detlev Mehlis, Commissioner UNIIIC, Beirut, 19 October 2005, hereafter referred to as the Mehlis Report

34   Mehlis Report, 19 October 2005, paragraphs 23–30

35   Sheikh Naim Qassem, interview with author, Beirut, 30 October 2004

36   Jamil Mroue, interview with author, Beirut, 26 October 2004

37   Lebanese intellectual, interview with author, Dubai, 28 October 2005

38   Mehlis Report, paragraphs 96 and 95

39   Mehlis Report, paragraph 103

40   The Mehlis report, the first of several by the UNIIIC, may be the tip of the iceberg. Some sources, albeit partisans of the Hariri camp, say a disc recording some five years of top-level conversations between Beirut and Damascus has been handed to the UN. If so, it will presumably come to light if and when the Hariri Tribunal convenes on 1 March 2009

41   State Department and Congress officials, interviews, Washington, 15 October 2005

42   Senior Arab official, 24 November 2005

43   Probably the best account of Hizbollah is *Hezbollah: A Short History*, by Augustus Richard Norton (Princeton University Press, 2007)

44 Lebanese political sources say that after the assassination of al-Hajj, Hizbollah acquired critical influence over army operations (interviews, Beirut, 17 and 19 May 2008)

Chapter VII: A Naked, Poor and Mangled Peace

1 *Lion of Jordan: The Life of King Hussein in War and Peace*, by Avi Shlaim, (Allen Lane, 2007), pp. 377–8; 652–3

2 On Qibya, see *The Iron Wall: Israel and the Arab World*, by Avi Shlaim (Allen Lane, 2000), pp. 89–92; on French relationship, see memoirs of Shimon Peres (*Battling for Peace*, 1995). In 1953, Eisenhower froze a $40 million aid package over the Jordan waters conflict, but only made this public after the Qibya massacre

3 See Shlaim, *Iron Wall* (ibid), pp. 95–182; on the Lavon Affair, see *Every Spy a Prince*, by Dan Raviv and Yossi Melman (Houghton Mifflin, 1990), pp. 54–61

4 See Shlaim, *Iron Wall* (ibid), pp. 95–182

5 Shlaim (ibid), p. 219

6 Nasser's military intentions in 1967, despite Israeli rhetoric, were not seen as offensive. Yitzhak Rabin, then army chief of staff, said: 'I do not think Nasser wanted war. The two divisions he sent to the Sinai would not have been sufficient to launch an offensive war. He knew it and we knew it' (*Le Monde*, 28 February 1968); even Menachem Begin, who was in the 1967 cabinet, called the Six Day War a war of choice: 'In June 1967, we again had a choice. The Egyptian army concentrations in the Sinai did not prove Nasser was really about to attack us. We must be honest with ourselves. We decided to attack him' (*New York Times*, 21 August 1982)

7 *Years of Upheaval*, by Henry Kissinger (Little Brown & Co., Boston, 1982), pp. 625–9 and 1,037

8 'Eternal Divide in the thrice Holy City', by David Gardner, *Financial Times*, 28 September 1996

9 Shlaim, *The Iron Wall: Israel and the Arab World* (Allen Lane, 2000), p. 555

10 Yitzhak Rabin, interview with author, Jerusalem, 9 August 1995; see 'Jerusalem and Beyond', by David Gardner, *Financial Times*, 10 August 1995

11 Benjamin Netanyahu, interview with author, Jerusalem, 11 February 1998

12 http://www.fmep.org/analysis/articles/statements_on_american_policy_toward_settlements_by_us_government_officials.html

13 My understanding of Camp David is based on 'Camp David: the Tragedy of Errors', by Robert Malley and Hussein Agha, *New York Review of Books*, Volume 48, Number 13, 9 August 2001; *Scars of War, Wounds of Peace*, by Shlomo Ben-Ami (Weidenfeld & Nicolson, 2005), pp. 240–84; 'The Camp David Papers', by Akram Haniyeh, *Journal of Palestine Studies*, winter 2001, Volume 30, Number 2; conversations with three Israeli officials, two American officials and one Palestinian official between 2003 and 2005; and a résumé of the paper by Miguel Angel Moratinos, the European Union peace envoy and current Spanish foreign minister, who kept an account of the peace process

14 'Want Security? End the Occupation', by Marwan Barghouti, *Washington Post*, 16 January 2002

15 See *Jerusalem: One City, Three Faiths*, by Karen Armstrong (Ballantine, 1997)

16 See *Islam, the West and Jerusalem*, by Walid Khalidi (Hood Books, 1996)

17 Faisal Husseini, interview with author, Jerusalem, 8 August 1996

18 See *Expulsion of the Palestinians* (Institute of Palestine Studies, 1992), and *Land without a People* (Faber & Faber, 1997), both by Nur Masalha; *All that Remains* (Institute of Palestine Studies, 1992), by Walid Khalidi; and *New York Times*, 23 October 1979

19 Interview with UN officials, Beirut, May 2002

20 See 'The Wandering Palestinian', *The Economist*, 10 May 2008

21 Ben-Ami, *Scars of War, Wounds of Peace* (Weidenfeld & Nicolson, 2005), pp. 270–2

22 Sharon's tactics recalled those of Netanyahu. In September 1997, Israel attempted to assassinate Hamas leader Khaled Mesha'al in Amman, three days after King Hussein had communicated to Netanyahu a Hamas offer of a 30-year truce with Israel. Hussein said he felt as though somebody had 'spat in his face'. The capture of the Mossad agents who carried out the attempt forced Israel to release Sheikh Yassin. See Shlaim, *Lion of Jordan* (Allen Lane, 2007), pp. 570–6

23 *Report on Israeli Settlement in the Occupied Territories*, Volume 15, Number 6, November–December 2005, Foundation for Middle East Peace, Washington

Chapter VIII: Pax Arabica: the Middle East and the West

1   'Does "Pro-Israel" mean anything?', by M. J. Rosenberg (*IPF Friday*, 25 July 2008)

2   *A Faustian Foreign Policy*, by Joan Hoff (Cambridge University Press, 2008)

3   Albright, *Washington Post*, 23 October 1999

4   *American Orientalism*, by Douglas Little (I.B.Tauris, 2003), p. 17

5   Little (ibid), pp. 9–43

6   See *Inventing the Barbarian*, by Edith Hall (Oxford University Press, 1989)

7   See *God's Crucible: Islam and the making of Europe, 570–1215*, by David Levering Lewis (W.W. Norton, 2008), Chapter XI

8   See Little, *American Orientalism* (I.B.Tauris, 2003), p. 31

9   The debt may already have been collected. Imad Mugniyeh, organizer of the truck bombings and much of the hostage-taking, was assassinated in Damascus in February 2008 (see Chapter VI)

10 Interview with Khatami aide, Tehran, 9 May 1998

11 Sheikh Hassan Nasrallah, interview with author, Bir al-Abed, Beirut, 4 September 1998

12 General Pervez Musharraf, interview with author, Rawalpindi, 22 February 2001

13 'Bush's quandary shaped by Pentagon', by Edward Luce and Daniel Dombey, *Financial Times*, 7 November 2007

14 Recep Tayyip Erdogan, interview with the author, Elazig and Malatya, 23 October 2002

15 Erdogan (ibid)

16 *On Identity*, by Amin Maalouf (Harvil Press, 2000; first published as *Les Identités Meurtrières*, Bernard Grasset, Paris, 1998)

Index